The People's Mandate

The People's Mandate

Referendums and a More Democratic Canada

PATRICK BOYER

Toronto and Oxford
Dundurn Press
1992

Editing: Erika Krolman
Design and Production: GSN
Cover Design: Ron and Ron Design
Printing and Binding: Gagné Printing Ltd., Louiseville, Quebec, Canada

The publisher wishes to acknowledge the generous assistance and ongoing support of **The Canada Council, The Book Publishing Industry Development Programme** of the **Department of Communications, The Ontario Arts Council,** and **The Ontario Publishing Centre of the Ministry of Culture and Communications.** The author neither sought nor received any government grants in connection with the writing of this book.

Care has been taken to trace the ownership of copyright material used in the text. Credit for each quotation is given at the end of the selection. The author and publisher welcome any information enabling them to rectify any reference or credit in subsequent editions.

J. Kirk Howard, Publisher

Canadian Cataloguing in Publication Data

Boyer, Patrick
    The people's mandate

Includes bibliographical references and index.
ISBN 1-55002-147-8

1. Referendum – Canada. 2. Plebiscite – Canada.
I. Title. II. Title: Lawmaking by the People.

JF493.C34B6 1992   328.271   C91-095603-0

Dundurn Press Limited	**Dundurn Distribution Limited**
2181 Queen Street East	73 Lime Walk
Suite 301	Headington, Oxford
Toronto, Canada	England
M4E 1E5	OX3 7AD

*This book is dedicated to Canada's First Peoples,
whose mandate is a simple one but has yet to be fully
heeded by all who now live in this land.*

Books by Patrick Boyer

The Egalitarian Option (contributor) (1975)

Political Rights: The Legal Framework of Elections in Canada (1981)

Lawmaking by the People: Referendums and Plebiscites in Canada (1982)

Money & Message: The Law Governing Election Financing, Advertising, Broadcasting and Campaigning in Canada (1983)

Election Law in Canada (1987)

Local Elections in Canada (1988)

Contents

Foreword

When I began work in the summer of 1984 on the project that was to become an international television series called "The Struggle for Democracy," I felt that we in Canada took democracy's benefits too much for granted and would be stimulated and perhaps provoked into a greater degree of participation in our own democracy by travelling through the struggles, the bloodshed, the intellectual labour, the whole very dramatic and often very dangerous theatre of real life that had won us the rights, freedoms, and powers that we enjoy. All over the world, I felt, democracy was bursting to get out of its bonds in nations that had never known it, or had known and lost it; so it seemed timely to ask through the medium of film where this political treasure had come from, what it was made of, and where it might go.

The funny thing is, I thought I was pretty clear about the nature of democracy before I began serious work on the project. It was only after I was irreversibly launched that I began to realize how deep and complex and contradictory the subject is, how resistant to definition, and how various in its expressions, as various as the hundreds of different cultures in which it is growing or yearning or striving for expression. But there was one overriding issue about which I held deep convictions from the start: citizen participation. Early in the 1970s, I had been privileged to head a national task force on citizen participation in the national decision-making process, under the direction of then undersecretary of state Bernard Ostry. My interest in the issue remained strong thereafter. And the deeper I went into the subject as "The Struggle for Democracy" evolved from a two-page proposal into a fifty-page series outline and then a whole production machine that was soon to roll out hundreds of thousands of feet of film and propel me and my team over hundreds of thousands of air miles, the more I became convinced that one dominant political theory of our time was wrong.

Many traditional liberal political theorists advocate a "democracy" in which the power is in the hands of élites and bureaucracies and the population consists of docile clients "*served*" by its governments rather than of genuine *citizens* deeply involved in the democratic process themselves.

"In Praise of Apathy," you might call it. Active citizens, the theory goes, mess things up; if citizens keep quiet, vote obediently from time to time to legitimize the process, and let the experts get on with good government, democracy will achieve its best objectives. I came to feel that this theory was not only wrong but vicious and in the end a serious threat to the survival of democracy itself.

I have since written and spoken publicly, in a number of forums, about the related danger of charismatic electoral politics in which candidates make impossible promises, and sadly sometimes convince voters of the reality of those promises. I felt that the political leader as hero or saviour could generate only disappointment, social anger, and cynicism.

We are seeing it now.

And I have come to believe that the antidote lies in changing our attitudes towards direct democracy; it lies in the greater participation of citizens through a number of mechanisms – including those discussed in this book.

I myself, however, yielded to cynicism (an attitude I characteristically deplore); I felt that the beneficiaries of the present system – policy élites and certainly members of Parliament – would be entrenched in hostility towards any reforms of this nature.

And now along comes this fascinating exploration of the same issues – by a practising parliamentarian!

How Patrick Boyer finds the time and energy to be an active parliamentarian, an amateur historian, and a political theorist all at once escapes my understanding, but I am glad he does so.

One of the things that gives Canada its distinction is our willingness to constantly re-examine what we have made and where we are going. The country is deeply into that process again as I write. Patrick Boyer's widely researched study and judicious display of the issues flowing from these great democratic questions, situated in the Canadian context, will be of service to Canada as we strive to carry forward the essential and characteristically Canadian political task of refashioning our society towards the always elusive but – thank God – always beckoning goals of greater civility, greater generosity, greater sensitivity, and – in the present context of prime importance – greater *citizenship*.

I write as a still-fascinated, still-bemused, and still hopeful observer of the long, tangled, messy, and unpredictable story of democracy. This book is timely, rich in texture, insightful, and not without surprises.

Patrick Watson

Toronto, 1992

Acknowledgments

The help of others always deserves recognition, and I especially wish to thank those who have assisted in the preparation of this book.

William R. Young, author, historian, and friend, read and commented on many of the chapters, and I am grateful for his contribution of time and intelligence.

Alison M. Stodin, a fellow graduate of Carleton University and now my assistant in Ottawa, volunteered her spare time in the evenings and on many weekends to both type the manuscript and make thoughtful suggestions from her own knowledge and experience of the operation of our parliamentary system.

Joan Hudson, chief librarian with my former law firm Fraser & Beatty in Toronto, helped with her legal research skills when I wrote *Lawmaking by the People,* a 1982 book about referendums and plebiscites in Canada, and I want to thank her for a continuing interest in election law and for the many detailed points she tracked down to help ensure accuracy in this book.

To the fine people in the Library of Parliament in Ottawa, I wish to express appreciation for the friendly professionalism with which they have helped me over the past seven years to locate articles and books and obscure facts on many diverse topics of interest to an MP. I would specifically like to acknowledge their help in bringing to hand a number of long-forgotten speeches from the pages of old *Hansards* where earlier debates, mentioned in this book, raged in the House of Commons over referendums and plebiscites.

To Patrick Watson, the thoughtful activist and intellectual catalyst who as broadcaster, writer, and promoter of good causes, has given so much to Canadians, I want to give special thanks for his foreword to this book. In his celebrated television series "The Struggle for Democracy," Patrick Watson, displaying the prescience for which he has deservedly earned a reputation, turned to the camera atop the Acropolis in Athens and spoke words I shall never forget. "I have been repeatedly struck by the fact," he said, "that some of the most corrosive cynicism about democracy, and some of the most leaden indifference towards it, are expressed by people who live in prosperous democratic countries."

My life partner Corinne, whose interest and encouragement in writing this book helped make it a reality, deserves full credit and recognition, too, for the total support she gives to my writing and political work. Corinne also gathered material from newspapers and radio broadcasts, read and helped revise pages of manuscript, and visited the archives. Her instinctive knowledge of what I am trying to accomplish makes collaboration on this book, as on all else, a joyful endeavour for us both.

Patrick Boyer
Etobicoke, 1992

Introduction

A Reality
Far Different

The present turmoil in Canada, while distressing to many, is actually a positive symptom of the necessary transmutation through which our country must now go. The Canadian story is essentially a tale of evolution and adaptation, and we are again moving to a new stage, into a reality far different from what we have known.

Culturally founded as the fragments of many societies, Canada is currently described as "multicultural" because of its pluralistic nature. Like Switzerland in nineteenth-century Europe, our country preserves its identity by having many identities.

Politically founded as colonies of European powers who occupied the lands of the Indians, our country has many structures of government, and concepts of sovereignty have changed dramatically over two centuries. These now await a reconciliation, and this process is under way.

Structurally, we are changing our institutions, values, laws, and practices from the model that Europeans first created for themselves and imposed on much of the world. We are moving to a new model that we are creating, not only for ourselves, but also as an example for the rest of the world. Canada is in transition, becoming a twenty-first-century international country from having been a nineteenth-century nation state.

Our changing nature as a democratic society is best seen within this context of far-reaching cultural, political, and structural change.

Some developments and political attitudes today seem instru-

1

mental, if not in making Canadian society democratic, in levelling it. Yet the egalitarian option, even when pursued to its ultimate end, will not in itself create a democratic Canada. A democratic society is defined more by how decisions are made, how people participate in the decision-making process, and how mandates for an agreed-upon course of action are achieved than by any effort to obliterate natural distinctions and hierarchies based on talent, merit, wealth, education, or cultural heritage. A democratic country is pre-eminently one in which everyone is *not* the same. For, if we were the same, it would follow that a single individual could set all the rules and make all the decisions and these would be acceptable to each of the rest of us. No, a democratic approach is made essential in a country or society like ours because of its great diversity, and the *process* by which a decision is reached can be as important, and is often more significant, than the decision itself. Canadians, in short, have no choice but to be democrats.

We have values in Canada that are worth preserving, including recognition of the spiritual nature of our existence, acceptance of the proper role of humans within the ecological system; conservation of the natural environment; respect for the many strands in our richly diverse cultural inheritance; the primacy of family and local community; a sense of duty to serve the country and a feeling of personal obligation to our fellow citizens; voluntarism; respect for time-tested traditions and institutions; the importance of individual self-reliance and of privacy of the individual; and government that works in partnership with the people.

The collective wisdom of a large body of well-informed people most reliably produces the best decisions. Therefore, the consensus deliberately reached by a large, diverse group ought to be trusted more than the conclusions or commands of a small, homogeneous group or a single individual. Pooled information and variety in experience can blend to produce not only a sound course of action, but also and as important, the underlying consensus necessary to implement it. We must find the courage to fully accept this truth and its consequences. It means trusting in democratic methods that enable collective wisdom to be accurately expressed.

Currently, a banality pervades much of our public life. An inhibition that it would be unseemly restrains us from robustly embracing our authentic Canadian reality. The body moves, but the soul within languishes, ignored and unnourished.

The conflict between the political and cultural ideas of Canada as a nation is slowly being faced. It is not political tinkering we need, but a more profound "cultural reconfederation," as Northrop Frye said in his last formal address at the University of Toronto in the fall of 1990. In a democracy there are no uncritical loyalties, he observed. Instead, he concluded, "There must always be a tension of loyalties, not in the sense of opposed forces pulling apart, but in the sense of one feeling of belonging attached to and complemented by another, which is very often the relating of a small ethnical community to a larger one . . . It is through some such process that the cultural development of Canada must make its way."[1]

Novelist Robertson Davies thinks that Canada has a soul, but that "it is a battered soul among souls" and "needs nourishment, exercise, fresh air, and, above all, love, if it is to reach maturity." Answering the question, what is Canada to do? Davies says, "As a beginning some vigorous goading of the national intelligence is essential. Sleazy education and unexamined, patiently accepted government along weary mixture-as-before lines must go. As these things go – not after, but concurrently – there will inevitably be an awakening to the numinous, in personal and national life."[2]

Canada has remained a timid democracy. The establishment that has run our country has proceeded comfortably – not always in the interests of the people, nor indeed of the country itself – supported by Canadians' deference to authority and a strange willingness to be passive spectators in our own land. We have become what anthropologists call "participant observers." When describing Canadians' attributes or practices, our historians, commentators, and politicians frequently refer to a disembodied third-person "they" rather than an inclusive "we." This linguistic distancing is a specious objectivity that has contributed over time to the eerie notion that nobody really lives here. We refer to "the system" or "the government" as if it were some autonomous entity, separate and far away, rather than part of us, something over which we do have power.

We Canadians have been strangely fugitive from our own reality and have engaged in massive conspiracies to bury our past and hide

3

from our history. Apart from the dwarfing vastness of our land and our inherited colonial preference for getting the answer from elsewhere, our political structures and practices of governance have also been partly responsible.

When we do look within, the range of vision is often too narrow and focuses on the obvious – our political leaders. It is customary, for example, for many Canadians to toss off a glib but spiteful denunciation of the current occupant of the prime minister's office, as if that completed their exercise of responsible citizenship. Canadians love to hate their prime minister. Before the current animosity towards Brian Mulroney, we had the frothing denunciations of Pierre Elliott Trudeau. In John Diefenbaker's time, anyone who seriously defended him was ostracized in polite company. Mackenzie King was not only booed by Canadian troops during World War II, but was also defeated several times when seeking re-election in his own constituency. R.B. Bennett personified the Depression in the eyes of many and was accordingly denounced. So the pattern goes – all the way back to John A. Macdonald. The reason for failure has not lain with these men, however, as much as with ourselves and our political culture. Educator and public commentator John Godfrey wrote recently, from his observation deck as editor of *The Financial Post,* that "one of the least attractive national characteristics of Canadians is our propensity, indeed even our delight, in finding fault."[3]

In a curious mutation of our colonial mentality, we *externalize* responsibility, rather than turning maturely to ourselves. Since the 1960s Quebeckers have shown the way, seeking to be "maître chez nous" (masters in our own house) and with this mentality developing a political culture where the soul truly is nourished and political activity is both germane and authentic. Yet in the rest of Canada we flounder because of a destructive frame of mind, weighed down by an attitude that charges with frustration and, like lightning, strikes the highest and most visible target – usually the prime minister of the day – with bolts of blame. For all their human frailties, our prime ministers have contended well with the challenges generated by the circumstances of their times. Canadian historian Frank Underhill once told me that "a great leader should be a one-man distillation of the country." But I suspect there is always a long time between great leaders, and what are we to do in the meantime? Are we to wait for the rare leader, the one who takes, as Norman Mailer suggests, "national anxieties so long buried and releases them to the surface where they belong"? Or, is there another way, one which we are groping towards but have not yet fully recognized?

Isn't the new image of democracy in Canada one in which greater popular participation is understood as being vital to our national well-being? Does personal involvement not become necessary in a country where the duties and responsibilities, as well as the "rights," of each citizen are being emphasized?

The role of direct voting by Canadian citizens on issues of transcendent national importance can be positive and constructive. We have already accumulated a rich, if little-known, Canadian experience on this subject of referendums. This story has had a poor chance of taking hold of the Canadian imagination, however, because the political élites who benefit from the present arrangements have largely played their part in suppressing and discrediting the relevance of direct democracy to our Canadian situation.

Wider use of referendums and plebiscites could help cure some of the present ailments in the Canadian body politic. At the same time, they are not magic elixirs or cure-alls: the role of referendums, while precise, is limited. There is the risk of overdosing on this medicine. Nonetheless, intelligent use of this instrument of direct popular participation is worthy of more than the usual out-of-hand dismissal given it by those individuals who conveniently and sometimes maliciously misinterpret our Canadian experience with referendums and plebiscites. Some of these people dress up their excuses with lofty principles about parliamentary democracy, while their objective is really that of maintaining the status quo.

Again, not every issue has to be "put to the people." The main work of enacting laws, resolving issues, and debating public concerns must continue in our elected and deliberative legislative bodies. Many Canadians seem at present to feel that elected representatives, of whatever party, cannot be counted on to make decisions and that constituent assemblies are needed – a return in a sense to the amphitheatre of Athens where direct democracy was born. As a member of Parliament, I obviously believe in the institutions of "representative democracy." But, on the basis of seven years' experience in Parliament and for reasons given in this book, I must conclude that serious imbalances created by rigid party discipline must be corrected if we are to keep on calling MPs elected "representatives." Even with their faults, our legislatures are still vital to our system of government.

Perhaps every decade, or maybe once in the life of each Parliament, one or two topics of overriding national importance should be subjected to the fullest expression of popular opinion. Certainly major constitutional amendments ought to be submitted for ratification by a direct vote of the people in a referendum. The reasons for doing so are developed in Chapter 7. Direct voting might also be especially appropriate where the government of the day lacks a "mandate" for a fundamental policy change that could significantly alter the nature or operation of our country. This approach of using the instrument of direct democracy for special purposes would neither threaten nor displace our institutions of representative democracy but could complement and actually enhance their role, as this book will show.

Our Canadian identity, further, could be strengthened through the use of plebiscites because we would be forced, in very specific terms, to speak out and debate with one another about the kind of country we want. To move beyond the vague generalities that too often pass for public discourse in our land would be refreshing. The plebiscite process could thus help us to define ourselves and supplement the "weary mixture-as-before" approach that is preventing the required interest in our national life. Instead of passively letting elected representatives in Parliament make all the decisions for us, or relying on editorial page writers and CBC commentators to do our thinking, it would be far more stimulating and productive to have everyone coming to terms with his or her own view about a public issue. That is what happened in Prince Edward Island in 1988, as the heritage and future of the Island were debated in relation to the question of building a fixed-link crossing to the mainland. It happened in Quebec in 1980 when the referendum forced every Quebecker to consider his or her individual future, as a resident in a province that either would become a separate entity or would

6

remain within a greater Canada. It also happened in 1982 in the Northwest Territories as northerners came to grips with the plebiscite question on whether to divide the region into two territories.

A larger dose of direct democracy could also counteract a number of other developments that have caused political life and the governing process in Canada to suffer in the past decade. Examples of such developments include the ascendant and unchecked role of opinion polling and pollsters, the increasing dominance of single-issue groups, the growing power and influence of professional lobbyists, the hardening partisanship and rigidity of party lines in Parliament, and the hijacking of decision making from the legislatures by what has been called "executive federalism."

In these days when we suffer a plague of opinion polls, it is worth recognizing the several ways that plebiscites are a superior method of divining the public mind. First, instead of the "representative sample" of an opinion poll, each citizen has his or her own say in a plebiscite. Second, plebiscites give the possibility of a well-considered opinion that polls do not. A person may be watching a hockey game, cooking a meal, working in the garden, or otherwise distracted, when a pollster phones and asks, out of the blue, for an on-the-spot opinion on some issue of the day. In a plebiscite everyone discusses and deliberates over the issue several weeks before expressing his or her verdict. We do not elect our representatives on the first day of a multi-week election campaign, but on the last. For the same good reason people ought also to have the chance to obtain information, to debate and to reflect, before "electing" one of several choices on important public issues.

A plebiscite, it is important to realize, is more than a large-scale, formalized opinion poll. With opinion polls, there can and will always be doubt about the wording of the pollster's question, quibbling as to the representativeness of the sample, and a feeling that it is "nothing more than an opinion poll" to be contradicted by someone else's poll tomorrow. Nothing, on the other hand, speaks with the same eloquence as a counting of ballots, deliberately cast on a question by the voting citizens of a province or the entire country, after a cathartic debate.

Single-issue groups and special interest organizations are a second concern. While they have long played a role in our political system, their recent emergence on centre stage has tended to distort the broader political agenda that pluralistic and industrialized countries like Canada must constantly address. Lobbyists have always been present wherever power is exercised, and in our system of government they do perform an important role. Yet, as they have come to much greater prominence during the 1980s, their role is one that many observers, quite rightly, are finding increasingly awkward. The sensation is something like seeing a football player appear on the ice at a hockey match. He may be a superb athlete, dressed in a colourfully handsome uniform, and capable of deftly executing complicated plays with great strength and aplomb, but his blocking and tackling is not part of hockey. His discordant performance is unsettling to the spectators. In the past decade, the emergence in Ottawa of the new breed of paid professional lobbyists (responded to, so far, by the Lobbyist Registration Act, in force since September 30, 1988) marks, in practical terms, a serious interference in the operation of government or, to put it in moral terms, a corruption of Canadian democracy.

The third phenomenon we should be wary of is excessive partisanship. In the Senate and the House of Commons, simple matters are blown out of proportion by political grandstanding for perceived partisan advantage. Major issues have sometimes been trivialized, again by the same destructiveness that substitutes party lines and a phoney adversarial stance for honest debate and intelligent analysis.

The fourth phenomenon, that of our legislatures being reduced to "rubber stamps" for decisions already taken by cabinet, has to be troubling to anyone concerned about maintaining the dynamic counterbalances essential to a parliamentary democracy. The firm control of government by the prime minister, and at the provincial level by the premiers, has been solidified in the emergence of "executive federalism" and includes cabinet and a committee system that gives contemporary Canada a tableau of governance where dissent is perceived as disloyalty, and even reasonable accommodation of differences becomes a struggle of the first order.

This book springs from the idea that we will benefit from making Canada a more democratic country where people participate in and have greater responsibility for decisions that affect them; direct voting to obtain a mandate from the people, is, therefore, its central focus. It is a rising theme in current political discussion in Canada, but the lack of information about Canadian experience with referendums and plebiscites has hobbled intelligent assessment of this important democratic instrument.

Like a general election, this specialized electoral procedure of direct popular voting is certainly not a neutral or antiseptic device for registering voter opinion. The controversial nature of referendum issues is almost a guarantee that the troops in the trenches will wage battle with all available weapons, as the Canadian experience recounted in this book illustrates. It has been observed that frequently referendums, "even in the most democratic countries, have to some degree been engineered to produce a popular endorsement for what those in power happen to want."[4] Yet precisely because of this, it is important to have in place a realistic and comprehensive statute to govern the holding of direct votes in Canada, just as we long ago enacted the Canada Elections Act to govern the general voting to elect our representatives and thus ensure the fairness of that process. The problems of conducting elections (people were killed in a number of nineteenth-century election riots) did not dissuade us from democratic elections but led to our embracing them more firmly and working to eliminate the abuses that threatened them. The risks (more perceived perhaps than real) of direct voting on issues should not now find us more timid than our forbears in creating an appropriate legal structure and procedure, and getting on with it. That is the subject of Chapter 8, "The Quest for a Canadian Direct-Vote Statute."

Canada's story is one of change and evolution. To help us remain clear-eyed and resolute amid the turmoil of change, we have had to retain strong images that encapsulate the values or vision we have of our country. Consider historian W.L. Morton's description of the character of Canada in earlier times. He recounted the visions Canadian people had in the first decade of this century "to bring in immigrants, to break new fields, to turn out the new machines, to fill the long trains rumbling day and night to the seaports, to fill the wilderness with the prosperous and comfortable homes of a simple, democratic people."[5] This vision of our country suggests, at least to me, the image of progress and prosperity that comes in concert with a thorough-going democracy that reaches and is embodied by every part of Canadian society. My dream is that we can re-express this Canadianism in contemporary terms, and that we can yet evolve into a robust democracy so that Canada will truly be the homeland "of a simple, democratic people."

Although the ideals of democracy can never be fully achieved, perhaps a continuing struggle for them is, as Canadian political theorist C.B. Macpherson once suggested, the only way we can even hope to approximate them.

The struggle to make Canada a more democratic country is driven not just by a desire for some abstract or intellectual state of being, but by the need to address, through a constructive process, several pragmatic and real challenges facing us in contemporary government. For example, impossible expectations can be moderated by showing people what the choices really are. Parts of the Spicer Commission report, certain publicity pamphlets of the Reform Party, and some of the mail from my constituents show me that a number of Canadians have unrealistic expectations and believe in simplistic solutions. In a recent address, Joe Clark said that quite apart from the worry over Quebec's separation, his concern is that Canada may be separating "from [its] own modern reality." Part of the explanation, he told his Toronto audience, "is that we do not realize what we have become. We have based our assumptions about Canada on facts which have changed. Our country has changed, but our vision of it hasn't and often our institutions haven't either."[6] One way to present the choices to people in a way that brings home "our own modern reality" is by referendums.

In order to participate and understand, people need information. This means having more rounded and thoroughly presented information than usually comes in a single article, speech, or news story. Information could be transmitted through a period in which there would be a focused, nationwide "teach-in," where all points of view would be heard and all data publicized, and, furthermore, the motivation to learn would be present because the process would culminate, within a fixed time frame, in a simple question for everybody to answer with a "yes" or a "no." One way to provide such an opportunity for citizens to inform themselves and participate is by referendums.

To bridge the credibility gap between the public and the government in modern society, people need to share the responsibilities of self-government more than just by voting infrequently to elect representatives. One way to share the responsibility of government more effectively is by referendums.

The case for a referendum on a singular and far-reaching matter is that it is the only way to maximize democracy while concentrating on the issue.

Yet this book is not only about referendums, a process of direct voting that has important Canadian roots. It is also about making our country more democratic, about finding the courage to accept a mandate from the people, about achieving in Canada a reality far different from the one that so perplexes and perturbs many good citizens at the present hour.

1

Our Democratic
Instinct

Moving with some uncertainty into the twentieth century's concluding decade, the world is experiencing unscripted confrontations both with new environmental and economic realities and with enduring problems, such as war, crime, racial prejudice, shortages of food, and religious fanaticism, that are sometimes dressed up in new ways. Accompanying this daunting phase of change, however, is an opportunity to involve people more directly in making decisions about the solutions to problems.

Using Democratic Means

Giving fuller reign to this democratic instinct is in itself a challenge, since over the years our decision-making process has jealously been guarded by the smooth hands of the political establishment. Yet such a transition is important if we are to successfully address the issues currently before us. As Nelson Mandela told members of Parliament when addressing us on June 18, 1990, just four months after his release from thirty years of imprisonment in South Africa, "We must use democratic means in our search for a democratic result."

A tide of democratic change has been sweeping the world, not only recently through the once-monolithic Communist bloc of countries in eastern Europe where the wave hit in a way as dramatic as it was sudden, but earlier in Mediterranean Europe in the mid-1970s after which it spread to Latin America, Asia, and Africa, and today is felt even in South Africa.

This historic transformation from totalitarian systems, which imposed a single view, to democratic regimes, which provide a process of choice, is bringing changes that allow for resolution of the very dilemmas that have ended numerous dictatorships. Democracy in these countries is largely a process of communication and an instrument of choice that offers alternative solutions to any given problem. In this context political scientist Dankwart A. Rustow has noted how "situations that confront rigid dictatorships with insoluble dilemmas thus allow democracies to show themselves at their best as mechanisms for change, specifically for orderly change among parties in power."[1]

Democratic Evolution in Canada

Although Canada has been an exemplary multi-party democratic state for well over a century, many Canadians today argue that the "democratic revolution" in other countries also needs to wash anew through our own institutions and political practices in order to take democracy, Canadian-style, to the next phase in its evolution.

Much can be done to democratize our society more fully: referendums could be held to ratify constitutional amendments (like the proposals now before the country, or previously the Meech Lake Accord, or before that, an entrenched Charter of Rights); plebiscites could be held from time to time on issues of great national importance (like converting the national system of measurement to metric or imposing a moratorium on government spending and taxation); native Canadians deserve powers and structures of self-government; election law requires further reforms; standards of ethical conduct in public affairs at all levels need a more balanced emphasis; and practices and programs in government must be re-tested against the democratic principle of "the greatest good to the greatest number," to ensure they cease serving only special interest groups with narrowly defined interests; shareholder democracy could reassert important accountability over companies; greater employee participation in the profits and decisions of the plants where they work will be a more beneficial form of industrial democracy; many of the 3,300,000 Canadians with varying degrees of mental and physical disability want to assume "the dignity of risk" and

14

experience a less paternalistic approach when it comes to their education, employment, transportation, recreation, and accommodation. These are only some examples. Quite apart from these and other specific measures, the real change must take place in a cultural dimension, a new attitude that is positive and accepting about what "to use democratic means" entails.

On many levels and in many ways, people can participate more in the decisions whose consequences affect their lives. Canadians can become less the passive spectators, and more the active participants. This fresh manifestation of the democratic instinct is strongly entrenching itself in Canada these days. Widespread support across the country for native goals is specific evidence of our new sensitivity to participation and accountability. In addition to a "healthy and well-justified sense of guilt," which has begun to take hold regarding the conditions of Canadian native peoples, John Dafoe also observed of western Canada in the summer of 1991 that "native claims these days are being viewed as more acceptable than Quebec's because they are expressed in terms that are more in harmony with the populist mood that has taken hold."[2]

Some Canadians have lamented the emphasis on *rights* in the new era of our Charter, saying that equal stress should be put on each citizen's *responsibilities*. Yet until we regenerate an attitude of self-reliance in our culture at all levels, until we are increasingly prepared to say to one another, "It is your decision – make it, and live with the consequences," we ought not to pretend such dismay over the anaemic state of people's interest in assuming duty and accepting responsibility. To become a healthier democracy where people's lives and values matter more, it will help to shed the traditional Canadian instinct of paternalism.

Accountability Depends on Participation

We Canadians – like the British, French, Americans, and Mexicans – live in a large country with representatives elected by the population at large. We all may exhibit a somewhat proprietorial attitude towards democracy. Yet many smaller countries (from Switzerland to the Netherlands, Iceland to Israel, and New Zealand to Papua New Guinea) also show, as Patrick Watson detected in his examination of the ageless struggle for democracy around the world, how "democracy and smallness go hand in hand." In some of these countries, Watson notes, "accountability depends more on the participation of citizens than on the conduct of leaders."[3]

Democracy, a concept born in the Greek city states, at its simplest means the rule of the *demos*, the citizens' body, or the citizens in full assembly together. It was the right of each citizen to decide what should be matters of public concern, and how those matters should be resolved. The evolution of modern nation states and the growth of populations necessarily resulted in democracy being converted from direct to indirect forms – through the election of representatives of the people.

Blending Representative and Direct Democracy

Most contemporary nation states calling themselves democracies not only incorporate into their constitutions the apparatus of representative legislative assemblies, but also balance this by maintaining some provision for direct democracy. Certainly the more successful democracies creatively combine a healthy mix of direct-voting procedures with representative assemblies, and use each approach according to its appropriateness for resolving the matter at hand. In Canada the uses of this device of direct democracy have been somewhat limited – we have held only two national plebiscites so far, although about sixty have been held at the provincial level, and several thousand in our various municipalities.

Before a detailed discussion of the who, what, where, when, why, and how of referendums, it would be best to face up to the rigid attitude which holds, quite simply, that direct voting by the people on major issues is incompatible with our system of representative democracy. In Canada's parliamentary democracy, goes this reasoning, we elect members of Parliament to make our decisions, and we do not want them passing the buck, or ducking an issue. Many eminent and eloquent Canadians express this line of thought. Some add that issues are too complex to be put to the (uninformed) people in a simple "yes or no" question decided by a single round of balloting. Still others support this with a "floodgates" argument, suggesting that if we start holding referendums on one or two issues, this will open the gate to the vast dam that currently holds back mob rule. What would be the point, they ask, of having MPs at all? Buttressing that with a final argument, some critics conclude that direct voting is simply "unparliamentary," or even worse, "un-British."

The answer to all this is that referendums and plebiscites are not meant to replace parliamentary rule, but rather to enhance it. Our system of government depends, ultimately, upon the consent of the people being governed. Canada is not a dictatorship where tyrannical force is used to obtain public acquiescence in the measures and programs of the government. Nor is it a theocracy where we follow the dictates of our leadership because of blindly obedient religious faith. Ours is a democracy, where, at the end of the day, there simply must be public consensus about where we are going, and general agreement on how to get there. Without consent, the whole elaborate superstructure – the legislatures, the courts, the financial system, the commercial marketplace, the acceptance of laws and norms of behaviour – will corrode until it collapses.

How are we to achieve consent, this indispensable glue of a democratic society? Elections every four or five years? Opinion polls? First ministers' meetings? One method, that of diffusing amongst the electorate a greater sense of personal responsibility for the actions of government, Vernon Bogdanor has noted, results in decisions of government acquiring greater authority and legitimacy because they are based upon a wider degree of support.[4]

Because the major issues facing Canada now are as much political and psychological as they are economic or technical, the all-important educative role of referendums and the consent that can be created by an inclusive and participatory approach are both vital. The environmental and social behaviour challenges currently facing our country, for example, cannot simply be resolved by a mechanical application of legal rules or precepts of the social sciences; they depend crucially upon the mobilization of popular consent.

"This consent requires that there be in the political system some focus for the public interest," says Bogdanor, adding that this interest would come about through "a feeling that the policies of a government reflect more than merely the interests of its supporters" and that such a community of interest "cannot be assumed, but must be constructed through intelligent political action."[5]

Of course, many of the issues of immediate concern to most Canadians in the social and economic sphere are not simple, and they could not be readily solved through a single direct vote of the people. Nor can such complex and interconnected decisions be separately referred to the voters. Direct voting – like everything else involving the exercise of statecraft – must be used intelligently. This book gives a number of examples of wise and unwise uses. Where referendums and plebiscites can be appropriately used, however, they additionally serve the fundamental role of creating consent for the actions of government, taken through parliamentary voting.

Our Democratic Instinct

The democratic instinct permeates Canadian life. Many laws and constitutional provisions within this broadly formed political milieu form the legal framework of our democratic system.

Ten fundamental political rights and freedoms present in Canadian law are: the right to elect governments periodically, the right to vote for one's representative, the right to vote on certain laws, the right to a secret ballot, the right to free speech, the right to assemble freely, the right to information about public policies, the right to be a candidate for public office, the freedom to participate in the political process, and the freedom to form a political party.[6] These freedoms and rights are accorded differing levels of constitutional and legal protection in our country, as the examination in this book of one of them – the people's right to vote on certain laws – will demonstrate.

In addition to these express legal provisions, many norms and practices of a democratic, populist, and favour-the-underdog or egalitarian nature are intrinsically, even instinctively, part of the "Canadian way." From tax laws to immigration practice, Canadians have a healthy abhorrence of a double standard. Our democratic instinct compels us to insist on fairness to all, special privileges for none.

Patterns of Anti-democratic Thought

Yet a countervailing attitude also operates within Canada today. This anti-democratic attitude accepts democracy if necessary, but not necessarily democracy.[7] Those having this outlook prefer a controlled democracy. This is the Canada that believes in deference to authority and that stresses the values of peace, order, and good government. Tourists from abroad marvel at how tidy and efficient our cities are. In government as in urban living, Canadians love orderliness. The same mindset that has bequeathed us a smothering thicket of laws to govern the minute details of our daily living has been present to keep us from the disorderly conduct of an easy-going democracy.

Puritanism, extended from religious dogmas into codes of personal conduct aimed at the moral uplift of society as a whole, was in turn carried through into political puritanism, which has produced a tangible expression of denial.

Some of our oldest institutions, such as the Senate, which still bedevils Canadian political and parliamentary life, were expressly designed to curb the popularly elected assemblies, to provide "sober second thought" after elected representatives, implicitly "intoxicated" by their power, may have acted rashly (that is, in a way in which the governing establishment did not approve).

Quite apart from institutional manifestations of anti-democratic thought, attitudes can be found in many quarters of Canada today which proceed from the unspoken premise that the people simply cannot be trusted. This denial of any genuine role for the people in our system of government is itself a betrayal or disavowal of the core given, that our society is a democracy. I listened in disbelief as a fellow MP, several years ago, explained why referendums were "not a good idea." "I was talking with some ladies in my constituency, and they had no clue about even basic aspects of government. How could they be entrusted to vote on an important issue facing the country?" he asked. This from a man who was sitting in Parliament because he had been elected by those same people!

Lamentably, it is at this superficial level that the assessment of participatory democracy usually ends. It is time to take the analysis a little deeper and show how these patterns of anti-democratic thought have actually served us poorly.

Three Criticisms of Democracy

Some critics of democracy are opposed to it, root and branch, on the basis that it is the least efficient form of government and one in which the stability of the state is threatened by factionalism; complex issues are distorted by popular discussion; difficult decisions are evaded or put off; and matters of judgment are decided according to what will be acceptable to the majority of the voters.[8] This attitude is not uncommon in totalitarian and fascist regimes, but probably a number of people in contemporary Canada would agree with this critique, not pausing to reflect on just how those "efficient" governments might deal with the same issues we face and whether those methods really ought to replace democratic untidiness.

A second group, whose critique is often based on Marxist analysis, argues that political democracy is ineffective unless it is carried into the economic sphere; otherwise, democracy is at best incomplete, at worst a sham, disguising the reality of class rule. Debate has raged for years between socialists and capitalists about which of their rival systems is more democratic. The socialist, Patrick Watson and Benjamin Barber note, argues that capitalism nourishes poverty and inequality in the name of freedom, wondering how "one man, one vote" can really mean much when millionaires and paupers exist side by side in the same society. Capitalists counter this view by saying that, in pursuing economic equality, socialism limits political freedom.[9] "Today," observe Watson and Barber, "we find capitalist democracies trying to become more egalitarian in the name of social justice, and we find socialist dictatorships aspiring to more competition and market freedom in the name of *glasnost* and *perestroika.*"[10]

A third line of criticism comes from those who think that the bureaucracy too often makes the decisions in a democracy. This belief gave rise, for instance, to demands for "participatory democracy" in the 1960s and fuelled abundant plots for the popular TV series "Yes Minister," based on Richard Crossman's diary from the 1980s, permitting people to laugh about what they fear is all too true in an age that tacitly accepts the establishment's premise that specialist bureaucrats are better than generalist politicians.

Avoiding the "Hamlet Syndrome"

As the democratic instinct stirs people anew in other countries, we Canadians owe it to ourselves and our country not to spend too much time either gazing at what others are doing, or succumbing to what R.D. Fullerton, chairman of the Canadian Imperial Bank of

Commerce, calls the "Hamlet Syndrome," by which he means the intense introspection and inner debate that ultimately paralyzes us.[11]

The next wave of democracy to help our country through its current malaise must include greater use of plebiscites and referendums. The renewal of Canada will come – not from lectures by our political leaders, nor by prescriptions from our country's media pundits – but rather from the people themselves. We must, to repeat, "use democratic means to achieve democratic results."

An Energizing Degree of Self-government

Other democratic countries have not been timid about using plebiscites and referendums. Australians resort to referendums on constitutional matters, and submitting questions to voters in the United States has long been an integral part of that country's system of government – one that occasionally sends seismic waves throughout the North American political culture, as with the 1978 "Taxpayers' Revolt" on Proposition 13 in California, when the sovereign public voted to impose ceilings on their government's spending. In the United States, most state constitutions contain provisions enshrining the right of citizens to vote on certain laws. Even in the United Kingdom, the "mother" of most of the world's *parliamentary* democracies, a final coming-of-age occurred when three plebiscites were held in the 1970s.

Canada's democratic process, under increasing criticism for not providing sufficient voice to the public at large, can be broadened and strengthened through greater use of referendums and plebiscites, not in a frivolous way, but as an effective means of helping Canadians achieve an energizing degree of self-government.

It is usually a wise practice, when facing uncertainty or having to choose among conflicting alternatives, to let intuition be one's guide. At this juncture, we Canadians can prove the wisdom of this approach by giving greater reign to our democratic instinct.

2

The Meaning of
Direct Democracy

In clarifying basic terms and concepts pertaining to direct democracy, four words in particular embrace the main doctrines involved: referendum, plebiscite, initiative, and recall. This chapter examines the vocabulary of direct democracy in its historical context, concluding with a fine Canadian example of what happens when purity encounters practice.

Distinctions between Plebiscites and Referendums

A plebiscite and a referendum are not the same, even though in popular usage, and indeed in the statutes of several provinces, the words are sometimes used interchangeably. Both processes appear the same, involving as they do the phenomena of a campaign and of voters going to polling stations to mark a "yes" or a "no" in answer to a specific question on a ballot paper.

French scholar Jean-Marie Denquin, in his book *Référendum et Plébiscite*,[1] makes numerous distinctions between the concept of a referendum and a plebiscite. Other scholars have not agreed with his separation of the two terms. David Butler and Austin Ranney, for instance, in *Referendums*, state that "since there does not seem to be any clear or generally acknowledged line that can be drawn to distinguish the subject matter, the intent or the conduct of a referendum from that of a plebiscite," the word "referendum" would be used exclusively throughout their book.[2]

Legally, a referendum is binding on a government, whereas a

plebiscite is not. Expressed in slightly broader terms, the distinction that ought to be drawn is that a referendum in its legal meaning is a binding verdict of the people that must be reflected in a law or action by the government, whereas a plebiscite is a formalized expression of public opinion that can serve to guide the government on a specific issue or question.

The referendum on sovereignty-association held in Quebec in 1980, for instance, was in fact a plebiscite, because it was without any direct consequences in law. The direct votes held in 1979 in both the City of Edmonton and the City of Calgary with respect to expensive public works projects were referendums, in that the results were legally binding on the respective municipal governments.

The word "plebiscite" originated in Roman law around the fourth century B.C. and described a law enacted by the vote of the plebeians (the common people) at the request or on the proposition of a plebeian magistrate. In modern constitutional law, it has come to mean a vote of the aggregate of enfranchised individuals composing a country, province, or electoral territory, expressing their choice for or against some specific issue or question submitted to them.

The word "referendum" identifies a similar method of submitting or "referring" an important legislative measure to a direct vote by the whole people and was apparently first used in Switzerland to describe this type of balloting. From the 1830s to the 1860s an obligatory type of referendum was developed under Swiss constitutional arrangements. This procedure required a legislature to refer certain classes of actions to a popular vote for approval or rejection.

Swiss experience with the devices of direct legislation in turn influenced its adoption in other countries such as the United States, Australia, and, to a lesser extent, Canada. In our case, Swiss experience has sometimes been invoked negatively to discourage greater democracy, rather than as a positive example to encourage more. A recent instance is that of the 1991 Parliamentary Committee on the Process for Amending the Constitution gently embracing a referendum as part of the amending procedure, while couching its recommendation in an expression of concern for how excessively referendums had been used in Switzerland. Accordingly, the committee refused to recommend that a referendum to ratify amendments be incorporated in the constitution itself, recommending instead that it just be used as a supplementary procedure if the powers that be decided that holding a referendum would be appropriate. The Swiss story had obviously carried greater weight with them than the more apt example of Australia, where the constitution requires a direct referendum to adopt an amendment to the constitution.[3]

A referendum is generally an established procedure provided for by existing constitutional or legislative provisions, while a plebiscite usually arises either by a special legislative act providing for it or by a special initiative of a government, utilizing procedures already provided by statute.

In a referendum, the right is reserved to the people to adopt or reject an act or measure that has been, or is about to be, passed by a legislative body and that, in most cases, would without action on the part of the electors become law. In a plebiscite, by contrast, the choice is exclusively with the government of the day as to whether the subject-matter should even be voted upon.

The distinction about the binding effect of referendums and the non-binding nature of plebiscites is, however, an oversimplification. For example, a government could say in advance that it will be bound by the results of the plebiscite. This has happened with several provincial plebiscites on liquor prohibition. Thus, while the government might have no constitutional or legal obligation to carry out the verdict of the electorate by enacting legislation, it would, because of its stated commitment to honour the results, at least have a strong moral and political obligation to do so. Also, there is a type of referendum that is only binding if it is turned down (whereupon the government must refrain from taking the proposed action). If it is accepted by the people, on the other hand, the government may pass a law at its option to then implement the measure.

Some confusion also arises due to the fact that in statutes of Newfoundland, Quebec, and Yukon, the term "referendum" means what in other Canadian electoral jurisdictions is considered a plebiscite. For example, nowhere in its twenty-five sections did the Newfoundland Referendum Act of 1948[4] contain any binding provisions to suggest what had to happen as a result of the outcome of voting on whether Newfoundlanders favoured "1. Commission of Government for a period of five years, 2. Confederation with

25

Canada, or 3. Responsible Government as it existed in 1933."

Quebec showed this tendency to use these terms interchangeably in 1969, when Bill 55 was introduced in the National Assembly. The purpose of the proposed legislation was "to enable the government to order that the electors of the Province of Quebec be consulted by referendum on any subject which it indicates and upon which it wishes to obtain their opinion." Likewise, Section 7 of the Referendum Act,[5] passed in 1978 states simply that "the electors be consulted by referendum." It contains no provision for making the results of such consultation binding. However, the Quebec statute does provide for a public vote both on a "question," which is traditionally the word used to identify a plebiscite, and on a "law," which conveys the meaning of referendum-type balloting. The obfuscation of the strict legal distinction between referendums and plebiscites is complete in Quebec, where the terms have been blended: there one refers to plebiscites as "consultative referendums."

Classification of Referendums and Plebiscites

Referendums[6] occur in several forms. First, there is a distinction to do with the manner in which the vote arises. Under an *obligatory referendum*, a government *must* refer a matter to popular vote for approval or rejection. This imperative provision is found in the legislative acts that themselves give rise to referendums, such as liquor control acts requiring local option votes, or municipal acts requiring voter approval of money by-laws.

An *optional referendum*, by contrast, arises under statutes that provide that a popular vote on a law may, but need not, be held. Once it is held, however, it will have certain binding consequences. An example is the Fluoridation Act of Ontario.[7] The act gives each council a choice: either vote on your own to introduce fluoride into the municipal water supply, or refer the decision to local voters. Once a council chooses to submit the matter to a popular vote, however, it is bound by the people's mandate.

Such *optional referendums* may also come about through application of the initiative technique, by which a direct vote is triggered as the result of an action initiated, not by government, but by the people themselves. (It is described more fully later in this chapter, and also in Chapter 6.) Normally, a municipal council would have the power to deal with a local question on its own; but, if a petition is received from local electors on their initiative in connection with matters such as local improvements, Sunday activity, or the availability of liquor, a general vote must take place that will bind the council (an obligatory referendum), and may, in some cases, even overrule the council.

A second distinction among referendums is their subject-matter. In this sense, two types appear: *constitutional referendums*, which affect the constitution of the country or province, and *legislative referendums*, which are confined to a specific subject, for example, questions concerning local boundaries and municipal status (such as whether a built-up area is to be designated as a village, town, or city), municipal franchises (for local utilities and transportation services), money by-laws, fluoridation, liquor, libraries, and permitted Sunday activity.

Plebiscites, in contrast to referendums, are not usefully subdivided into any categories. They originate either with a government or with electors, who can cause a non-binding vote to be held in certain limited instances. Because plebiscites simply require the submission of a question to the voters, they can be on any topic. (Although, in the case of municipalities, they must be limited to a question within the jurisdictional competence of local government.) Consequently, there is no basis for categorizing plebiscites on the basis of subject-matter.

The Initiative Technique

The initiative technique, mentioned earlier, is frequently associated with plebiscites and referendums because it springs from the same direct democracy theory of government. On the initiative of a specified number of voters, a popular vote on a proposed law may be provoked. In Canada today this special device in the legislative process is found only at the municipal level and is used for matters such as authorizing Sunday activities under the Lord's Day acts in British Columbia, Alberta, Saskatchewan, Manitoba, Yukon, and the Northwest Territories; introducing fluoride into a municipality's water supply in Ontario; and changing the ward basis for municipal elections in the same province. Formerly, the power of initiative existed at the provincial level as well, but only briefly, and only in western Canada.

In its direct form, an initiative, which is usually a petition, often leads to submitting a by-law straightaway to a popular vote. Under the indirect form, by comparison, the local council has an opportunity on its own simply to enact what is being sought by the petition, rather than taking the step of putting it to the people.

Where a council receives a petition signed by the requisite number of voters and is required by statute to submit a by-law to the electors (dealing, for instance, with annexation of an area in an adjacent urban municipality, or on a question under liquor control legislation) but refuses to do so, the council can be compelled by mandamus to submit such a by-law to the electors in accordance with the terms of the petition or requisition.[8]

In its pure form, the initiative represents a power vested in the people to propose bills and laws, and to enact them at the polls, independent of the legislative assembly or the municipal council. The form of initiative available at the municipal level in Canada is more constrained than that, however; the council also plays a role in the law-making process, and there is usually a further provision allowing the provincial government (through its municipal affairs board or department) to overrule such an enactment according to certain criteria.

From a constitutional point of view, this practice of voters enacting their own laws is somewhat less controversial at the local government level than at the provincial or federal levels, since no royal assent is required for municipal by-laws. Because royal assent is necessary at the provincial and federal levels, however, the initiative process requires a further specific step. This point of constitutional law was clarified in 1916 when the Manitoba legislature enacted the Initiative and Referendum Act, a statute subsequently declared unconstitutional by the courts ostensibly because the constitution requires provincial laws to receive royal assent, and the act did not provide for that procedure.

The Power of Recall

Recall, which is the removal of an elected representative by means of a ballot, has been alien to the Canadian political system.

The power of recall, constitutionally, is either granted to or reserved by the people, depending on the theory of government and sovereignty of the country in question. These procedures for voting to "retire" members of legislatures whom the voters feel have not strictly represented their views, means that such voters can "de-elect" legislators when a departure by the elected representatives from the voters' views is detected.

After the turn of the century, a number of American states, particularly in the west and midwest, adopted this direct democracy procedure. By 1912, eleven states had added general recall provisions to their constitutions, and five had even adopted provisions for recall of elected judges. There are no constitutional or legislative mechanisms allowing for recall at the federal level in the United States, but at the state level, Americans have developed extensive experience with the principles and operation of recall, and today approximately fifteen states provide for recall of state officials, while thirty-six allow for recall of local officials. Only one successful attempt has been made to recall a state governor, while several have succeeded in recalling state officials. Many more unsuccessful state-level attempts have been made. At the municipal level, some 2,000 recalls have succeeded to date.

To institute a recall procedure in the United States, a significant number of signatures from disgruntled people within the electoral district of the official in question is typically obtained. Commonly, 25 percent of eligible voters must sign the recall petition. California requires more signatures for certain offices than for others (for instance, 12 percent for state officers and 20 percent for state legislators or judges). Once the formal petition requirements are completed, a recall election is normally held quite promptly. In some states, the same ballot is used for both the recall and replacement election, a process that certainly seems to prejudge the results as far as the incumbent official is concerned. In other states, two separate votes are held, a method that is certainly more reflective of due process. The first determines whether the office-holder is to be recalled, and the second is held to elect a replacement if he or she has in fact been recalled by the electors. Most states prohibit the recalled individual from running again for the same office. Should the elected official resign from office prior to completion of the recall procedure, most statutes in the United States stipulate that the recall is then automatically terminated, and the vacancy is to be filled according to normal election procedures. In the state of California, the constitution stipulates that the election expenses of the state official who survives an attempt at recall be reimbursed.

Recall is not a legal impeachment process, but more akin to the firing of a representative, and, on this basis in the United States, the courts have generally held that recall is a "political," rather than a "judicial," process. Judicial guarantees protecting the rights of defendants do not apply, therefore, when the recall process is initiated, nor is there any requirement that an official subject to recall be charged with any offence, unless the state legislation (for instance, in Florida and Washington) requires the charging of cause against the office-holder.[9]

This American idea has never caught on in Canada, essentially for three reasons. The first is that it is the monarch, not "the people," who is sovereign here. Secondly, the political theory in our country concerning the role of elected legislators holds that they are not just "representatives" of their constituents, but also "members" of Parliament or of a legislative assembly, and as such have a duty to both. The third and most practical reason is that the interests of constituents are seldom so uniform that an elected representative can be said to be at variance with them. On any given issue an MP's stand will please some constituents and antagonize others.

A world of difference exists between seeking to oust an elected representative because of his or her views or because of the poor quality of representation provided, and trying to remove one who has committed some offence under the criminal code or is guilty of corrupt practices. Criminal prosecution procedures in such cases in Canada are clear and are governed by the statute that deals with disqualification from office. These procedures can give rise to a vacant seat in the House of Commons or legislature. Much of the U.S. experience with recall relates to the removal of corrupt or incompetent elected officials who would otherwise hold office until expiration of their fixed term. In Canada, provisions in statutes such as the Senate and the House of Commons Act, or the various provincial statutes pertaining to the legislative assemblies and provincial constitutions, govern disqualification from office of an elected representative. Legislation relating to conflict of interest may also serve to remove elected officials who have breached the rules of conduct related to holding office. In either case, it should be strongly emphasized that these provisions for removal apply to legal procedures of impeachment, not to political procedures of recall.

Only one real experiment with the recall technique has taken place in Canada, and the story of its fate tells all that need be said about the alien nature of such a procedure to the Canadian political system. In the years following World War I, many members of the United Farmers of Alberta favoured recall. When the United Farmers formed the government of Alberta in 1921, however, their experience soon tempered their view of this device: they were themselves facing the possibility of recall. Because they had achieved direct control of the government apparatus, these United Farmer MLAs rationalized, it was no longer imperative to be able to recall an elected member who voted against agrarian interests. Enthusiasm for the concept faded as a consequence. At the 1924 party conference of the United Farmers of Alberta, a motion calling for the legalization of recall was actually defeated.

The concept of recall was next adopted as part of the platform of the Social Credit movement. During the 1935 general election campaign in Alberta, Social Credit leader William Aberhart pledged to introduce legislation that would provide for the recall of any member of the legislature. Once elected, the Social Credit government duly carried out its pledge, and in April 1936 the Legislative Assembly (Recall) Act[10] was passed by the Alberta legislature – the only such law in Canada.

This statute, consisting of twenty sections and three forms (including the form of petition), provided detailed procedures for unseating a member, but was absolutely silent about the grounds on which electors could petition for a member's recall. Any member who had been recalled could, by virtue of Section 3 of the act, stand for re-election. Only one motion could be made against a member for the same electoral district during the life of a legislature. Perhaps it is worth summarizing how this unique recall procedure actually worked, since the idea is again being promoted in some quarters of Canada today, and is even a plank in the political platform of Preston Manning's Reform Party.

The procedures in Alberta's Recall Act were quite strict and formal, which was fair enough, since the rules specified in the Election Act for electing a representative in the first place were equally precise and designed to weed out frivolity.

The first step involved an application for a recall petition, which had to be signed by at least ten persons whose names were on the voters' list for the last election. These applicants, referred to as the "promoters," had to set out in the application the reason for the recall of the member, and pay a fee of $200. The application was lodged with the clerk of the Legislative Assembly in Edmonton, who took the second step of providing forms of petition to the promoters.

During the next stage the promoters had to obtain the requisite number of signatures on the petition, and the act posed eight hurdles for this requirement. First, the petition had to be signed by more than 66 2/3 percent of the total number of electors on the voters' list for the last election in the electoral division concerned. Second, each signature had to be written in ink. Third, each signature had to be verified by the declaration of an attesting witness on a form provided. Fourth, each attesting witness had to be over the age of twenty-one. Fifth, the petition had to be signed on the forms issued by the clerk of the Executive Council, which were specially marked by him. Sixth, the petitioners not only had to have had their names on the voters' list for the last election but had to be, at the time of signing, duly qualified electors within the meaning of the Alberta Election Act in the electoral division to which the petition related. Seventh, the petition had to be lodged with the clerk of the Executive Council within forty days of its being delivered to the promoters. Eighth, the promoters had to post a true copy of the petition, including all the signatures, in various conspicuous places at or near each post office in the electoral division within ten days of lodging it with the clerk of the Executive Council.

The act also stipulated, in Section 12, that giving or lending any money or money's worth to an elector or any other person on behalf of an elector in connection with signing the petition, or corruptly doing any such act on account of an elector having signed the petition, would cause the petition to be void. Again, just as it was an offence to bribe anyone in connection with an election, the same standard of behaviour applied to the process in reverse, in other words, the recall of a member.

Once the petitions had been delivered by the promoters to the clerk of the Executive Council, the procedure that had to be followed next was also specified in the act. The clerk had to give notice to the chief justice of Alberta, who then fixed a time (not sooner than forty days after the clerk received the petition) and a place for holding an inquiry into the regularity of the petition. Detailed provisions governed the procedure at such an inquiry. In essence, the chief justice had the powers conferred upon a commissioner appointed under the Public

Inquiries Act. The promoters of the petition, as well as the member of the Alberta legislature affected by the petition, were entitled to appear at the inquiry either in person or by counsel. The hearing, as befitted the spirit of democracies, was open to the public.

After hearing all the evidence at an inquiry, if the chief justice was satisfied that the requirements of the act in relation to the petition had been complied with, he would transmit a written report to the clerk of the Legislative Assembly and the clerk of the Executive Council, declaring that a petition had been duly lodged which conformed with the requirements, and that the seat of the member to which the petition related was vacant. Such were the provisions of Canada's first, and so far only, law on recall.

When Purity Encounters Practice

Alberta's Premier William Aberhart came soon enough to regret his bold move in the direction of direct democracy. The Legislative Assembly (Recall) Act proved to be a political boomerang: the first Canadian attempt to recall an elected member of the government was made in 1937, in the electoral district of Okotoks-High River, where the MLA was Premier Aberhart himself.

The intended victim struck back quickly. In October 1937, as historian Agar Adamson explains, the legislature repealed the Legislative Assembly (Recall) Act retroactive to April 3, 1936, the day the original act had received royal assent.[11] All pending proceedings in connection with the recall of any member were declared null and void. "With this," notes Adamson wryly, "the principle of the recall vanished from Alberta and from Canadian politics."[12]

Although the Alberta statute was the only law to enable recall of members of a legislative assembly, several laws that specifically prohibited such a device were also enacted. For instance, Section 104 of the Canada Elections Act[13] was first enacted in 1938 as Section 106 of the new Dominion Elections Act that year. This provision made it an illegal practice and an offence against the Canada Elections Act

> for any candidate for election as a member to serve in the House
> of Commons to sign any written document presented to him by
> way of demand or claim made upon him by any person, persons,
> or association of persons, between the date of the issue of the writ
> of election and the date of polling, if the document requires the

candidate to follow any course of action that will prevent him from exercising freedom of action in Parliament, if elected, or to resign as such member if called upon to do so by any person, persons or associations of persons.

A number of members elected to western Canadian legislatures had signed various types of recall statements in the early decades of this century. These statements, however, like those signed by the Progressive Party MPs elected to the House of Commons in 1921, were unofficial and, notes Adamson, would have had no legal standing if they were ever presented to the speaker of the legislature.[14] After 1938, as noted, they were even prohibited by law.

Elsewhere, when proponents of the recall, initiative, and other direct democracy methods came to power, for instance in Ontario, no such enabling legislation was passed because the leadership of these governments found such measures anathema to the parliamentary system after coming to power. Back in the 1919 general election, for example, the United Farmers of Ontario (UFO) had more candidates elected to the legislature than any other group, and formed a coalition government with a handful of Labour Party members. The UFO, however, being an agrarian movement and not wanting to be seen as a political party, had no "leader." Finally, though, Ernest Charles Drury, a prominent figure in the agrarian movement, was selected to head the United Farmers government and be the province's premier. He flatly rejected recall and other related direct democracy procedures such as the initiative, however. A proud man, the new Ontario premier shifted quickly to defend his position from procedures that could leave him open to attack or criticism. Drury, who soon proved himself to be most maladroit as a politician, was more a farmers' spokesman than a democrat. Observed historian Joseph Schull, "He could work for his friends' goals, but not with his friends' tools."[15]

Semi-direct Democracy

Referendums, plebiscites, and initiatives are voting procedures whereby citizens – in concert with their elected representatives in Parliament, provincial legislatures, and municipal councils – may play a role in making public decisions and enacting laws. Because the traditional law-making procedures remain part of the process, a more accurate expression to describe this form of government is probably "semi-direct democracy," which is the term customarily used by Swiss constitutional lawyers to reflect that country's democratic process. The use of this term, notes Peter Studer, editor of the Zurich newspaper *Tages-Anzeiger*, is appropriate because the Swiss system is bound by a unique combination of representative and direct components.[16] Although it may be too cumbersome an expression to gain popular usage, semi-direct democracy is an accurate description of the actual practices in, as well as the theory behind, most modern democracies.

These instruments of direct or semi-direct democracy, which are sometimes coupled with the concept of recall, may be seen to constitute a challenge in some respects to the traditional pattern of representative government. Although they are variants of the political and legislative processes, the limited extent to which people resort to them indicates, in part, a favourable verdict on the effectiveness of Canada's traditional law-making and political procedures. They can, however, also be seen as an important adjunct to those existing procedures, as a way to supplement and reinforce them for the betterment of all concerned.

That betterment is the extent of what is being advocated in this book. The approach is not an either-or proposition where we must choose *only* representative legislatures or *only* direct voting, but rather an intelligent blending of the two, so that on truly significant issues the people can complement or supplement the process normally engaged in by the representatives they have elected.

The Present Picture

Is present-day support for measures such as recall a symptom of the anger and envy many Canadians feel towards our contemporary political system and our elected representatives, or do we genuinely see them as part of a solution? The seventh annual *Maclean's/ Decima* poll, published January 7, 1991, painted, using the dramatic sorts of expressions so cherished by pollsters and publishers, "an unsettling portrait of a nation that has lost its way," revealing "a massive loss of confidence in politicians and in the political system itself."[17] The poll showed that many Canadians "may now be more ready than ever before to accept fundamental and radical changes in the makeup of their country and its system of government."[18]

The answer to a specific question about "recall" (though the term was not used) showed a majority in favour of a mechanism to remove politicians from office during their term. Pollsters explained how, in the current system, we elect politicians who stay in power until the next election, and then asked some 1,500 Canadians whether they thought this was best, or would they "rather see a system where a majority of voters could sign a petition and remove their elected member any time they wanted?" To this, 44 percent replied they felt politicians should remain in power until an election, 1 percent had no opinion and 55 percent preferred a system where politicians could be removed by petition.

The Reform Party of Canada, meanwhile, true to its western Canadian roots, and representing a further cycle in the rise-and-fall popularity of direct democracy, has advocated the recall of MPs as part of its reform package for the Parliament of Canada. "Reformers believe," stated a 1991 policy pamphlet of the party, under the heading "Recall," "that voters should have a mechanism to remove MPs who will not represent their interests in Parliament."

The Social Credit government of British Columbia under Premier Rita Johnston certainly felt the public mood favoured recall to a degree that warranted putting the question on a referendum ballot. When, therefore, British Columbians went to the polls in the general election of October 17, 1991, they also answered the question: "Should voters be given the right, by legislation, to vote between elections for the removal of their Member of the Legislative Assembly?" The B.C. Referendum Office, in the background information it distributed on the issue to British Columbians prior to the referendum, summarized both the strengths and weaknesses of recall mechanisms by citing the views of several experts on the subject. Four strengths were noted: recall provides one method of removing elected officials who do not meet established standards for public office; recall may encourage increased accountability to constituents and improved performance of elected officials; recall may give citizens an additional reason to become better informed of political issues; and recall may enhance standards of public service and trust expected of elected officials. Conversely, four weaknesses identified were: recall may discourage elected officials from making long-term decisions of province-wide interest or from using personal judgment and experience on behalf of all voters; the threat of recall may induce elected officials to refrain from action so as to avoid conflict or controversy; recall elections may be disruptive, divisive, and costly; and recall mechanisms may require adjustments to a parliamentary system of government.

Determining the suitability of the recall mechanism to the British Columbia government, concluded the background paper issued by the B.C. Referendum Office, "is a complex matter." Simple reference to the use of recall in other countries, it cautioned, does not fully address the issue: "Each country has a unique political system, history and culture." For this reason, it goes on to say, it "is necessary to consider the general strengths and weaknesses of recall, its intended purpose and effect, its history and the unique considerations presented by combining recall with parliamentary government."[19]

The editors of the Victoria *Times Colonist* doubted that recall would generate "a higher quality of democracy in action" and cited the example of the riding of Oak Bay–Gordon Head. If the recall rules required a by-election whenever 20 percent of the electorate in the riding signed a petition requesting one, the 32,000 eligible voters in the riding of Oak Bay–Gordon Head, suggested the *Times Colonist*, could force a by-election – "on any MLA for any reason" – if about 6,200 voters in the riding signed a recall petition. In the previous by-election in the constituency, noted the newspaper, New Democrat Elizabeth Cull, with 10,751 votes, narrowly beat Socred candidate Susan Brice, who had 10,392. Given the polarized politics of the province, collecting signatures from 6,200 voters whose candidate lost may not be all that difficult, and, consequently, "a loser could harass the majority's choice throughout her term in office, no matter what she did or didn't do,"[20] concluded the editors.

To date, initiatives and recall have proven to be fragile seeds on the barren ground of a Canadian political culture dedicated to the stolid precepts of "peace, order and good government" and have been sacrificed to the realities of a representative democracy, not to mention the self-interest of public office holders, epitomized in the complete reversal by true believer William Aberhart himself, when his promotion of the recall idea came full circle. This vignette from our history is worth recalling in the 1990s, as once again some Canadians, especially certain western Canadians, are speaking favourably about the device of recall, and a considerable level of public opinion also appears to favour it.

The more important story of the core concept of direct democracy – holding referendums and plebiscites – has been quite different, however. The quest for direct voting has been relatively much more successful and, as the rest of this book will make clear, now shows far greater promise in being accepted as one means of helping invigorate and restore Canadian democratic life.

3

The Pros and Cons
of Direct Democracy

Although the holding of a public vote on important but controversial matters has itself proven controversial, methods for registering the opinion of citizens on public questions and legislation have existed in a number of forms in Canada in both the nineteenth and twentieth centuries.

The theory of referendums and plebiscites has been advanced and debated in a number of works, most of which date from the time of a progressive movement in Canada and the United States in the late nineteenth and early twentieth centuries. This movement enshrined the concept of "direct democracy" as one of the methods for introducing a new age of reformed, open, and direct public interest politics and government.With the creation of the Progressive Party in 1920 by Ontario and prairie farmers and dissident Liberals led by former cabinet minister Thomas Crerar, a new political formation on the Canadian political landscape championed free trade, nationalization of the railways, and direct democracy. The next year, when the Progressives won sixty-five seats (in the west, Ontario, and New Brunswick) in the general election of 1921, they broke forever the two-party pattern of Canadian politics. Through the 1920s, some Progressives drifted back to the Liberal fold, by 1932 others joined the Co-operative Commonwealth Federation (CCF), and in 1942 still others joined the Liberal-Conservative Party when it changed its name to Progressive Conservative. Lost in this diaspora of Progressives was a single political party championing as one of its fundamental planks the reforms inherent in "direct democracy." Since those days, democrats have found themselves scattered among Canada's several political parties, where they have struggled and often faced great frustration in seeking to advance procedures and programs of a more democratic nature. For many, it seemed as if the quest for direct democracy had become a lost cause, especially when confronted with modern techniques of party control and slick electioneering.

Yet these "old" ideas continue to have currency. They have become enshrined as standard procedures, laws, and institutions in many other democratic countries, and their popularity is again ascending in Canada, a reflection of the growing dissatisfaction and frustration with the workings of today's democratic institutions.

As well as setting the coming Canadian debate on this subject in context and providing tools for analyzing past and present experiences with direct democracy, this chapter considers some of the arguments for and some of those against direct democracy at a theoretical level, several of which have already been touched on in the two preceding chapters.

Compatibility with Representative Parliamentary Government

The reasons Canada is a timid democracy include our tradition of deference to authority, our constitutional precept that sovereignty resides not in the people but in the Crown, and the widespread feeling among the political élite of our country that direct voting by the people on specific measures is an ill-fitting overlay in a parliamentary democracy where citizens elect members of Parliament and governments to run their public affairs and decide issues for them on the basis of the mandate given at the last election. Government, these people feel, should not be so weak that, when facing a difficult question, it throws the issue back to the electors. Those electors have, after all, put the government in office in order to deal with such problems as they arise, they assert, as if that were all there was to the question. The democratic universe for these people consists of two worlds, the rulers and the ruled, and the more the line between each can be kept separate the better.

Such a view came thundering from the bench in 1889 in the case

40

of *Darby v. Toronto*, when Osler J.A. referred to the "pernicious practice . . . of taking a *plebiscite* upon a subject wholly within the discretion of the council, which it is their duty to decide and to take the responsibility of deciding, themselves, without putting the public to expense."[1]

At that time, to be sure, uncertainty as to the validity of municipal plebiscites existed, because the legislature had not expressly provided for them. Clear statutory authority for taking the opinion of the electors in cases in which the vote has no statutory effect was first conferred under the Municipal Act of Ontario in 1903. Before the enactment of this provision there had been some doubt expressed (quite apart from the hostility to such proceedings as conveyed by Judge Osler) as to the legality of such votes.[2] In 1902 Judge Britton said: "There is nothing in the Municipal Act permitting the council to take a *plebiscite*, and there is no express prohibition against their doing so."[3] Prior to that time courts had refused to restrain the taking of a vote on the ground that it was ultra vires, there being no statutory prohibition thereof and no injustice or injury being shown.[4]

A view from the same perspective as Osler's was that of W.B. Munro, who wrote in 1929 that a referendum "asks an opinion from people whose prejudices or emotions or passions are stirred up because an issue is isolated, and whose judgment accordingly lacks the soundness which usually comes during a general election when governmental policy as a whole is under consideration." Munro considered it a "self-evident proposition" that the use of referendums "on any considerable scale would inevitably weaken and demoralize the scheme of parliamentary government which Canada has inherited and developed." Using the metaphor of a horse and buggy, he said that it would be impossible to "drive in double harness responsible government and plebiscites of any sort without getting ditched," for a "ministry cannot serve two masters – the legislative body insisting on one thing and the electorate requiring something different."[5]

Members of this school of thought believe that even where a referendum is constitutional, it is unparliamentary. Neither the plebiscite nor the referendum is seen to be the least bit relevant to the operation of a parliamentary system of government. Decisions in such a system are, and ought to be, made by Parliament, not by the people. Although it is up to a government in a parliamentary system whether to declare that it will be bound by the result of a plebiscite, these people feel it would be unwise for a government to do so on a question about which it cannot be sure. The virtue of the parliamentary system, they say, is that it permits a government to change its mind as circumstances change, without having to go to the people each time to get approval. In contemporary political society, moreover, with the widespread dissemination of information in the news media and the availability of results from public opinion polls, governments can keep in step with public wishes better than the advocates of direct democracy, who were responsible many decades ago for grafting the plebiscite technique onto the Canadian lawmaking system, might have hoped.

The British Precedent Reconsidered

Those Canadians who are quick to assert that direct democracy is incompatible with our system of representative parliamentary government, often add that it is at variance with our inherited British parliamentary practices and undermines the model of Westminster. They assume, in citing such authority and precedence, not only that they bolster their argument, but also that they are correct.

In fact, they are wrong on two counts – failure to take account of democratic evolution in the United Kingdom, where three plebiscites have now been held, and failure to understand that the concept of the referendum has, as noted by Vernon Bogdanor, "a perfectly respectable place in the British political tradition, having been advocated by some of the most perceptive political thinkers this country has seen in the last hundred years."[6]

Throughout the mid-twentieth century, many leading British Conservatives advocated the use of the referendum device in specific circumstances. In 1930, for instance, Stanley Baldwin, leader of the Conservative Opposition, agreed to the proposal made by Lord Beaverbrook (a Canadian, who hailed, ironically, from the only Canadian province never to have sponsored a direct vote) that a referendum be held before a British Conservative government introduce tariff protection legislation.

Winston Churchill also saw an occasional and important role for direct voting on specific questions of transcending importance. In the spring of 1945, Britain's wartime prime minister still hoped to maintain the Coalition in power until the defeat of Japan. It had been ten years since the previous general election, the British Parliament having voted on an annual basis to extend its life by one year as World War II continued. On May 18, 1945, Churchill's hope was enhanced when Labour leader Clement Atlee told him that he was "favourably disposed" to persuading the Labour Party to remain in the Coalition until Japan was defeated.[7] Senior Labour ministers in the Coalition were similarly agreeable to continuing the arrangement. As the next step, Churchill formally wrote to the leaders of both the Labour and Liberal parties, proposing a national referendum be held to ascertain if it was the will of the people that the life of the current Parliament continue until the end of the Japanese war. So firm was the agreement between Atlee and Churchill on holding a referendum that "Atlee asked if, in Churchill's formal letter proposing the continuation of the Coalition, a sentence could be added that the Government would do its utmost 'to implement the proposals for social security and full employment contained in the White Paper which we have laid before Parliament.'"[8] Churchill accordingly did so.

But, later that same month, at the Labour Party's annual conference, the party activists were more anxious "to return to the cut and thrust of Party politics, and the possibility of the first Labour government since 1931. That effectively made sure the Coalition would come to an end."[9] When Atlee telephoned Churchill from Blackpool on the evening of May 21 to tell him there could be no agreement to a referendum, Churchill realized that nothing could save the wartime Coalition. Atlee's letter to Churchill, replying to the prime minister's earlier letter, as part of their agreed-upon correspondence to formally record their referendum plan, arrived a few days later. Atlee now wrote that he "could not consent to the introduction into our national life of a device so alien to all our traditions as the referendum, which has only too often been the instrument of Nazism and Fascism. Hitler's practices in the field of referenda and plebiscites can hardly have endeared these expedients to the British heart."[10]

The British Labour Party and, to a large extent, the New Democratic Party in Canada have opposed direct democracy. One of the premises of socialism, notes Vernon Bogdanor, is that the policies required to secure a socialist order in society "formed a total package, the ingredients of which could not be separated and presented seriatim for inspection by the electorate. It was for this reason that most socialists were opposed to the introduction of the referendum."[11] During much of this century, as British politics proceeded according to the separate theories and sets of policies of the two major parties, Conservative and Labour, support for referendums on specific elements of either party's programs was low. It was only when their ideologically coherent programs began to break on the shoals of hard new issues – such as joining the Common Market or "Devolution" (a mild form of "sovereignty-association," in Canadian terms) for Scotland and Wales – that the parties' supporters could no longer be controlled by the party machines and their whips as in the past. The referendum then became a device, particularly for the British Labour Party, for preserving unity on issues that many MPs considered subordinate. Referendums therefore would allow the party system to continue, but on a more flexible basis.

As the question of British membership in the European Common Market drove ever deeper wedges between the practitioners of British politics and the British public, the argument for increasing public participation in the process was convincingly argued by Conservative MP Philip Goodheart. In his 1971 book, *Referendum,* the respected Tory backbencher, whose sympathy lay with the pro-market forces, expressed his anger at the fact that the voice of the electorate was not to be heard on an issue of such fundamental importance. He argued that the referendum was not an alien device suited only to continental countries and irrelevant to Britain's problems. Goodheart documented how referendums had a perfectly respectable place in Britain's political tradition, having been advocated by Conservative leaders such as Balfour, Baldwin, and Winston Churchill. He further showed, according to Bogdanor, "that referendums, far from being the plaything of dictators and demagogues, had been used by almost all democracies at some time or other without in any way weakening their parliamentary institutions. He demonstrated, therefore, that two of the central arguments against using the referendum in Britain were entirely without substance."[12]

Thus, in 1975 the British came to vote in their first referendum. Adoption of the referendum was in harmony, notes Bogdanor, with the feeling in the country that some form of popular endorsement of the European Economic Community was necessary if the decision to enter was to attain legitimacy. It "defused what could have been a deep populist resentment against politicians who were denying to the electorate the right to decide so central an issue."[13]

In addition to the 1975 vote on Common Market membership, the British have used referendums twice in recent years. In 1973, in an attempt at a new settlement to the problems of government in Ulster, a referendum ballot asked the voters of Northern Ireland whether they wanted the province to remain part of the United Kingdom. In 1979, another was held, as mentioned, to decide on proposals for devolution of government powers to Scotland and Wales.

To point out these facts to British-minded Canadian opponents of referendums often produces tight-lipped nodding, akin to that of a lawyer who has slavishly followed a precedent until someone using common sense points out how and why he is wrong. Such opponents or resisters may consider these three direct votes in the United Kingdom a major departure from accepted constitutional practice by the "mother" of most of the world's parliamentary democracies. Yet those seeking solace from British practice would gain even less succour from British theory. When Bogdanor refers to referendum advocates as "some of the most perceptive thinkers," he means such influential individuals as the great constitutional lawyer A.V. Dicey and such parliamentary leaders as Joseph Chamberlain, Arthur Balfour, James Bryce, and Benjamin Disraeli.

An Offset to Intermediary Organizations

To the proponents of direct democracy, the use of referendums is the preferred technique for bringing about direct rule by face-to-face assemblies of all citizens. While everyone obviously could not participate in the same gathering, the freedom and possibility of holding many town-hall-style meetings would permit far greater interaction and discussion among thoughtful citizens on specific issues – just as we have witnessed in countless gatherings across Canada in late 1991 and early 1992 to discuss the pros and cons of the government's twenty-eight constitutional proposals. Today, using our communications abilities and technology, we have evolved beyond earlier forms of assembly in some respects, but the central concept remains the same.

In a 1911 Fabian Society tract, British publicist C.D. Sharp explained why this line of reasoning in support of public meetings in the community had been especially persuasive in Switzerland and the United States:

> Historically the Referendum is the offspring by unbroken descent of the primitive mass meeting of self-governing citizens. Both in Switzerland and the United States, the only countries where it flourishes today, the whole body of citizens were from the earliest times (in the Swiss cantons from the thirteenth century, and in the American colonies from their foundation) accustomed to exercise all the functions of government for themselves in open assembly.

This direct control over the affairs of state was never entirely surrendered, Sharp contended, and when the assemblies of all the citizens became impracticable and more and more powers had to be delegated to representative councils, "the referendum came into being gradually and naturally, not as an accession of popular power, but as a mere retention by the sovereign people of certain important powers in their own hands."[14]

This vital concept that in a democratic society people retain ultimate power clearly places intermediary organizations in their proper context, and was one of the organizing principles a century ago in the "Progressive Era." During the 1890s, in Canada and elsewhere, the cumulative effects of the evils and abuses of industrialism led many people to recognize the failures of political democracy as it had developed. This was the start of a concerted effort for basic political, economic, and social reforms. The "progressives" spoke about the public interest rather than private interests, and focused their reforms on the abusive aspects of child labour, slums, sweat shops, alcohol, concentration of economic power, business monopolies, wasteful consumption of natural resources, despoliation of the landscape, maldistribution of wealth, limited voting rights, bribery and corruption of public officials, lobbying, worker protests, and farmers' dissent. A wide array of proposals, advanced through the 1890s and up to the start of war in 1914, became new laws and practices at the federal, provincial, and municipal levels – from child welfare, public service reform, educational modernization, factory laws, housing, nationalization of some key companies for the public benefit, election law reform, and use of the plebiscite to counteract the "intermediary organizations" through direct voting by the people.

Progressives not only believed in the importance to society of the unorganized, free individual, but were also hostile to intermediary organizations that distorted the expression of the individual's will and imposed on society governmental policies and practices that represented established, special, or private interests. As summarized by Butler and Ranney: "They believed that truly democratic government consists of all the John and Jane Q. Publics observing, discussing, pondering, deciding, and, finally, voting. The public interest is discovered by their discussions and ponderings, and it is served by the measures which majorities of them adopt when the deliberations have run their course." These authors conclude that for progressives, any intermediary organization seeking to interpose itself between the people and their government "is bound to subvert democracy and the public interest to some degree . . . Only when the power of all intermediary organizations is broken and all obstructions between John Q. Public and his government are removed can true democracy flourish and the public interest triumph."[15]

In contemporary Canada, an offsetting role is especially necessary in the face of intermediary organizations, such as lobbyists and special interest groups, which have gained unwarranted prominence recently.

Legitimization by the People of Major Decisions

Another important feature of referendums is that they can serve to legitimize political decisions a government has taken or proposes to take. A basic argument in favour of referendums, therefore, rests on the dual proposition that all political decisions should be as legitimate as possible and that the highest degree of legitimacy is achieved through decisions made by the direct, unmediated vote of the people. "It is not surprising," say Butler and Ranney, "that perhaps the most widely accepted case for referendums concludes that decisions by referendums are the most legitimate of all."[16]

The particular advantage of the referendum, according to Audrey Marilyn Adams in her study of the use of plebiscites and referendums in British Columbia, is that it "permits the severance of specific issues from political parties and enables the electorate to reject them even though they may have been enacted by the political party which enjoys the support of a majority of the electorate." In this way it becomes "a convenient device from the viewpoint of both the elector and the political party for deciding contentious issues, which might because of their nature be avoided by the party, or, if made a subject of party politics, face the elector with the difficult situation of voting for an issue and against the party which otherwise represents his choice."[17] Adams, moreover, concludes, "On the theory that only the electors' direct vote can effectively commit the electors' consciences, the referendum has a unique advantage for all moral issues."[18]

Elected representatives themselves have different attitudes to their personal duties in cases where laws are submitted for popular assent. With particular reference to municipal councillors, for example, Kenneth Grant Crawford has reported that some believe it is their duty to support or oppose the proposals publicly and to give leadership to the voters, while others take the attitude that the electors should be left to make their own decisions. Some councillors take the position that, where the matters involved will result in expenditures or the granting of franchises, the representatives should strive in council to work out the best possible plan and then allow the people to endorse or reject it. Others believe that in such cases, unless the proposal is a sound one in their opinion, the representatives should not approve of its submission to the electors, on the ground that the electors are entitled to assume that it would not be placed before them for approval if it were not satisfactory to the council.[19]

Seven More Points in Favour of Referendums

Butler and Ranney have found seven positive points for the holding of referendums:

All issues are faced. Through the initiative and referendum, issues which may be divisive or offensive to those in power, and which

48

would not therefore ordinarily be brought into the public forum for debate and resolution, can be put on the law-making agenda by concerned citizens and brought to decision.

Decisions are brought close to the people. When an issue must be resolved by the direct, unmediated votes of the people, rather than at a geographically and psychologically distant legislature, "the government moves close to home and the mystery disappears."

Public decisions are publicly arrived at. Rather than in the sometimes private and often internal procedures by which governments and legislatures make decisions, decisions by referendum are always made in the "clean open air of true democracy" because the signatures on the petitions, the propositions on the ballots, the speeches on the issues, and the results of the votes are all matters of public record, freely available to all.

Popular will is accurately expressed. If government decisions are filtered through a political party or a legislature or any other intermediary organization, they are bound to be distorted to some degree, but when matters are settled by direct legislation it is certain that the government is acting in accordance with the popular will.

Apathy and alienation come to an end. When governments are dominated by special interest groups, boss-controlled parties, and corrupt legislatures, widespread apathy and alienation among citizens result, but if people can control the law-making process through referendums and initiatives and know that they control it, their belief in its value will grow.

The public interest is served. When the people rather than the politicians vote on laws, they will be more concerned for the next generation than the next election.

Citizens' human potentials are maximized. When voting truly controls government, as it does in initiative and referendum elections, it can lead to other forms of popular participation by citizens in the affairs of society and government.[20]

Some Arguments against Referendums

Not surprisingly, there are a range of arguments opposing referendums. Chief among them is that because referendums are open to emotional oratory and to misrepresentation by interested parties, the electorate may, out of confusion, vote on the issue without being aware of its real merits or demerits. Thus, no single party can be held responsible for the consequences of the decision. (The same, of course, can be said of elections and of issues dealt with in an election campaign.) The plebiscite, according to Adams, "also suffers from this defect," and, from the point of view of the electorate, has "the additional defect of permitting the government to get rid of a contentious issue without providing a solution for it." After the plebiscitary vote is taken, the government, while responsible for the consequences if it orders the vote, is nevertheless free to treat the results as nothing more than an expression of opinion and is under no legal obligation to enact legislation on the issue, she suggests.[21]

Another problem is that if a government chooses to hold a plebiscite on a difficult moral issue – for instance, capital punishment – on what logical basis could it then refuse to hold another plebiscite on some other moral issue – say, abortion – which other groups in society consider equally important? The dilemma is, once you start, how and where do you stop?

The fact that in most modern democratic nations referendums are held either infrequently and in unusual circumstances or not at all suggests to Butler and Ranney that "the case against any general use of referendums and initiatives as substitutes for representative assemblies, cabinets, and other elected agencies has had substantially more acceptance and influence than the direct-democracy pro-referendum case."[22]

Lack of Control and Unpredictability

Another of the concerns about referendums is that, because they represent an alternative method of reaching political decisions on important matters, they pose a threat to the established political system and to the control of elected and other established authorities.

There is anxiety, too, because the outcome of a referendum cannot be guaranteed. The 1972 referendum on the European Economic Community in Norway shows two examples of this: first, the verdict of the people ran counter to the consensus of those who held public office; second, the referendum results "badly split both the Liberal and Labor parties, forced the Labor government to resign, and may well have led to a permanent reordering of the Norwegian party spectrum."[23]

Risk of Inconclusive Outcome

That the results of a referendum are not always clear is another cause for concern. Before Newfoundland joined Confederation in 1949, for example, three alternative relationships and systems of government had been considered. The results of the June 3, 1948 plebiscite, however, showed that no majority of voters were in favour of any of these choices. The British government had stipulated that a clear majority would be required for victory, and said that if a second ballot were necessary the form of government receiving the smallest number of votes on the first round would be dropped from the second ballot paper. A run-off referendum was accordingly held on July 22, 1948, since a procedure to resolve the problem of uncertainty had happily been provided.

Another example of an uncertain outcome involves Quebec. In the late 1970s debate about the separation of Quebec from Canada, Premier René Lévesque suggested successive votes on the question be held until an affirmative vote had been received from the electors of Quebec. During the campaign for the April 1981 Quebec general election, which came one year after the sovereignty-association option had been rejected by the voters of Quebec in the first of such referendums on the question, however, Premier Lévesque clarified this point somewhat. He indicated that another vote would at least not be held during the life of the next National Assembly. In response to Lévesque's suggestion that a succession of referendums be held until the desired result had been obtained by the Parti Québécois, Prime Minister Pierre Trudeau stated that if the negative votes in a referendum were not binding on the government of Quebec, then neither would the positive votes in such a referendum be binding on any of the other governments.

The recommendation in 1991 by the Bélanger-Campeau Commission that another referendum on Quebec independence be held prior to October 1992 recalls Lévesque's plan.

Illustrative of the uncertainty problem at the local government level was the plebiscite held in Ottawa in the 1930s when several choices were given as to changes in the nature of the elected council. None of the choices won a majority, the results were quite contradictory, and the whole exercise became a farce.

Such mixed results reflect the ambiguities in Canadian society itself. While the plebiscite in Saskatchewan on the question of time zones, which is discussed in detail in Chapter 4, is a classic example of inconclusive results, another illustration common to many provinces is that of plebiscites on the question of liquor. Severe social and economic problems associated with the abuse of alcohol in Canada's early years, and the resulting efforts to establish liquor control, created a major political issue in virtually every Canadian community. The uneven experience with prohibition plebiscites, which is also examined in Chapter 4, shows how a reference of the liquor question to the voters could be inconclusive. This, again, reflects the ambiguities that existed in Canadian society as it grappled for more than half a century with the problems of alcohol abuse and with questions regarding the appropriateness of prohibition and government control.

Our history reveals that, in referring matters to voters in a plebiscite, not just once or twice but even three times, complex issues that cannot be resolved in a speedy, clearcut fashion, can eventually just become worn out. To suggest that an inconclusive outcome denotes the failure of the referendum technique, however, rather than being a reflection of deep ambiguities in society or of the fact that an issue is not yet ripe for resolution, or even simply the consequence of a poorly worded question, is an unnecessarily harsh judgment of this instrument of direct democracy. After all, one could also condemn general elections, which frequently produce inconclusive results, either by returning a minority government or by failing to give a clear "mandate" on some issue, and yet no one seriously suggests we stop holding elections.

Can Ordinary People Decide an Important Issue Wisely?

A third concern of those opposed to referendums is the supposed inability of ordinary citizens to make wise decisions. This thought seems born of an anti-democratic instinct, although it may simply be based on the idea that "elected representatives are better qualified to make such decisions, not because they are necessarily more intelligent or more public spirited, but because they are paid to spend full time on government affairs."[24]

Forcing the Issue

Whereas pro-referendum theorists speak about the "popular will being accurately expressed," the opposition says that the inherent nature of a referendum is in fact to divide an issue simplistically into two camps: pro or con, yes or no. Thus the ultimate goal of decision making in a truly democratic society may not be, as Butler and Ranney say, "a vote which identifies how many citizens support each of two irreconcilable alternatives" but rather a "consensus, a sense of the meeting, a general agreement that a particular course of action is the best way of promoting the interests of all the citizens. This ideal solution can be realized only by discussion among people who know and respect each other and who seek the truth, not forensic triumphs over their neighbours."[25]

In her study of the referendum and plebiscite experience in Saskatchewan, Elizabeth Chambers concluded that resorting to a popular vote, even if only an advisory plebiscite, "while it may make it possible for a government to gain time and thus perhaps avoid a party split or the loss of substantial electoral support, does not enable it to escape entirely from an awkward situation arising from being subjected to strong conflicting pressures."[26]

How an appeal to the voters is handled can thus be an important matter of high politics. The vote sometimes becomes a means to defeat or delay a proposal, or to gain popular support. At the municipal level when a councillor finds he cannot secure sufficient votes in council to defeat or to carry a proposal, Kenneth Grant Crawford explains, "he may move that the people be consulted . . . a very difficult request to oppose in a popularly elected body." The member who proposes the appeal to the electors may do so, suggests Crawford, in the hope that the electors will vote for the action for which he could not secure sufficient support in council. "If his purpose is to defeat the proposal, particularly where it involves the expenditure of money, he may attain that end by having several other money expending issues submitted at the same election so that the voters, confused and frightened by the grand total, will vote against all of them."[27]

Influence of Mass Media on Referendums

For proponents of direct democracy, the referendum is seen as a direct link between the people and government, a modern-day equivalent of the town meeting, where all citizens gather to discuss and resolve public policy. Critics, however, point out that since all voters could not possibly meet face to face, much of the discussion in a referendum campaign takes place through the mass media. There is still an intermediary between the public and the government, but instead of its being the politicians and bureaucracy, it is the news media.

Legislative Process in Contrast to Referendums

The important attributes of a legislature, in comparison with those of a referendum, have been ably summarized by Butler and Ranney:

> Representative assemblies are far from perfect, but they have several crucial advantages over referendums: their members meet face to face regularly; they do not immediately or necessarily vote up or down every measure that comes before them; they discuss, refer, study, delay, amend, and give and take. Their decisions only occasionally approach unanimity, but their discussions approach the small-group ideal far more closely than the discussions preceding referendums. Even in national legislatures votes are mainly expedients to get decisions when the time available for discussion has run out. In referendums votes are the very essence of the decision process.[28]

Many of the other arguments one finds in the literature on direct democracy are more relevant to countries where "initiative" provisions are established by law, permitting a group of citizens to initiate referendums on particular subjects. This is clearly not the case in Canada, where initiatives are only available at the municipal level or, rarely, on a province-wide basis to selected economic groups (such as farmers), on particular issues and under specific statutes.

Often the questions submitted to the electors are quite controversial, such as prohibition of liquor, conscription of men for military service, introduction of a chemical (fluoride) into the local water supply, and the question of separation of one province from the rest of the federation. These questions are complex, and it is often hard to state them simply or adequately in a single ballot question for the electors. So the issue may be simplified, or only stated in part. Anger and frustration sometimes result among voters who feel there is no scope for the proper reflection of their views on the question. Yet this is the same dynamic that operates in a legislature, around a cabinet table, or in a prime minister's mind. At the end of the day, a decision must be made. Is it yes, or no? Is it stay, or go? Do we have a trade treaty? Do we go to war? Do we change the tax system? The argument of complexity can be a convenient excuse for temporizing, or delaying a hard decision. Yet for all – a leader or an entire society – the final question is the same: yes or no?

"Generally speaking," concludes Agar Adamson, writing more than a decade ago,

> the concept of direct legislation appealed to those who had a special case to advance – a class interest, a moral reform such as temperance, or a "grand idea" to remedy the West's problems. The Canadian advocates of referendum politics today are in many respects the rightful heirs of the devotees of direct legislation in 1911.[29]

For better or for worse, referendums and plebiscites have long been and remain a fact of Canadian political and legal life. For better, say those who see a referendum as a means of giving a greater, clearer voice to the people; for worse, counter those who see referendums as a pernicious unparliamentary practice.

For better, too, say those who see the occasional necessity of extracting a highly controversial issue from the normal parliamentary processes (which might be badly ruptured if members are forced to deal with the issue by the traditional non-compromising means of party discipline and cabinet solidarity) and turning it over to the people as a whole for a verdict by means of voting.

For worse, would respond those who instead see such appeals to the public as highly dangerous and unpredictable devices for resolving an issue, given that battle lines must be simplistically drawn between "yes" and "no," rather than permitting the usual compromising procedures of Parliament.

Others, though, more critical of the practice and operation of governments and legislatures, and imbued with a deeper faith in democracy, contend that referendums and plebiscites mean issues are squarely faced; public decisions are publicly arrived at; popular will is accurately expressed; apathy and alienation are reduced; and people have a greater voice in major political decisions. For these reasons, they argue, the use of referendums should be encouraged and extended.

In considering a number of the disadvantages and advantages of direct voting, Butler and Ranney summarize several key arguments. Referendums by their very nature set up confrontation rather than encouraging compromise. They divide the populace into victors and vanquished. They force decisions often before the discussion process has had a chance to work itself out fully. Surely, they conclude, this is a great deficiency. "Yet," they say,

> in every polity there are times and circumstances when some decision is better than no decision, when continuing delay is itself disruptive of consensus and good temper, when the likelihood of working out a just compromise that will please everyone is slim or nonexistent. In such a situation the referendum has at least one great virtue: not only will it produce a decision, but the decision it produces is, in this democratic age, more likely to be regarded as legitimate and therefore acceptable than is a decision produced indirectly by elected officials.[30]

4

Some Fundamentals of Fair Referendums

Once the decision is made to hold a plebiscite, as has been done in Canada twice on a country-wide basis and over sixty times in the provinces, some basic issues arise about how to conduct the vote. Since practical considerations of holding fair referendums and plebiscites loom with new urgency in Canada these days, this chapter focuses on six of these fundamentals.

The six subjects are (1) the impartial administration of, and sincerity of purpose in holding, the vote; (2) the nature and validity of the question being voted on; (3) the wording of the question; (4) the timing of the vote; (5) the provision of information to voters; and (6) the financing of the campaigns. By examining each of these, some standards and criteria can be clarified prior to considering other important aspects of direct voting, dealt with in subsequent chapters.

Impartial Administration of the Referendum, and Sincerity of Purpose in Consulting the People

The right of a citizen to vote on a law is meaningless unless the balloting is protected by impartial administration, and the government is sincere in seeking a real expression of popular thinking on the matter in question. This, of course, was not the case in 1930s Germany, for example, when Hitler's plebiscites, with their 99-percent affirmatives, "cast a cloud over the whole idea of referring specific questions to the voters."[1] Similarly, between 1956 and 1976, Egypt held nine referendums that never yielded less than 99.8

percent "yes" votes, although in May 1978 a referendum was reported to have produced only a 97.8 percent "yes" result.

Overwhelmingly lopsided referendum results are not necessarily the result of manipulation, especially if a referendum is *required* by law, although one ought to be sceptical about extreme results One might, suggest Butler and Ranney, take at face value, for example, the results in 1905 when Norway voted 99.9 percent for separation from Sweden, in 1944 when Iceland voted 99.5 percent for separation from Denmark, and in 1967 when Gibraltar voted 99.6 percent to keep its ties with the United Kingdom.[2] Yet because these numbers so favour one side of the question, one is at least entitled to ask a few questions. More reflective of the normal diversity one might expect, even on a question the answer to which seems a foregone conclusion, were the 1990 and 1991 votes in Estonia, Latvia, and Lithuania, when each of these Baltic republics, which had been forcibly annexed in 1940 by the Soviet Union, voted 79, 77, and 90 percent, respectively, for independence from the U.S.S.R.

The closely controlled and hegemonic referendums used by communist and fascist regimes and by many new states where competitive democratic processes have not taken root are obviously different in all fundamental respects from the relatively open voting procedures in effect when laws or questions are submitted to voters in Canada. Perhaps their only common feature is the general purpose of giving a special legitimacy to a particular institution or to a specific course of action.

The best recent example in Canada of a plebiscite illustrating the importance of impartiality is the 1980 Quebec vote on sovereignty-association. The Referendum Act of Quebec requires the creation of "national committees," which are umbrella organizations set up to represent each of the two options or sides in a plebiscite. All those who wish to participate in the campaign – including members of the Quebec National Assembly, groups, and organizations – must register with the committee of their choice. The act imposes restrictions on the campaign activities of the two umbrella committees. Each receives financial assistance from the Quebec government, in the amount voted by the Assembly, on an equal basis.[3]

Administratively, the 1980 referendum in Quebec was conducted efficiently and, in general, fairly. The electoral lists were comprehensive and the voting was carried out smoothly and fairly. Even if the victory had been a narrow one – the result was 60 percent to 40 percent – the referendum would not have been open to any serious challenges on technical grounds. The care and forethought of those responsible for organizing the referendum, combined with the responsible spirit of the electors who participated in the process, made the exercise an admirable example of democratic decision making. A traumatic issue that aroused strong emotions was, at the end of a long debate, put to the people.

In all aspects of administering plebiscites, from the preparation of voters' lists to scrutiny of the balloting, from enforcing the spending limits to the wording of the question, the greater the impartiality of the process, the clearer the mandate from the people will be.

In cases where a public vote on a question either cannot be brought about by the positive action of citizens or is not required by law, but rather depends entirely on a decision by the government, the motivation of the government in so acting may well form a context in which an impartial process will be difficult. The people may simply be called in as a standing jury to register a verdict when, for reasons sufficient to the government of the day, it is felt that the political and decision-making process requires this public seal of approval. The governments of many countries with optional referendums have chosen to invoke them only infrequently, and in special circumstances.

As will be shown later, some Canadian plebiscites were not motivated by a sincere interest in obtaining a public verdict on an issue, but more to help a government get out of a predicament, or to perfunctorily honour a promise too easily made in an election campaign. Insincerity of purpose is a poor basis for a referendum.

Nature and Validity of Questions Voted Upon

The destinies of populations and territories is perhaps one of the most profound questions dealt with by plebiscites. In Europe, the plebiscite was first used during the French Revolution to legitimize wholesale annexations of territories made by the conquering French republic and subsequently employed by Napoleon I for similar purposes.

This practice, which has continued into this century, also shows how the direct-vote procedure cannot be isolated from the broad political context in which it takes place. In one case, the ebbing and flowing power and rivalries between France and Germany set the broader stage for a plebiscite held January 14, 1935. Citizens of the Saar region between France and Germany, which had been administered by the League of Nations since 1920, voted to return the region to Germany. Another plebiscite in the Saar in 1947 favoured a return to France. Finally, on October 25, 1955, a third plebiscite rejected a Europeanization proposal and led to a Franco-German agreement in 1956 that reunited the Saar with Germany.[4]

In Canada, questions to settle the destinies of peoples and territories have usually been dealt with directly by government, but have occasionally been submitted to the people for a direct vote. A major example is the Newfoundland plebiscite in 1948 on entering Confederation. The 1980 vote in Quebec on continuation in Confederation and the proposals by non-separatist groups or peoples in areas within Quebec to hold their own plebiscites about remaining part of Canada in the event of Quebec separation are other examples of citizens' asserting their right to vote on territorial matters. In 1982, the question of whether the Northwest Territories ought to be divided in two was put directly to its people in a plebiscite.

The questions submitted to provincial plebiscites have covered an interesting range of topics. The mixture reflects the same diversity of issues that come before legislatures: from ownership of power companies, women's suffrage, public health insurance, and time zones, to prohibition and control of alcohol, marketing of grains, sovereignty-association, and large-scale construction projects.

Municipal-level votes sometimes also concern territorial boundaries and status questions. For instance, they may deal with the formation of a local government, the granting of municipal status (as a village, a town, or a city), or annexation of one territory by another. These arise under various provincial statutes and often are of a plebiscitary (or non-binding) nature, although in certain instances the outcome of such a vote does settle the question, making it, legally, a referendum. Other municipal questions range from Sunday sports to liquor sales, from fluoridation of the water supply to bond issues, from utility franchises to matters affecting roads or the structure of a local council. Beyond this, the nature of local plebiscites has varied considerably because of the power to submit "any question" over which a council has jurisdiction to the electors directly. This power has even been extended (wrongly, in my view) to permit municipal plebiscites on global nuclear disarmament.

As to the validity of laws enacted at the municipal level where voters must assent by a vote, a considerable body of Canadian jurisprudence has developed. Many such cases grew out of the squirming efforts of local councils to avoid compliance with the statutory provisions that required a vote to be held on certain questions or by-laws. In these instances, the local government tried to deny citizens their statutory right and was quite properly taken to court by the offended local citizenry. This anti-democratic action by some councils stands in sharp contrast to that of others whose members actively sought to give greater scope to direct democracy than the provincial legislation governing municipalities in fact allowed. Thus our jurisprudence also includes cases at this other end of the democratic spectrum, involving the submission of matters to a vote by electors in a plebiscite where there was no authority for doing so. In these instances, not surprisingly, the courts held such proposed plebiscites to be constitutionally beyond the powers of the municipality, and therefore invalid.[5]

Even where the submission of a "question" to voters is proper, other court cases have examined the subject-matter being voted on, and as a result judges have established several important principles. For instance, as to what constitutes a "municipal question," the courts have ruled that what goes on the ballot in a local plebiscite need not be confined to matters over which municipal councils are expressly assigned jurisdiction, although the questions cannot be too far-ranging or nebulous.

The leading case in this area of interpreting what constitutes a "municipal question" is *Re Jones and Toronto*,[6] in which Chief Justice J.C. McRuer of the High Court of Ontario found it very doubtful that a question submitted to the voters was truly a "municipal question" within the meaning required by the Municipal Act, since it amounted to "little more than a canvass of the electors as to their views on a matter of provincial legislative policy as applied to the City of Toronto." No proposed course of municipal action was supported by the by-law, explained McRuer, nor was the council asking for the opinion of the electors on a matter on which it proposed to take action itself.

Chief Justice McRuer outlined, in a passage which has been quoted and relied on in a number of subsequent judicial decisions relating to municipal plebiscites, a test for determining municipal plebiscite subject-matter. While he felt it was not necessary for him to define exactly what is or is not a municipal question, McRuer noted that, "viewed in one aspect, the matter of what action a municipal council may wish to take concerning proposed steps to get power to restrict or control the sale of intoxicating liquor in the municipality might well be a municipal question." This approach had been suggested, he observed, by the late chief justice of the High Court in 1938 in the case of *Re Thomas and Hamilton*.[7] McRuer hesitated to hold that the meaning ascribed to the words "municipal question" in Section 404(11)[8] was restricted to those questions over which the municipality had jurisdiction expressly conferred on it by statute. McRuer concluded,

> I think that if a municipal council wishes to have an expression of the views of the municipal electors on a matter over which the council proposes to apply for legislative power, it might well have power to submit such a question to the electors; or if the municipal council desires to have an expression of the views of the electors on some proposed course to be followed, even though further legis-lative power may be necessary, it might well be considered to be a municipal question.

In the case of *Lippert v. Greenock*,[9] a decision of Mr. Justice Wells, the question for the voters was whether a certain road in the township should be transferred to the county system. The judge simply stated that "the matter of a county road system is one that is within the jurisdiction of the county and not the township council."[10] He quoted the criteria set down by Chief Justice McRuer, saying,

It might well be that, if such consent were necessary, the question proposed to be asked the electors of Greenock Township would be a municipal question within the meaning of s. 386(19) of The Municipal Act, but I do not think that it can be said in the present instance that that section has been invoked by any of the legislative authorities concerned. It may be that it can be fairly said that the subject-matter of the by-law before me is very close to the border-line of the powers of the township council, but in my view it is outside them. Moreover, the question asked is not asked pursuant to any action which the township council may take.[11]

Where the course taken by the County Council of Bruce is concerned, he felt, the township council obviously is not entitled to be consulted as to what roads are to be county roads. The by-law did not, Wells thought, using the criteria of McRuer, support "any proposed course of municipal action."

In the 1949 case of *Re Lillis and Kingston*,[12] the rather loaded question on the municipal ballot was: "Are you in favour of having the salaries, holidays and other working conditions of Kingston City employees fixed by a person appointed by the provincial Government rather than by the City Council which is responsible to the municipal electors?" In this case, Mr. Justice Urquart also followed the test devised by Chief Justice McRuer.

The criteria established by McRuer were again applied in 1980 by Mr. Justice Hollingworth in *Attorney General of Ontario ex rel. Dorion v. Penetanguishene*.[13] This case involved the submission of a question to electors in the Penetanguishene area of Ontario, pursuant to the Municipal Act of Ontario, asking whether they supported the decision of the Ministry of Education and County Board of Education to build a separate French-language school in the area. The court held that a by-law passed by a municipal council that provides for asking electors such a question was not one that the council could submit to electors pursuant to the Municipal Act. Hollingworth concluded that the matter is not within the legislative jurisdiction of the municipal council, nor is it one over which the council proposes to or can apply for legislative power. Matters of education policy are for the board, not the council. Consequently, the by-law was held to be ultra vires, or beyond the council's constitutional powers.

Another principle, established in a 1965 British Columbia case, is that the courts may restrain further action on a plebiscite question if there has been an irregularity in the vote.[14] It has also been judicially determined that if, in submitting a ballot question on a matter for which the council has power to act, council attempts to substitute the direct decision of the electors for that of the council to which the law has assigned it,[15] the vote is illegal. In such circumstances it is seen as an invalid delegation to the voters of the council's power to make the decision. It is beyond the scope of this book, however, to examine in detail the requirements for valid municipal law making. The main point here is that citizens do have a legal right to an intermittent role in the law-making process, and that it is a right that Canadian courts have protected and clarified.[16]

In addition to legal rules and the statutory framework for municipal plebiscites, questions of political judgment also enter the picture in deciding the nature and validity of questions voted upon. As mentioned, municipal votes to create "nuclear-free zones" came into vogue in the late 1970s and early 1980s. That they did displays how this instrument of democracy can be misused in the sense that the question was simply not a valid one to be submitted by a municipality according to the constitutional division of powers between levels of government in Canada, any more than the Parliament of Canada ought to busy itself creating a series of one-way streets in a particular municipality.

"Do you support the goal of general disarmament and mandate your government to negotiate and implement, with other governments, the balanced steps that would lead to the earliest possible achievement of this goal? Yes? No?" That was the plebiscite question, or at least one version of it. Like responding to the adroitly worded questions in referendums submitted to the citizens of the Fifth French Republic by President Charles de Gaulle, or to those of Adolf Hitler's plebiscites, which invariably generated affirmative responses, it was hard to say no to this proposition.

The disarmament question was posed to voters in municipalities ranging from large cities such as Toronto and Ottawa to small towns such as Paris, Ontario, and Mount Waddington and Zebalos, both in British Columbia. I wondered at the time whether the leaders of the United States and the Soviet Union were to meet with the Council of Zebalos as it sought to implement its mandate. No, I learned upon inquiry, the plebiscite results from Zebalos would simply be sent to Prime Minister Pierre Trudeau, the Parliament of Canada, and the United Nations.

Impetus for these plebiscites came in some measure from the Ottawa-based organization Operation Dismantle, led by former university professor James Stark. Then Ontario Liberal leader David Peterson sent a letter to 515 Ontario municipalities urging them to include a question on global nuclear disarmament on municipal election ballots. Although inclusion of this issue on the ballot had been approved by several dozen municipalities, others held back, awaiting legal clarification.

The legal issue was simple: global disarmament is not a proper matter of municipal government. Section 208(25) of the Municipal Act of Ontario, for example, only authorizes the holding of a plebiscite on a "municipal question." If the holding of such a plebiscite were to have been challenged in court, a judge presumably would have wasted little time deciding that disarmament did not satisfy the McRuer test of a municipal council jurisdiction. Legal opinion seemed settled on this point. What was unsettled, and in some respects unsettling, was the response by a number of elected representatives. City councils in Ottawa and Toronto voted to hold disarmament plebiscites in the face of legal opinions from their solicitors advising that council had no legal authority for doing so. According to press reports at the time, Toronto Alderman Anthony O'Donohue, supporting the resolution, called it "a good idea, irrespective of whether it's legal or illegal" and Alderman June Rowlands said the issue was so important it was worth taking the risk of breaking the law.

Others were more mindful of the rule of law and the concept that there can be no exemption for officials from the duty of obedience to a law which governs others in the same circumstances. Some councils, although desiring a plebiscite, had nevertheless decided to restrain themselves until the law was changed, not wanting to set a bad example by acting outside the legal framework that governed them. In this vein, an effort was made to change the law. At Queen's Park, Herbert Epp, Liberal MPP for Waterloo North at the time, introduced a private member's bill to amend Section

208(25) of the Municipal Act so as to authorize municipalities to include a question concerning nuclear disarmament on election ballots. The bill did not pass, so the legal obstacle remained.

While holding such a plebiscite would not have invalidated the general election of councillors, taking place at the same balloting (as the Ontario Ministry of the Attorney-General had incorrectly suggested it would initially), the holding of the plebiscite could have been open to challenge by disgruntled taxpayers. For example, the nuclear disarmament plebiscite in Toronto would have added an estimated $10,000 to the cost of the election.

Indeed a legal challenge was made in the County Court by a number of Toronto residents and voters, against the City of Toronto, who were seeking a declaration that the plebiscite about support for nuclear disarmament was void. In a decision rendered July 6, 1984, however, Judge Hoilett failed to address the substantive issue of whether a plebiscite on the issue of nuclear disarmament was a proper "municipal question" to appear on a City of Toronto ballot. Instead he dismissed the case on the grounds of the "threshold" stipulation, which required the plaintiffs to have had the by-law itself quashed as invalid within the statutory time limit. In short, the issue was thrown out of court on procedural grounds.[17]

Earlier in British Columbia the same issue had come before that province's Supreme Court in the Oak Bay nuclear disarmament plebiscite case. A disarmament referendum committee had been at work in Oak Bay, as in other municipalities of British Columbia, and the propriety of direct voting in a plebiscite on nuclear disarmament in conjunction with municipal elections had already received close attention. At the September 22, 1982, meeting of the Union of B.C. Municipalities Convention, for example, the province's minister of municipal affairs had advised against passage of municipal by-laws to hold referendums on nuclear disarmament because he had concluded that legally it was not a municipal matter. A similar conclusion had been reached by W.E. Cochrane, the returning officer who would be called upon to conduct such a vote if the council of Oak Bay authorized it.[18] The Municipal Act of B.C., in Section 283, empowered a municipal council to pass a by-law which would "provide for a referendum at the time prescribed for elections . . . to obtain the electors' opinion on a question that affects the municipality and with which the council has power to deal." On October 28, 1982, Oak Bay Council met and gave first, second, and third readings to "Referendum By-law (Disarmament) 1982." On November 1, 1982, council again met, reconsidered, adopted, and finally passed the by-law. In spite of the express requirement of the Municipal Act that the referendum be on a subject "with which the Council has power to deal," the referendum which Oak Bay Council had decided to submit to municipal voters was the following:

> Do you support the goal of general disarmament and encourage your federal government to continue its efforts to negotiate and implement, with other governments, a progressive mutual reduction in the world's stockpile of nuclear and other weapons of mass destruction, subject to effective verification, and implemented in such a way as to sustain a stable balance between the nations of the world?

A significant and rather startling development relating to this plebiscite was the fact that the costs of the referendum were to an extent underwritten by the disarmament referendum committee, rather than by the municipality of Oak Bay itself. In other words, a special interest organization had been able, working through members of the council, to purchase the use and operation of public law and a public electoral process, and had succeeded in doing so against the legal advice of the provincial minister of municipal affairs and the returning officer.

Important legal issues relating to the holding of this plebiscite clearly needed to be confronted. Soon enough, Bruce Douglas Baird, an elector residing in Oak Bay, filed a petition in the British Columbia Supreme Court asking for an injunction prohibiting the proposed referendum. Mr. Justice Proudfoot, giving his decision orally on November 18, 1982, just two days before the municipal election when the referendum would be held, concluded that the question of nuclear disarmament is a matter that affects the municipality. "When dealing with a subject of the magnitude of nuclear disarmament which affects not only a municipality but the entire universe and the possible devastation of large portions, the section[19] should have a broad and liberal interpretation," he said. Proudfoot

J. could see "no reason why it would not be within the power of the municipal council of Oak Bay to make representations to other levels of government concerning nuclear disarmament if the electors' opinion gives the municipal council that mandate." The judge did not think that the rule of law would "be damaged, tarnished, or undermined if such a by-law to deal with these particular and very special circumstances" were allowed to stand. He dismissed Baird's application, and the plebiscite took place.[20]

Unlike the Toronto nuclear disarmament plebiscite case, the Oak Bay case addressed the substantive issue, but in a judgment singularly lacking in legal analysis, and gave an extraordinarily broad approach to the lawful use of municipal referendums. In contrast to this ruling are such cases as *In Re: Dorion and Penetanguishene,*[21] which, as described above, took a much narrower approach and held that even a by-law providing for a referendum on the building of a French-language school in the municipality was not a municipal question. If the school board wished to build a French-language school, there was nothing the council could do about it legally. This, the Ontario Supreme Court suggested, was a purely political question to assist the municipalities in intervening with the authorities. On that ground, the court held that the by-law providing for the referendum was ultra vires. Unlike the British Columbia Supreme Court, its Ontario counterpart was not prepared to look kindly on "a purely political question" and confined itself to a court's more traditional and more appropriate role of just interpreting the law.

As it turned out, some 132 municipalities across Canada held plebiscites on nuclear disarmament in late 1982. Predictably, given the wording of the question, the anti-nuclear voters outnumbered by nearly four to one voters who supported the use of nuclear weapons. Legal aspects about holding a municipal plebiscite on a national and international issue were shunted aside in the well-orchestrated campaign. James Stark, who, as already mentioned, was the leader of Operation Dismantle, said the results showed "a tremendous concern among Canadians and a dissatisfaction with what our Government is doing. Canadians want leadership out of their government and they're not getting it."[22] Operation Dismantle would use plebiscite results "to press the United Nations for a world-wide referendum on disarmament," Mr. Stark said. "The issue is too damn important to be left in the hands of generals and politicians. We want to establish a mandate from the whole human race for global disarmament." Significantly, some 137 federal MPs joined forces in this effort to convince the 4.6 million Canadians eligible to vote on the matter, because they lived in the municipalities where the question would appear on the ballot, to support disarmament.

A municipal plebiscite on this subject of disarmament misleads a great many people, abuses the direct voting technique which has a limited but useful role in our system of government, and provides an imperfect signal to Ottawa. For instance, the vote across Canada was held not on a nationwide basis – as it was being done at that same time in Spain, for example – but on a fragmented basis where some municipalities held a plebiscite on the nuclear question but most did not. Further, given that the question was so worded that it was virtually impossible to vote against it, the result was that the electors had probably made no decision on the matter.

The municipal plebiscite on nuclear disarmament was judged by University of Toronto political science professor Peter Silcox to be a "misuse of power" by municipal politicians. Municipal governments "already have enough to worry about without taking on issues which have no clear relation to their role," he said.[23]

Nuclear questions have not been the only areas, however, in which municipalities strayed across the line in their enthusiasm to put questions on the ballot. For instance, in the same 1982 Ontario municipal elections when disarmament was addressed, voters in Gloucester, near Ottawa, also voted on how they felt about capital punishment, tougher criminal laws, and a reform of prison sentences to fight violent crime – all matters of federal jurisdiction.

Nuclear disarmament was not a bad idea, or unimportant; just the opposite. Nor was a plebiscite itself inappropriate for seeking such an expression of public opinion in Canada, since "direct democracy" clearly has a place in the Canadian political system. Within the Canadian constitutional framework, however, a vote on disarmament could only properly have been held at the national level, given the reality of the federal system's division of powers, where Ottawa alone deals with such international and military matters. Having jurisdictional power to do something concrete with the people's mandate, once it is rendered, is a vital element in deciding the nature and validity of questions voted upon in plebiscites.

Wording of Questions

The courts, as well as common sense, dictate that any question submitted to electors be stated in the clearest possible terms if voters are to respond intelligently and the legislative body concerned is to understand their wishes. The question in a plebiscite should be clear, simple, and direct, explained an Alberta court early in this century, and should not refer to considerations which might influence the voters or contain uncertainties, probabilities, and possibilities which might tend to confuse them.[24]

When the wording of the plebiscite question makes it virtually impossible to vote any way but one, the result is that the electors in fact probably make no decision on the matter.

The "loaded" question is perhaps the greatest risk. A minor example was cited above in the case of a question in the city of Kingston, the wording of which played to sentiments that would have made it hard for any self-respecting, civic-minded Kingstonian to vote "yes." Ambiguity in the wording that allows for more than one interpretation of the question (and consequently of the result) can likewise defeat the purpose of the vote, unless this is the intent of sponsors of the plebiscite, who are, therefore, being insincere with voters about their motives for holding it.

An example of ambiguity in the wording of the question that produced an uncertain reply from the electors arose at the municipal level in Ottawa in 1933. The city's electors, when asked whether they favoured having a council composed of a mayor and six councillors, or having a council composed of a mayor, four councillors, and eleven aldermen, or retaining the existing system, voted in favour of all three choices. After this understandably ambiguous outcome, the Ottawa City Council took no action.[25]

Confusing questions and uncertain results are also found at the provincial level. One example is the case of the Saskatchewan plebiscite on the time zone issue. Because the province's easterly and westerly boundaries are not within a single time zone, Saskatchewanians were puzzled over how they should set their clocks. In 1956, the electors went to the polls to express their opinion on this subject pursuant to the Time Question Plebiscite Act, 1956,[26] but when they got there they found the ballot confusing. Saskatchewan voters had been asked to vote for or against Central Standard Time for the whole province, and also to show their personal preference for the time to be used in their own locality. Only 34.2 per cent of the electorate voted, and on the first question 101,292 favoured Central Standard Time, 19,380 Central Daylight Saving, and 83,267 Mountain Standard.[27] These results were, of course, impossible to interpret in a single policy, so the government referred the question to a legislative committee, accepting its eventual recommendation to put Saskatchewan on Mountain Standard Time in winter and Central Standard Time in summer, a solution that split the cabinet, the legislature, and the population.

Confusion reigned in the province until 1959 as a result of each locality having proceeded to adopt its own time. In that year the statute producing this result by permitting each municipality to hold local plebiscites on time zones was repealed. The matter was then further considered in 1962 by a legislative committee, whose recommendation resulted in the province being bisected into two time zones in 1966 – Central Standard in the east and Mountain Standard in the west, with numerous exceptions.[28]

Today, everyone in Saskatchewan operates on Central Standard Time in the summer. In winter, western Saskatchewan is on Mountain Standard Time officially, unless electors have held a local plebiscite vote to put a particular municipality on Central Standard Time. While direct voting has played its part in this Saskatchewan time story, it has only helped solve the problem with about the same success as all the other methods tried. Although the results are confusing to many, everyone at least understands the problem thanks to direct voting.

Adams notes another example of confusion at the provincial level; she demonstrates that the "vagueness in wording" in each of the 1920, 1924, and 1952 liquor plebiscites in British Columbia "encouraged misrepresentation by pressure groups."[29]

A basic lesson emerges from these examples of how to choose

the words for a plebiscite ballot: ask a simple question, get a simple answer; ask an ambiguous or overly clever question, and who knows what the people will do with it. One should not shortchange the referendum process by concluding that people are too dumb to understand and decide on important issues. The framers of the ballot question will both have insulted the voters' intelligence and denigrated the process by their inane or inept wording of the "question." Indeed, all aspects of direct democracy considered, the wording of the ballot question is one of the most crucial – along with timing – and represents one of the high arts of statecraft.

Research indicates that in a plebiscite voters approach the polling place knowing whether they will vote "yes" or "no," based on the discussions they have heard during the campaign rather than the wording of the plebiscite question. This suggests that the question should be as straightforward as possible, and that it is not necessary to summarize the entire issue in the wording of the ballot. A model of simplicity, for instance, was the 1975 British vote on EEC membership. The form of ballot paper contained only a simple sentence and a single question: "The Government have announced the results of the renegotiation of the United Kingdom's terms of membership of the European Community. DO YOU THINK THAT THE UNITED KINGDOM SHOULD STAY IN THE EUROPEAN COMMUNITY (THE COMMON MARKET)? YES . . . No . . . "

The wording of Canada's 1942 plebiscite on conscription for overseas military service was also admirably brief. Prime Minister Mackenzie King took a number of runs at drafting the most politically suitable wording, including a number that were discarded. One was "Are you in favour of the government's having power to send men beyond Canada?" In the end, rather than asking straight out about conscription for overseas military service, the question was framed in terms that referred to the election pledge given in 1940 by Mackenzie King's Liberal Party to Canadians (and in particular to Quebeckers) that there would be no conscription for overseas purposes. Consistent with this promise, his efforts to move ever so gradually on the explosive issue of conscription, and his oft-repeated approach of "conscription if necessary, but not necessarily conscription," the wording finally chosen by King and approved by Parliament was: "Are you in favour of releasing the Government from any obligation arising out of any past commitments restricting the methods of raising men for military service? Yes... No..."

Certainly the 1980 referendum in Quebec employed one of the longest questions. For months the Quebec cabinet minister who had masterminded the referendum strategy, Jacques-Yvan Morin, scribbled out plebiscite questions, mused on them, then burned them in his fireplace. Others, too, suggested appropriate wording. Morin's ultimate handiwork, as approved by Premier René Lévesque, read as follows:

> The Government of Québec has made public its proposal to negotiate a new agreement with the rest of Canada, based on the equality of nations; this agreement would enable Québec to acquire the exclusive power to make its laws, levy its taxes and establish relations abroad — in other words, sovereignty — and at the same time, to maintain with Canada an economic association including a common currency; no change in political status resulting from these negotiations will be effected without approval by the people through another referendum; on these terms, do you give the Government of Québec the mandate to negotiate the proposed agreement between Québec and Canada?

This question, running to more than 100 words, is a contrast to the brief, clear British question on the Common Market quoted above.

Length is not the only cause of a question's appearing ambiguous. Another example of the poor wording of a ballot question is the one given by the municipalities of Manitoba in which electors were asked to vote in a plebiscite on French-language services in October 1983. Quite apart from the problem that the issue was not in their municipal jurisdiction, the wording of the question on the ballot in most municipalities violated even the simplest rules of fairness and simplicity. While the question was not quite the same in each municipality, the dilemma of wording can be easily grasped by considering the question voters in Winnipeg had to answer: "Should the provincial government withdraw its proposed constitutional amendment and allow the Bilodeau case to proceed to be heard and decided by the Supreme Court of Canada on the validity of the English-only laws passed by the Legislature of Manitoba since 1890?" This question, noted Don Sellar of Southam News, was "legalistic in tone, double-barrelled in construction, and dynamite in content."[30]

Winnipeggers were being asked to agree with two statements at the same time: whether the provincial government's resolution to amend the constitution should be withdrawn, and whether the Bilodeau case should proceed to the Supreme Court of Canada. In the United States, courts assess the constitutionality of plebiscite questions by applying several criteria, one of which is the "single issue" test. A ballot question ought to ask but one question and deal with one issue, since a voter can only give a single yes or no answer.

Deciding to present voters with a "neutral" question in a plebiscite is certainly problematic. This was demonstrated during the fierce debate in 1897 and 1898, when the Laurier government was under pressure to add to its main question about prohibition a second one about how the government should make up the $7-million shortfall in excise revenues to the public coffers that would result. The issue was debated in the Commons, and on May 13, 1897, a deputation representing the liquor interests of Canada met with leaders of the government in Ottawa and expressed a desire that the proposed plebiscite not take the form of a vote only on the abstract question of prohibition. The deputation argued that if prohibition were enacted it would involve a loss of revenue that would have to be replaced by direct taxation, and that the question to be submitted to the people should be so framed that those voting in favour of prohibition would also vote for direct taxation. A statement was published in some newspapers to the effect that the government agreed with the liquor sellers' proposition and intended to frame the question in the plebiscite so that electors would vote upon both matters.

This called forth strong expressions of concern.[31] From mid-May 1897 to February 1898 many large ecclesiastical organizations forcibly voiced their view that the prohibition plebiscite, to be "untrammelled and fair," had to be on a question "separate from all other questions of public policy."[32] The General Assembly of the Presbyterian Church in Winnipeg urged the government to submit the question "untrammelled by any other political or financial issue."[33] The Montreal Methodist Conference resolution of January 3, 1898, expressed the conviction that introduction of any other issue than the direct and sole issue of prohibition in the plebiscite "would be a direct subversion of the distinct pledge given by the political party now in power in the platform on which it appealed to the country, and on which it secured the people's mandate in the general elections of 1896." The Toronto Methodists, on June 9, 1897, expressed their "profound regret" that the government had already postponed consideration of the plebiscite during the current session of Parliament, and reminding the government of its "solemn pledge," confidently expected, "that this question, when submitted, [would] not be rendered confusing by the addition of other questions in reference to modes of taxation or anything else."

Turning up the heat in a well-orchestrated campaign to head off the second question about costs, which the prohibitionists feared would be fatal to the plebiscite's outcome, Methodists, Baptists, Congregationalists, Presbyterians, Sons of Temperance, Women's Christian Temperance Union, the Grand Lodge, and other fraternal societies, representing numerous conferences, synods, chapters, councils, and divisions across Canada, began passing resolutions that urged that the plebiscite question not be confused with any other considerations. These resolutions received local publicity and were soon dispatched to Prime Minister Laurier. The wording of the plebiscite question on the ballot, which Canadians marked on September 29, 1898, was duly confined to a single issue: "Are you in favour of the passing of an Act prohibiting the importation, manufacture or sale of spirits, wine, ale, beer, cider and all other alcoholic liquors for use as beverages?"

One sure way of reducing the risk of poor wording on a ballot question is for the legislature to set out the exact wording to be used by the municipality in the governing statute. For instance, in the province of Ontario, under the Fluoridation Act[34] the wording on the ballot is stipulated as: "Are you in favour of the fluoridation of the public water supply of this municipality?" Similarly, the province of Quebec requires that the question on the ballot paper must begin with the words "Do you approve," then state the number, title, or object of the by-law, resolution, or ordinance that is the subject of the referendum (or, in the case of a plebiscite, the question defined by the municipal council); and the word "yes" must appear above the word "no," with circles intended for the mark of the voter opposite each of these words. Likewise, fairly detailed instructions are set out in statutes in Saskatchewan, Ontario, Manitoba, and other provinces, which give the municipal councils strict guidance (and often little choice) in the phrasing of the ballot question. This is particularly so with respect to local option votes on liquor.

Timing of the Vote

It seems a Kafkaesque exercise to conduct opinion polls in order to determine the timing of a plebiscite, yet such steps are understandable when a matter of great consequence is involved, and where the results of the balloting will lead to real law making by the people.

If the referendum is one initiated by public petition, so that the government really has no choice but to submit the matter to a vote within a statutorily specified time limit, public opinion samplings taken by the government may have little more than academic value. However, if the referendum is one that the government is required to submit to the people at a time of its own choosing, a judicious testing of the political waters in advance may be of greater importance in the outcome of the vote.

In the spring of 1991, for instance, Quebec's Bélanger-Campeau Commission struggled with the issue of whether to recommend a referendum on separation, and especially whether to determine the nature of the question to be asked regarding the relationship between Quebec and the rest of Canada. The timing of such a vote was also a crucial consideration for the commissioners. Current opinion polls showed a high level of popular support for sovereignty-association, and this encouraged strong nationalists to push for a referendum at the earliest possible date. By contrast, federalist Quebeckers, still intent on achieving a new relationship with Canada and hopeful that the heated sentiment of Quebeckers would cool down as memory of the loss of the Meech Lake Accord receded, urged delay in calling the referendum.

Referendum provisions in a number of provincial municipal acts impose constraints on timing by requiring that the balloting take place in conjunction with the regular elections for municipal council. This is essentially a cost-saving measure, but also helps ensure that voter turnout is high enough to give legitimacy to the results.

Another constraint on timing is found in statutory provisions that "deem" something to have happened at a time when it has not. Typical is the Lord's Day Act of Yukon, which provides that a question about Sunday activities can be submitted by a municipal council to a plebiscite "at any time," but adds that if a petition from voters seeking such a plebiscite is presented in the month of November or December in any year, "it shall be deemed to be presented in the month of February next following." The reason for this constraint is to prevent having to campaign for and conduct the voting on a petition presented too close to local council elections, which in Yukon are held every second year in mid-December.

Whether to hold a plebiscite at the same time as a general election is an intriguing question both for democratic theorists and political strategists. In some provinces, such as Quebec, a referendum cannot by law be held at the same time as a general election; Section 15 of the Referendum Act stipulates that a writ for a general election voids a writ for a referendum. Yet in British Columbia and Saskatchewan, in conjunction with their provincial elections of October 17, 1991, and October 21, 1991, then premiers Johnston and Devine initiated, through their province's respective legislatures, plebiscites timed to coincide with the general elections. The B.C. referendum posed two questions to voters, one on the power of "recall," the other on creating a citizen's right of "initiative." Saskatchewan's plebiscite put non-binding questions to the electorate on abortion, deficit spending, and the constitution.

Yet at the national level, the preferred view is to keep the two voting processes separate. The Canada Temperance Act, in force from 1878 to 1990, stipulated that a prohibition plebiscite could not be held on the same day as any election for a member of Parliament or the legislature of the province concerned. The Canada Referendum Act, introduced in Parliament by the Trudeau government in 1978 but never fully enacted, stipulated in Section 6(3) that *no* writs of referendum were to be issued during a general election, and that if a referendum had been started and a general election were subsequently called, the writs of referendum would be deemed to be withdrawn. The private member's bill that I have had before Parliament since 1988, the Canada Referendum and Plebiscite Act, likewise precludes holding a plebiscite and general election simultaneously.

Holding an election and a plebiscite at the same time permits voters to give a mandate on a specific issue, quite separate from the broader question of passing judgment on the past performance of a government and one's elected representative. It can also save money by combining the electoral procedures. It is the requirement, indeed, of municipal plebiscites that they be held in conjunction with the balloting to elect the local council. On the other hand, to keep the plebiscite and the general election separate avoids confusion.[35]

Providing Information to Voters

Some early drafts of the referendum acts in western Canada provided for an official "publicity pamphlet." This would typically contain the text of each measure to be voted on, the arguments prepared by committees appointed to represent the promoters and opponents of each question, and a sample copy of the official ballot. The pamphlet had to be mailed to each voter sixty days before the poll so that it could be studied at leisure. The only law in Canada to contain this admirable provision at present is the Referendum Act of Quebec, which in Section 26 provides for a booklet to be sent to the electors at least ten days before the holding of a poll.

In Quebec the plebiscite of October 1, 1987, pertaining to the evolution of a Northern government, represented a further advance in providing balanced information to electors in the fourteen widely separated communities of the region in question. In addition to a poster prepared by the chief electoral officer (CEO) summarizing the important stages in the referendum, a pamphlet was prepared giving the position of the pro and con groups. The text was prepared by each side for its case, in three languages, and the CEO printed and distributed it far enough in advance of the voting to give electors time to study and reflect on its contents. Additionally, a videotaped documentary was prepared and shown in the settlements, and a taped message was broadcast on the northern FM radio stations.

Municipal councils, when submitting a by-law or question to electors, have limited means of presenting the case. The only paid publicity is the official advertisement of the by-law or question. The case of *Parent v. Ottawa*[36] held that a municipal council is not entitled to make use of public funds for the purpose of advertising its views on a question being submitted to voters. Still, depending on the complexity of the issue, referral to the people may not be fair unless the electors have as much detailed knowledge of the facts as that possessed by the government or local council. Indeed, the courts may even restrain a plebiscite if the voters have not been provided with enough information.[37] When municipal voters in Calgary were asked in 1979 to indicate their support for or opposition to borrowing $201,960,000 to build the proposed Calgary Civic Centre, the City of Calgary prepared and distributed a twelve-page information bulletin about the Civic Centre, the need for such a facility, and a breakdown of the costs involved.

An enduring challenge in this area is how to differentiate between information and advocacy. The problem of a municipal council in effect telling people how to vote in a plebiscite arose in 1991 when Toronto City Council decided to include a ballot question in the November municipal election on the concept of market-value assessment. Prior to the election, council's executive committee indicated it would like the city to mount a campaign urging voters to say "no," while Metro Council had already voted in favour of market-value assessment. The City of Toronto is just one of six cities making up Metropolitan Toronto. The metropolitan level of government proposed updating the system used to assess property taxes for the six municipalities within its jurisdiction. The reassessment, which was to be completed in mid-1992, would allow Metro politicians to gauge the impact of switching to 1988 market-value assessments from the current system, in use since 1954 and based on 1940 property values.[38]

Toronto councillors, fearing their electors would face the largest tax increases of the six cities because property values had risen most sharply in their city, decided to put a question about the concept of market-value assessment to City of Toronto electors in a plebiscite, and backed this up with a strong campaign urging a "no" vote. The communications strategy developed for this purpose was, reported *The Globe and Mail,* to state that "market-value assessment is an unjust and regressive tax masquerading as reform which . . . will have dire economic consequences for the City of Toronto including job losses, bankruptcies, and relocation of businesses" to other areas.

It is not hard, in this case, to see where information ended and advocacy began. City solicitor Dennis Perlin advised the executive committee that this message "goes much too far for what a council can do directly." It was not what he expected to see "as presenting the electorate with an informed choice." His view was that it would be illegal for the city to engage in such a lopsided presentation of the issue. "Council should not be telling the electorate what the answer should be," he said.[39]

City council, as representative of the corporation of the municipality, should not be putting forward a particular point of view, Mr. Perlin correctly stated, adding that council's role in such matters is to educate the public from as neutral a position as possible. Against this backdrop, an interesting question arises. As Councillor Kay Gardner asked, what is the distinction between the Council's opposition and individual opposition to the plan? In Councillor Gardner's words, "Do I not have the right as a representative of my ward to ask my constituents to support the position I have taken and that we have taken?" Clearly she did. The point, however, is that the question electors must vote on, and the information *officially* provided to them, should be as neutral as possible. Once the plebiscite campaign is under way, anyone – including city councillors such as Kay Gardner – is perfectly free to advocate strongly for one side or the other. The legal obligation, beforehand, however, is to put the issue fairly to the people. Slanting the question and disseminating biased information about the issue cannot but render the entire plebiscite exercise as bogus as the manipulated referendums generated in countries with military dictatorships.

Another issue concerning provision of information in the City of Toronto's market-value assessment referendum arose from the contribution made by the Toronto Council Executive Committee of $55,000 to the Committee for Fair Taxation to promote a strategy against market-value assessment. At issue here was the legal one of just how far a city council could go in spending public money on promoting, or opposing, one particular side of the plebiscite question. Normally where any public money is to be made available for the advocacy of the plebiscite options, it must be provided in equal amounts to both sides, to ensure impartiality.

Apart from the balance and neutrality expected from governments in providing basic information, advocates on both sides of an issue are free to oppose and promote the question by all known forms of political advertising and campaigning to the extent their resources allow. These are subject to certain general laws of advertising and campaigning and, in the case of Quebec provincial plebiscites, to the spending limits specified in the Referendum Act. Thus the information received by voters in most cases will – as in an election campaign – be coloured to benefit the group presenting it.

The general laws on advertising and campaigning just referred to include those on defamation, those that restrict locations in which posters and banners may be fastened (primarily municipal by-laws), laws regulating public assemblies, street parades, and demonstrations (again, most of which are municipal enactments), and, until they were repealed in 1991,[40] provisions in the Broadcasting Act[41] required a "blackout" of political broadcasting on the day of voting and the day preceding voting in a referendum.[42]

Providing information to voters is essential in order for a plebiscite to provide a collective expression of "informed" opinion. But, important as it is to have information about an issue freely available, it is just as vital that a citizen has the desire to read it. During the 1988 general election campaign, the hunger for information about "free trade" became palpable. As debate increasingly focused on this issue, demand for information about the Canada-U.S. treaty rose dramatically. *The Globe and Mail,* having written a series of six editorials to express its support earlier in the year when interest had not yet reached its fevered pitch, took the unprecedented step of reprinting all six towards the end of the campaign. Four days before election day, *The Financial Post* produced an eight-page special supplement: "Everything you want to know about free trade, but *no one's* telling you." In truth, as political observer and columnist George Bain noted at the time, dozens of books, hundreds of periodical articles, and thousands of newspaper stories had been published over the preceding several years – as evidenced by his own bulging files on the subject, and by the Library of Parliament index, which lists page after page of entries on the topic. The interest to learn can sometimes only be sparked, perhaps, by the intensity of an election – or by a referendum – campaign.

Late on a Friday afternoon in the 1988 general election campaign, one of my canvassers and I were walking down a street with copies of the *Financial Post* supplement, which we'd taken to distributing because I felt it was more factual, balanced, and readable than anything produced by any of the political parties on the subject. A car pulled over, and a young man in working clothes stepped out and approached us. "Is that about free trade?" he inquired intently. Told that it was, he asked, "Could I have a copy?" He took it, and drove off.

From my campaign office, one chap worked exclusively on preparing information kits addressed to individual electors who had expressed an interest in free trade. This feeling Canadians had on the eve of the election, that they needed to be informed about free trade before casting a ballot, hints at what a plebiscite dealing exclusively with one transcending issue could achieve – quite apart from its outcome – as an instrument for self-awareness and self-definition, and as a catalyst for education.

Financing of Campaigns

Everyone knows that the financing of a campaign is one of the underpinnings of its success, yet the means for financially promoting a plebiscite or referendum is something that is totally ignored in Canadian statutes. Virtually all legislative acts providing for such votes are silent on the question of money, except for the routine matter of how the actual costs of carrying out the vote itself (salaries of plebiscite officials, the expenses of preparing the voters' lists, and the like) are to be paid out of public revenues.

No restrictions are placed on the amount of money that can be spent by the factions favouring or opposing the question on the ballot, with the notable exception of those contained in the Referendum Act of Quebec. Like that province's Election Act, this law establishes limits on contributions and expenditures, and provides reimbursement from public funds for at least part of the expenses of the two campaigning groups.

Elsewhere in Canada, it seems, where something is not prohibited by law, it is allowed, and therefore anyone can raise and spend as much money as he or she wants during the plebiscite or referendum campaign.

The financing issues that must be addressed soon, in light of the increased prospects for Canada-wide plebiscites, include public disclosure, expenditure ceilings, prohibition of donations from certain contributors, restrictions on contributions, and public subsidies. The Quebec Referendum Act will provide a good model for that task. Chapter 8, "The Quest for a Canadian Direct-Vote Statute," outlines a number of the necessary provisions relating to balanced funding and fair expenditure control.

Many of the matters dealt with in the campaign-financing legislation that regulates parties and candidates have similar applications to the case of referendums and plebiscites, although, as Austin Ranney notes, "enough significant differences between candidate election campaigns and referendum campaigns warrant special attention." He finds four areas of distinction. First, political parties are usually much less active and prominent in referendum campaigns, which creates something of an organizational vacuum. Second, the special nature and requirements of the media, especially television, pose challenges and expenditure needs in setting out the pros and cons of ballot propositions that differ from those of candidates' records and personalities. Third, the absence of party labels in referendums deprive these campaigns of much of the structure and continuity that characterize candidate elections. Fourth, referendums offer "much less opportunity than candidate elections for direct and secret *quid pro quo* payoffs by the winners to their financial supporters."[43] This latter point is rather dependent, however, on the nature of the plebiscite itself. For instance, in the prohibition plebiscites, it was clear how the liquor interests stood to benefit by their direct financial support for the "wet" side of the proposition.

These issues have also been considered by the Royal Commission on Electoral Reform and Party Financing, which commissioned a separate study on the role of referendums in the Canadian political system that is expected to be published in 1992.

There are basically two approaches to controlling plebiscite finances – limiting the amount of contributions that may be made to either "side" of the question and limiting the total amount that each group may spend. The first is simply a method of restricting the amount of money going into the system; the second, the amount coming out. The theory of the former is that the best way to prevent abuse is to keep down the amount of money available for referendum campaign activities; the latter holds that there is no effective way to regulate money going into the system, so control must be on the amount of money spent and the manner in which it is used.

However, there are a number of techniques for implementing or refining these two basic approaches. Such techniques are: restrictions on the source of financial contributions; restrictions on the size of financial contributions; disclosure of the source of contributions; restrictions on the amount of political campaign expenditures; restrictions on the types of campaign expenditures; and disclosure of expenditures.

Three methods by which restrictions can be enforced are: the concept of agency, whereby one person is exclusively authorized to receive contributions or spend funds on behalf of an organization; the establishment of an independent body to oversee and enforce the regulatory provisions; and a method whereby certain public subsidies for the costs of campaigns are paid only on proof of compliance with the rules. Where Parliament and the provincial legislatures have used these methods for enforcing restrictions in *election* campaigns, however, they have adopted variations and combinations of all of them, since none of them is exclusive, and since a more comprehensive and effective regime of financial control is achieved by the interaction of all these techniques. Dealing with plebiscite expenses and contributions has not yet (again, with the exception of Quebec) evolved nearly so far; but, as the legal regime for direct voting does develop, it will no doubt parallel the general principles and specific techniques employed for controlling the contributions and expenses in election campaigns.[44]

Most of the controversy about direct voting by citizens centres on whether such procedures are appropriate in our system of democratic government. Yet one thing is certain: once a plebiscite or referendum is under way, everyone, except perhaps the most calculating or cynical of people, would want to see it proceed fairly and be successful. For this reason, the six fundamentals discussed above – impartiality of the process, validity and nature of the question, wording of the question, timing of the vote, balanced information, and the financing of the campaign – are each crucially important. Canadian experience with direct voting has already amply demonstrated how things can run amok when these guidelines for fairness and common sense are ignored.

5

Mandate, Mandate –
Who's Got the Mandate?

Powerful governments have long promoted a doctrine of parliamentary democracy that brazenly holds that once elected by virtue of winning the most seats in a general election, regardless of the size of their party's popular vote, they have a mandate to deal with any issue that comes up during the life of that Parliament. Most political scientists and media commentators operate within this accepted view, and have, along with many compliant politicians, reinforced its popularity by their teachings, commentaries, and behaviour.

While this doctrine makes sense as a practical approach to the many details and issues that could never have been aired and debated or even anticipated in an election campaign, it nevertheless enshrines a bold fiction. Because of the attitudes and practices that have come to cluster around the mandate doctrine, it has become one of the major factors in the loss of credibility suffered by Canadian governments and has led to a general disrespect for Canadian legislatures, shared even by many of us who are members of them. This chapter seeks to look, with fresh eyes, at the parliamentary dimension of "the people's mandate."

Tempering the Bold Fiction of a Mandate

To assert that a government can go to war, amend the country's constitution, or reverse a whole pattern of trade policies or immigration programs, when such courses of action had not even been talked

87

about in the election from which it received its "mandate," is to stretch a doctrine further than is reasonable in a democracy. To act in a way that expressly reverses aspects of the "mandate," such as freezing prices and wages or cancelling the acquisition of nuclear-powered submarines when promises to the contrary were made during the campaign, is to deny, or at least stretch to the point of meaninglessness, the doctrine on which that government depends for its very authority.

Governments most assuredly are elected to govern. Yet the defiant government that says, "We can do this because we have a mandate to govern" on an issue of transcending importance that was never broached in the previous election, is making as extreme a distortion of things as was made in the assertion after the 1988 general election, that because 57 percent of voters had voted other than Tory, a majority of Canadians had voted against the free trade agreement for which the Tories had campaigned and, therefore, government members had no mandate to vote in Parliament to ratify the free trade agreement. Both these extremes display a certain silliness, and Canadians, faced with such assertions, may understandably be uncertain of exactly what they have decided, as far as specific issues go, in a general election.

Election campaigns are a grab-bag of issues, and it is impossible to separate from the voting returns a clear mandate for a specific project. After the November 21, 1988, general election, which had been fought extensively but by no means exclusively on the single, yet multi-dimensional, issue of the Canada-U.S. trade treaty, did the contention that a majority of the voters specifically voted against free trade upset people? Clearly it did. To those who believe in electoral mandates, the Liberals' resolution, put forward in the House of Commons in December 1988, to the effect that the government lacked a mandate to proceed with free trade, was an example of democratic revisionism of a most troublesome sort. Letters to the editor showed that many Canadians were troubled on this score – some by the challenge to our traditional doctrine of an electoral mandate, others by the extent to which that doctrine could be used for supporting a policy of which they strongly disapproved. When Council of Canadians Chairman Maude Barlow cautioned the prime minister that a "majority of Canadians voted for parties opposed to the free-trade agreement,"[1] Paul Grant, a citizen of Mount Forest, Ontario, wrote to *The Globe and Mail*, saying that she was "exhibiting disdain for democracy when it doesn't suit her purposes."[2] Barlow would like to draw inferences from the "popular vote," he said, but they would be "based on fallacious assumptions, namely that every vote for a Progressive Conservative candidate was a vote for the free trade agreement and every vote for another candidate was against it." What was interesting, Grant added, was

> to extend Ms. Barlow's thinking to the voting in the ridings held by the leaders of the three main parties. More people voted against New Democratic Party leader Ed Broadbent than for him (22,994 to 18,410) and against Liberal leader John Turner than for him (30,953 to 24,167). According to Ms. Barlow's logic, does this taint or disqualify them in any way? In case she could not find the figures, 33,729 voted for Prime Minister Brian Mulroney, compared with 8,423 for his rivals.[3]

So much energy had been unleashed by the 1988 election campaign that it could not be expected to dissipate as soon as the votes were counted. Yet these post-election debates about the nature of a mandate, even when the Mulroney-led Progressive Conservatives had scored an impressive majority of seats in the Commons, revealed more than just a continuation of the intense national debate that had raged over free trade. It showed that our conventional wisdom about electoral mandates could, as will any fiction, cause us to suspend reason and reality only so far.

A mandate – the political authority supposedly given by electors to Parliament, or at least given to the party that wins the most seats or support in the House of Commons, which in turn enables it to form a government – is one of those concepts in Canadian politics everyone understands in broad terms, but disputes in specific application.

Nowhere does this dispute have greater relevance than in the assessment of the relationship between elections and referendums. Understanding that relationship is, in turn, most crucial in charting the future course of Canadian parliamentary democracy. This chapter accordingly brings into focus several aspects of the electoral mandate. Likewise, part of this effort to understand the real nature of a mandate from the people requires getting to the root of the confusion which curiously exists between the nature of elections and referendums.

The Moral and Legal Authority to Govern

An initial clarification is perhaps important. Canadians have increasingly come to use the word "mandate" as shorthand for "term of office," as in: "The Trudeau government had two years left to run in its mandate." The meaning of mandate I am using, however, is the one pertaining to the authority – both moral and legal – to govern.

By examining both current realities and history it will be easier to see why Canadians have for so long made the assumption, derived and developed from British parliamentary doctrines and practice, that a party in power has received a mandate from the public to govern. This doctrine, however, is increasingly untenable for the many Canadians who have lost their traditional deference to authority and who are now more than ever prepared to challenge it by declaring that a mandate does *not* empower a government to deal over the years of its term in office with any and all issues or crises that arise, including those never discussed in the previous election campaign either because they could not have been anticipated or were studiously avoided.

All political parties, of course, campaign on the basis of a program, and often the party that forms the government will even try to implement some of it. Yet many Canadians have grown sceptical about election promises of parties right across the political spectrum and realize issues not addressed in an election campaign may later emerge and influence the stated positions of the party in office. So, we have come to accept that a government in office basically has a mandate, received from the electorate in the most recent election, to govern as it must and as it chooses, for up to the constitutional time-limit of five years, provided it can maintain majority support in the Commons.

At the point when the constitution insists a fresh mandate be given by the people through the process of re-electing their representatives or electing new ones and, in the process, choosing a government, we have also come to understand that an election is no longer principally an accountability session. Elements of renewal and accountability assuredly are part of an election, but only a part. So the doctrine of a mandate continues to be a loose-fitting dress over a generously proportioned body, concealing bumps here, revealing some shape there, and generally giving, at a casual glance, the impression of having the whole thing covered.

The different ways in which a majority government mandate can cover vastly different practices and policies are admirably revealed by the contrast between two Liberal majority governments, both headed by Pierre Trudeau, elected in 1974 and 1980. When the Liberals won a convincing majority in the 1974 general election, we saw how the parliamentary theories about an electoral mandate camouflaged the actual practices of the government that had received the public's "blank cheque" to govern. Trudeau, Richard Gwyn suggests in his biography of him, "interpreted a majority victory as a mandate to goof off."[4] When the Conservatives led by Joe Clark defeated the Trudeau Liberals in May 1979, Marc Lalonde, a principal minister in the Trudeau cabinet, looked back bleakly and saw really no significant achievement of the Trudeau government in many portfolios, especially the economic ones. "It was quite clear in our minds that, if we came back, it would have to mean something," Lalonde later explained in a 1981 interview.[5]

Back in power following the 1980 election, the Liberals were convinced, according to Robert Sheppard and Michael Valpy, that Ottawa "must reassert itself in a number of key fields – energy, regional economic development, fiscal transfers and constitutional reform," and the revived Trudeau government "embarked on a new age of confrontational politics – competitive rather than cooperative federalism."[6] In the spring of 1980, the same writers say, Trudeau was "probably wielding more raw prime ministerial power than any of his predecessors. He had a majority government and was facing a dispirited opposition . . . his caucus and party were beholden to him for leading them out of the wilderness; and . . . his few promises in the winter campaign effectively gave him a free hand to pursue the national interest in his own fashion."[7]

This lesson about the vast discrepancy between an electoral mandate and the unheralded major policies that a strong-willed prime minister then imposes on the country through his majority government, and the consequent disaffection and alienation that develops across the country in response to policies flagrantly beyond the implicit terms of any electoral mandate, seemed not to have been understood by Trudeau's successor Brian Mulroney. Using the "licence to govern" of his 1984 majority government "mandate," Prime Minister Mulroney initiated a free trade treaty with the United States, thereby in fact reversing the traditional and historic position of the Conservative Party and his own earlier specific statements opposing "continentalism." The Tory government began to get into real trouble on this issue. It was "not because they had promised more than they had delivered," observed Michael Adams, "but because they had delivered more than they had promised, namely the free trade agreement with the United States."[8] Free trade, which had not even been mentioned during the 1984 election campaign and thus could not in any sense be considered part of the people's mandate to the new Mulroney Conservatives, became the most important initiative of the Mulroney government and consequently the central issue in the 1988 campaign.

These policy reversals prove that, at a theoretical and policy level, anyone wishing to believe in a mandate theory ought not to examine the correlation between election campaigns and subsequent government actions too closely. Indeed, this flip-flop approach seems more endemic to recent decades, when one considers party programs in elections and subsequent action from government in Canada's earlier days. The variance between promise and performance since the 1960s cannot be ignored as a factor contributing to the decline in the credibility of our political and governmental processes with the Canadian public.

The principle of our parliamentary system that holds that a correlation between election campaign promises and subsequent government actions should exist serves a practical purpose, however: the political party that can command the confidence of the House of Commons because more MPs support rather than oppose it on major issues has both the right to form the government and a general mandate to govern the country. It serves as a rationale for creating order out of potential chaos, and if the working of the numbers that justify its application sometimes seems crude, most of us still prefer to live with this constitutional fiction on the grounds that it is better to "count heads than to break them."

We are also prepared to go along with the mandate theory because we recognize that in practice it is subject to a number of constraints. Governing the country means doing so, for example, against such fundamental restraints on power as: the accountability to an Official Opposition in the House of Commons; the enactment of any new laws, including taxes, through Parliament; an obligation to meet Parliament every year; the necessity to submit a budget and all spending estimates to Parliament annually; the requirement to hold a general election at least every five years; the scrutiny by an independent judiciary of the government's laws and actions whenever they are challenged in court; the countervailing operations of provincial governments under our federal system; and the examination of the government's exercise of power by a competitive and generally critical news media.

Even so, a disquiet exists among many thoughtful Canadians who sense that our government operates at a remove from any genuine methods of accountability. Ever since television cameras began to broadcast proceedings in the House of Commons, a deep and accelerating shift has been under way across Canada as people realized that responsible government had in some important respects become a farce. The previously hollow theatrics of Question Period, propelled into a new form of sham confrontation by the nature of television coverage itself, is leaving an ever-increasing number of Canadians dismayed. Parliamentarians may have turned new attention to sartorial presentation because of television cameras, but the child's voice in Hans Christian Andersen's folk tale "The Emperor's New Clothes" now echoes across Canada.

Authorization and Accountability through Elections

In the contemporary Canadian political scene, the chain of communication and control required to make authorization and accountability function effectively has several weak links. The most obvious of these, suggest political analysts Allan Kornberg, William Mishler, and Harold Clarke, is the electoral connection. They write that the election process "enables an electorate to signal either pleasure or displeasure with an incumbent government by re-electing it or rejecting its candidates in favour of those of a competing party."[9] In a democracy, they observe, this is a powerful and authoritative message. Nonetheless, they say, as many political theorists have noted, electoral mechanisms, as they currently operate in Canada and other Western countries, constitute very imperfect communications channels and very blunt instruments of popular control. Both in logic and in fact, "elections frequently fail to convey clear signals about either the content of public policy preferences or the priorities voters assign to these preferences."[10]

Another critique by academics written in 1984 concluded that Canadians were disillusioned with their political parties and put the blame on "brokerage politics," which, they said, prevents our political parties from enunciating clear policy alternatives out of fear of exacerbating the country's regional and linguistic divisions.[11] The overriding concern of party leaders to simply hold the country together induces a cautiousness that prevents, or at least greatly discourages, innovative approaches to economic and social policies. The four authors, basing their views on results from surveys they conducted at the time of the general elections of 1974, 1979, and 1980, conclude that election campaigns have become nothing more than horse races between contending leaders. From this analysis came their book's title, *Absent Mandate*.

Since the electorate does not have opposing policies to choose from, they write, it cannot give a clear policy mandate to any government nor judge its record accordingly when the next election comes.[12] Thus the present workings of the Canadian party system cannot produce any clear mandate for the development of policies to deal with the country's serious problems.

This evanescence of a Canadian political dialogue contributes to frustration about "the uninspiring level of policy debate in this country, especially during election campaigns," according to Joseph Wearing, a political science professor at Trent University. Instead of presenting carefully developed policy programs, he contends, "all three major parties continually reiterate a few simple 'themes,' which change from one election to another depending on which issues are current and which are not."[13]

94

Perhaps as an MP I have been too close to the scene since 1984 to judge objectively, but I would argue that the elections of 1984 and 1988, to which most of the comments and criticism of these political scientists can be applied, did offer Canadians a wide range of policy choices, as outlined in the platforms of the contending political parties, in addition to the "simple themes," which, I agree, also formed part of the offering. Yet, this does not diminish the chief argument these critics are advancing, which is that, as Vernon Bogdanor expresses it, the voter can at best give a judgment only "on the general political colour of the government" and could only rarely "make his views felt on particular issues."[14]

General elections are difficult forums in which to provide opportunities for policy mandates, or indeed even meaningful discussion. I have heard it adamantly asserted by several highly successful political organizers that election campaigns are *not* the time to engage in political education, but are rather the time for bringing to the polls those individuals identified as supporting the candidate or party. In short, election-time democracy from the parties' point of view is a numbers game and not a public issues teach-in or policy colloquium.

It can be demonstrated that issues are important in election campaigns and central to the voting decisions of a considerable number of Canadian voters, but as Jon H. Pammett has accurately observed, "these issues are infrequently defined with a degree of precision that might approximate public policy." Adding that "voting patterns based on issues are frequently not in any concerted direction," and this causes "difficulties in trying to connect an issue mandate with any particular group of representatives."[15]

The broad problems that strike many voters as most important and that each of the parties promise to attack if elected, according to the authors of the book *Absent Mandate*, "are so diffuse as to defy any specific interpretation of a public judgement based on them." They also note that while the cost of living, the lack of growth, the need for jobs, and the price of energy were all important election issues during the 1970s and 1980s, no particular party was "decisively linked by the electorate with any preferred solutions."[16] Even when the political parties do advance specific policies to deal with general problems, these political scientists have found that

> the electorate often divides down the middle as to whether the idea is sound, again frustrating attempts to assign a mandate to the party which wins the election. As if recognizing this, parties are quite prepared to adopt the policies put forward by their rivals only a short time before, thus further complicating the question of electoral mandates.[17]

Brokerage Politics and Electoral Mandates

While *Absent Mandate* provides perhaps the best and most current statement of the brokerage theory of Canadian political parties, the idea has been expounded for many years and undergoes revision and reformulation every few decades.

In 1906, for example, André Siegfried's book *The Race Question in Canada* first appeared. In it, he analyzed in depth the operations of Canada's political system with an admirable detachment and described how extensively the two major parties worked to accommodate the diverse interests of Canadians – so much so that between the Liberals and the Conservatives "the difference" had "come at times to be imperceptible."[18] In 1943, Frank H. Underhill, adapting the theories of American Pendleton Herring,[19] said that a democracy

> is simply a society in which all interest groups have an equal chance to present their claims for benefits from the gains of civilization and to get them adjusted. It follows from this analysis that the pressure-group organizations which conduct their business with the party organizations are as essential to the working of democratic politics as the parties themselves.[20]

Underhill's thesis was that, with the breaking of the two-party monopoly over our political life during World War I, the Canadian party system passed into a stage of transition. It was to him a "paradox of the two-party system that it works best when there are more than two parties, for the challenge of new parties preserves flexibility in the old ones."[21] He saw too that it was the function of the minor parties "to formulate issues before the major parties were ready to take them up, to agitate and educate, to present new points of view, and to leave the great responsibility of adjusting conflicts and working out a national policy to the major parties."

Canadian sociologist John Porter, writing in 1965 and using the analysis of brokerage politics developed by Pendleton Herring as a point of departure, closely analyzed the interaction of political élites in Canada with the economic élites and interest groups, the fashion in which they accommodate one another, and the balances and compromises struck within the bureaucracy that bear no particular relationship to the governing political party's official policies and even less to any supposed electoral mandate. He noted that, as a result of the functioning of Canada's major political parties as brokers, "dynamic politics to mobilize the creative energies of the society were still absent."[22]

In 1968 political scientist Gad Horowitz joined the attack on brokerage politics.[23] Pointing out that we do not have the rule of the people but rather "the rule of the politician," Horowitz felt we had "not even approximated democracy" and suggested that, among the roles that the party system in Canada can and should play, the most important would be "to move our society toward democracy – not the 'utopian' democracy in which the people rule, but the 'attainable' democracy in which an élite accountable to the people rules."[24] For this to happen, in Horowitz's view, the political élite in Canada would have to be strengthened "to the point where it" could replace "the corporate and bureaucratic élites as the source of the most important social decisions."[25] He thought this would require both that our party system be polarized on a left-right basis and that the main issues discussed in the political arena be class issues. The conceptual approach of Horowitz was particularized and elaborated on in *Absent Mandate* and elsewhere.[26]

H.D. Forbes, a professor of political science at the University of Toronto, writing in 1990, finds the brokerage theory "complicated" but "basically sound" and explains how the theory's interpretation "begins from an observation about Canada's three main political parties: they are not divided by clear differences of principle, nor do they speak for distinct social groups. They are not like the socialist or other doctrinaire parties of the past, with their detailed programs for

97

broad social change rooted in elaborate ideologies."[27] Canadian parties are rather "catch-all" parties, trying to offer something to every group in the electorate, and sticking to the middle of the road ideologically.[28]

The brokerage role of Canadian political parties has been viewed, if not with enthusiasm, at least with tolerant understanding by those who recognize the integrative function parties perform in putting together coalitions in which all the diverse forces of such a country can be represented. "National unity is preserved," argued Frank Underhill, "by having every interest-group effectively inside the party which controls the government."[29] Brokerage politicians, suggests Forbes, "put party loyalty ahead of doctrinal purity or devotion to abstract principles." He believes that Stephen Leacock admirably caught the spirit of brokerage politics when he said, "pledges first, principles afterwards."[30]

Brokerage parties and the old brokerage theory of Canadian politics that viewed the process with approbation may, Forbes thinks, "be parts of an ideological apparatus for suppressing consideration of issues that would threaten the dominant classes in modern society."[31] Even the New Democratic Party, which has presented itself as the socialist alternative, has increasingly been co-opted into the system of brokerage politics, softening its doctrine, developing election platforms based on opinion polling as is done by the Progressive Conservatives and the Liberals, and moderating its positions as it seeks greater support in the so-called political mainstream. As socialists, they have become "backsliders."

By virtue of an "iron triangle," involving politicians, bureaucrats, and special interest groups, our political parties no longer serve as neutral brokers of all legitimate interests. Instead, they "arrange compromises among long-established élite groups," Forbes suggests, "neglecting the interests of the masses."[32] Certainly this may help explain the continuing preoccupation by our political parties and the political élites in Canada with the constitution.

A defining difference between the United States and Canada is that American solutions to social problems tend to be seen in economic terms, whereas ours are viewed politically. This approach certainly typifies the Canadian political élites' thinking on most issues and has been an important element in the operation of our brokerage politics system in this country. As John Porter observed in 1965, "To obscure social divisions through brokerage politics is to remove from the political system that element of dialectic which is the sole source of creative politics."[33]

The Myth of True Choice

The authors of *Absent Mandate* see a solution to this problem of the lack of true choice in elections. Following Horowitz, they point optimistically to the possibilities inherent in ideological, class-based politics, such as those that exist in more mature democracies. Perhaps a better answer, however, can be found closer to home. It is two-part in nature.

The first part of this answer depends on the recognition that the currently dominant concept of brokerage politics actually obscures a reality of Canadian politics and elections. The authors of *Absent Mandate*, for example, develop the theory that brokerage competition produces a volatile electorate. Voters react in this way because they are unable to see fundamental differences between the parties (because none exist) and, therefore, have no reason to develop long-term loyalties to one of them. *Absent Mandate* also views brokerage competition as shifting the focus of election campaigns from issues to leadership, with parties serving simply as vehicles for their leaders, and the election campaign consisting not of policy debate but of image politics: "Lacking ideological or continuing policy differences," the authors say, "the parties take on, in a sense, the personality of their leaders."[34] Because this brokerage system fails to mobilize popular support for broad policies, they contend, it is inevitable that an election will almost never "deliver a mandate for policy innovation designed to cope with economic problems of a fundamental nature." In these circumstances, they conclude, political parties cannot emerge from an electoral victory feeling or acting "as if they had a mandate from the public to implement a comprehensive economic policy. In times of severe difficulty, when a mandate to engage in long-term innovative economic engineering is most needed, it is in fact least likely to be forthcoming."[35]

Yet, as Forbes notes, the 1988 election campaign was "strikingly different from the sort of campaign that one is led to expect by the theory of brokerage politics found in *Absent Mandate*." The parties "championed different long-term strategies of economic development, which were thought by many to have profound implications for social programs."[36] The free trade agreement triggered a debate about the welfare state and economic management. As to the question of leadership domination of the political parties, he reviews past contests and finds that "elections in which the main parties have taken contrasting stands on issues generally considered important have been as common as elections in which only leadership has been in question."[37]

What Forbes finds most debatable in *Absent Mandate* and other recent studies on the issue is the suggestion "that elections would yield clear mandates about how to deal with the big questions of public policy if only the parties would cease to be brokerage parties and would take principled stands on all the issues of the day" and the further implication that if this change were made,"people would then really be able to control the government, big and complicated as it is, because the parties would give them real questions to decide."[38] I agree with Forbes that even if parties outline with impeccable precision their policies on 12 or 80 or 160 different issues, it would still be impossible to infer from the voting results which policies had been approved and which rejected. It is certainly arguable that some parties are elected to office in spite of, rather than because of, some of their policies.

The first part of the answer to the problem of the "brokerage" role, therefore, is to take a less ideological, more balanced view of Canada's political parties. It is more realistic, suggests Forbes, "to say they never were brokerage parties in exactly the sense implied by the contemporary use of the term, but still are the brokerage parties they have always been."[39]

Secondly, a more intelligent use of the referendum device might be the best medicine for this ailment of Canadian electoral politics. Certainly, it would be more compatible with our system than would the introduction of ideological, class-based parties.

A number of experienced Canadian politicians clearly understand this. For instance, former Liberal cabinet minister John Roberts, in his 1985 book *Agenda for Canada*, persuasively argues the case for the desirability of brokerage politics in a country with such geographic, social, and economic diversity as we have in Canada. Pointing out how "a brokerage party, when successful, disperses power to the various interests in society" and how "an ideological party, when successful, captures power for one interest in society . . . and tends to deny to other interests the hope that government will be sensitive to their points of view," Roberts makes the case that "participatory democracy" is consistent with brokerage politics.[40]

It is the brokerage role that allows Canadian political parties to accommodate our country's varied interests. Since it is, therefore, one of the most central and valid roles for Canadian political parties, it follows that the acknowledged shortcomings of this system can be resolved more readily through better occasional use of referendums to obtain a clear and specific policy mandate, rather than by a shift to class-based and ideological politics.

The Plebiscitary and Parliamentary Theories of Mandates

One reason perhaps for so much ambiguity about the concept of a parliamentary mandate is that the doctrine itself is based on two rather different premises. One is the plebiscitary theory of democracy, under which a government receives its authority directly from the people, while the other is the older theory of parliamentary government. The latter theory is grounded in the idea that the executive or ministry derives its authority from the House of Commons, and holds that its mandate is a parliamentary mandate and only indirectly a popular mandate. Parliamentary government is older than democracy, and, according to Robert Mackay, the "democratic theory has in effect been grafted onto the older and still legally correct theory of the sovereignty of parliament."[41]

The Canadian Senate serves as a useful model for describing the differences in practice between these two sometimes incompatible theories. The unelected Senate must deal with legislation emanating from the elected House of Commons which, under at least one of these theories, has proceeded to enact laws on the basis of a popular mandate. For this reason the Senate is the forum where the notion of a popular mandate often comes into sharpest focus. The recent turmoil in the Canadian Senate, when the Liberal-dominated upper house led by Allan MacEachen cast itself as an often obstreperous blockade across the pathway of government legislation, is only one chapter in a long and complicated saga.

In 1957 and 1958, the Progressive Conservative government of Prime Minister John Diefenbaker also faced an upper house dominated by Liberal senators, and the relationship raised all the same theoretical issues about Parliament and democracy so hotly argued during the past several years of the Mulroney government. The Progressive Conservative Party had come to office under Diefenbaker in the election of 1957 after twenty-two years in opposition as a minority government. By that time the Liberal majority in the Senate had grown to be the largest of any party since Confederation. The following year, however, the Progressive Conservative Party was returned to office in the election of 1958 with what was the largest majority of any government in Canadian history. In the next election in 1962, the Diefenbaker government lost its majority, but was sustained in office by the support in Parliament of the Social Credit Party. Throughout this time the Liberal Party retained its substantial majority in the Senate.

These three elections, says Robert Mackay, with their differing results, "inevitably raised questions as to the extent and validity of the mandate enjoyed by the Progressive Conservative government and about the responsibilities of the Senate majority (and hence of the Senate as a House) under such circumstances."[42]

The Liberal leader in the Senate of the day, the Honourable W. Ross Macdonald, endeavoured to define the Senate's role in these circumstances. Following the change of government in 1957, he said, "The over-riding responsibility of the Senate [is] to make the constitution work." He did not propose that senators "assert [their] legal rights and prerogatives to the prejudice of common sense or reason, or to the sacrifice of the proper functioning of our constitutional machinery . . . [nor] automatically resist every government measure which comes before us. To do so purely out of party considerations would be to hamper any effective government of our nation." Senator Macdonald reiterated this position following the general elections in 1958 and 1962, and it was a position in accord with the approach generally taken over the years by Senate opposition leaders, even those who later found themselves heads of Senate majorities.

Departures from this approach have occasionally occurred. The Liberal-dominated Senate rejected the Borden government's Naval Bill in 1911, and also turned back its legislation for redistribution of seats in both the Commons and the Senate in 1914. Contemporary examples include the Liberal-dominated Senate's treatment of the Mulroney government's legislation dealing with the Canada-U.S. trade treaty, the goods and services tax (GST), Unemployment Insurance Act reforms, the patent drug legislation, and borrowing bills.

In these instances, consternation results both within the government and to a degree among the Canadian public, because the Senate majority begins to act in the same fashion as the Opposition in the Commons. The Opposition generally conceives its role and constitutional duty to be that of defeating the government or forcing a new election. Response to this challenge to the mandate of the popularly elected government has tended to follow a consistent pattern over the years. From Prime Minister Robert Borden to Prime Minister Brian Mulroney, the senatorial challenge has involved various threats and excitement about reforming or abolishing the upper house. After a bit, the noise dies down and the powerful inertia of the system crushes the timid effort at reform.

Since reform efforts so far have always come to naught, the Senate remains. So too, therefore, has the issue of how far the Senate can properly go in fulfilling its constitutional role. Even if it were changed along the lines proposed in the Mulroney government's constitutional suggestions of September 25, 1991, the experiences of the past and present are still instructive regarding the nature of a popular mandate. Indeed, if Canada is to be saddled with a re-vamped and elected Senate, a number of these earlier concerns regarding a popular mandate and the upper house's role as a check or a balance on the House of Commons will become more, not less, germane.

A "Sober Second Thought" for the Electorate

"There is no question of a mandate at all in the case of at least ninety-eight per cent of the measures which come to either House,"

Arthur Meighen, a former Conservative prime minister of Canada, wrote in 1937.[43] Even with respect to such legislation, suggested Meighen, which came not from a popular mandate but merely from the routine working of government over the term of its life, he felt the Senate might improve it, but certainly should never refuse it. He added,

> If it is a subject naturally within the purview of Government, something to do with administration; if it is a reflection in a bill of what the Government should be and feels itself best suited to handle, and if it does not affect positive principle going to the root of our institutions, then I would say that even though it was thought a better way might be devised, even though it was thought that on a balance of merits the bill failed, it would be wiser for the Senate, if it can, after making such remedial amendments as will improve the measure, to allow the government to have its way.[44]

Significantly, however, Meighen made an exception for legislation that would "affect positive principle going to the root of our institutions." He also came to believe that the government ought to have held a general election to obtain a clear popular mandate before dispatching troops overseas in World War I. An outstanding parliamentarian, Meighen reflected deeply upon his experiences in government and in Parliament during the years after he had stepped back from the heated political battles. Having done so he came increasingly to articulate the values of a democratic conservative.

In the above-quoted article on the Senate, for instance, Meighen the parliamentarian had distilled, and Meighen the democrat had synthesized, a dictum about the upper house and the popular mandate, which since 1937 has been reiterated by others, including Liberal Senate leader Ross Macdonald in the late 1950s and early 1960s. Meighen's idea about a reserved power by which the people could authorize fundamental change – indeed by which they must be given the chance to authorize it, or even to reconsider it – flowed from earlier, similar doctrines about Parliament and the people's mandate.

In Meighen's words,

> Where there is a mandate for legislation which comes before the Senate, where such legislation was clearly discussed and placed on

the platform of the successful party in an election, then only in most exceptional circumstances should there be any attempt or desire on the part of the Upper House to refuse to implement a mandate by its concurring imprimatur. No one, however, who has thought the subject out can say under no circumstances should legislation coming to the Senate from the Commons, though clearly supported by a popular mandate in an election, fail of support in the Second Chamber.[45]

In other words, there could in rare cases be an exception to the rule that the Senate not refuse legislation that came about in clear fulfilment of the people's mandate.

Meighen invoked the names of earlier leaders such as Sir John A. Macdonald, George Brown, Étienne-Paschal Taché of Quebec, and those of various Maritime statesmen who had also enunciated the view that one of the Senate's duties

is to see not that wise legislation, having for its purpose nothing but the public good, is allowed, irrespective of mandate, to become law, but in certain conceivable events to see to it as well that the public of Canada, which may at one election have endorsed extraordinary proposals, has opportunity, if such proposals are of a particularly dangerous or revolutionary character, to think the subject over again.

Meighen was arguing, in short, that the Senate may, "under certain circumstance, be allowed to appeal from the electorate of yesterday to the electorate of to-morrow."[46]

This was the voice of Tory democracy, or what now might be called democratic conservatism. In the narrow cases where Meighen's dictum would apply, it was a radical challenge to the traditional doctrine of a mandate. Meighen argued not only for allowing the Senate to exercise "sober second thought," as John A. Macdonald envisaged it, but indeed for allowing the exercise of senatorial powers to permit, in turn, the Canadian electorate itself to have a "sober second thought" about its previous mandate to the government.

Yet, as Robert Mackay pointed out in *The Unreformed Senate*, the Canadian upper house is in a singularly weak position politically to make such appeals against the people's mandate. This, in its deepest sense, was the core issue in the debate about our institutional arrangements during the Liberal senators' efforts to block the free trade legislation in 1988 long enough to force a general election on the issue. In 1926, when Mackay first wrote his classic work on the Senate, he observed what remains as the case today: "there are no constitutional arrangements to enable the Senate to call for a plebiscite in which an issue could be fairly and clearly stated; any appeal against the mandate thus becomes in effect an appeal against the Government."[47]

In this context it would be for the government of the day to take up the challenge from the Senate, to choose the time of the plebiscite, and to phrase the wording of the question appearing on the ballot. In practice the appeal would appear to be coming from an Opposition majority in the Senate, noted Mackay, and only formally of the Senate as a whole. It would in effect be seen as "an appeal to the people to turn one political party out and to put another into office. This is the dilemma of the theory of an appeal against the mandate."[48] Of course it is a dilemma if one sees the "appeal to the people" taking only the form of a general election; it is not a problem at all the moment one allows for the possibility of a clear and specific appeal to the people on the issue in question through a direct vote in a referendum. Even though the Senate had not invoked this power, Mackay concluded, its right to make such an appeal could only be regarded as being in suspense, and not as an obsolete power or right.

The Validity of Measures in Relation to a Mandate

Following the 1962 general election, when the Diefenbaker government was returned with only minority support in the House of Commons, Liberal Senate leader Ross Macdonald returned once more to the question of the popular mandate, in light of the changed circumstances. He wondered whether they posed any further or special responsibilities on the Senate. The government has "no clear mandate from the people, either as to general policy or as to specific measures," he declared, concluding that the Senate must accordingly take the general attitude that no governmental legislation coming before the upper house had behind it a clear popular mandate.[49] Under these circumstances, said Mackay, in reviewing

Macdonald's position, it would be necessary for the Senate "to give all legislation more searching investigation than had been the custom following a conclusive popular verdict."[50]

Progressive Conservative senators, who supported the Diefenbaker government, understandably took a different view. They did not think the senators should be either sloppy in their work if a government had a majority in the House of Commons, nor stringently attentive only if a bill came from a House where a minority government was in office. They took a reasonably objective interpretation of the role of the Senate, seeing its function as being free of the constitutional fiction of a popular mandate. "It makes no difference by whom a bill is introduced in the other place," asserted Senator Brooks, the government leader in the Senate, "if it receives a majority there it comes to us as a measure endorsed by the elected representatives of the people of Canada. The fact that it was sponsored by a minority government gives no cause to consider it differently than we would a measure introduced by the strongest of governments."[51] Similarly, Senator Wallace McCutcheon asserted that the obligation of the Senate "at all times" was "to speak to the question and not to the electorate."[52]

This is where, as Mackay pointed out, the two different premises for the concept of a mandate – the plebiscitary mandate from the people and the parliamentary mandate derived internally from the Commons – converge. It is usually the case that a government receives its authority directly from the people, when one party or another is returned to the House of Commons with a clear majority. Yet minority governments resulted after the general elections of 1921, 1925, 1957, 1962, 1963, 1965, 1972, and 1979. If one believes that governments should constitutionally have a clear majority, "the implication is that any minority government is necessarily in the position of a caretaker government, with limited authority derived from, or assented to by, the House of Commons. Such authority would not extend to the introduction of unusual legislation which would constitutionally require a popular mandate," noted Mackay.[53]

In contrast, if one adopts the theory of parliamentary government advanced by Senator A.J. Brooks, that the government's mandate was a parliamentary mandate, and only indirectly a popular mandate, then, according to Mackay, the minority status of the government ought to be a matter of indifference to senators. From a strict constitutional point of view, concluded Mackay, Senator Brooks's argument was no doubt sound, and thus "any bill coming up from the House of Commons was of equal validity with any other precisely because it had behind it the parliamentary mandate."[54]

From this brief examination of the history of institutional relations between the Canada's elected Commons and its appointed Senate, what emerges is affirmation of the idea that when an election produces a clear result, the governing party in fact receives a direct mandate from the people. This broadly accepted notion has generally permeated all discussion on the subject. Governments facing defeat, moreover, or with a view to receiving a popular mandate when parliamentary support was doubtful or withdrawn, according to Mackay, have always appealed directly to the people.[55] What also emerges from this examination, however, is that the government's mandate is spoken of in terms that have virtually everything to do with the authority to govern, and almost nothing to do with specific policies. It remains true, as Meighen noted over a half-century ago, that "at least ninety-eight per cent," to use his estimate, of the measures being brought before Parliament by the government of the day have received no mandate for action from the people at all.

The Exaggeration of a Mandate

Consideration of an electoral mandate must next turn to this crucial point about the tendency to convert a mandate that merely gives authority to govern into a supposed mandate for specific policies. This significant distinction is mostly assumed in the sweeping and usually vague statements about a mandate's being virtually an authority to govern.

Once a government has been elected, says political science professor Robert Jackson, it can claim a mandate from the voters to rule on their behalf. "Thus," he says, "the electoral process helps to legitimate the government of the day and, although this may be exaggerated, to legitimate the policies that the government has been elected to carry out."[56]

It is this exaggeration or distortion of the mandate that is of concern here. There are fundamental issues on which the Canadian public cannot be said to have properly concentrated its attention before voting, and in respect of which a government at the peril of losing credibility may stretch the concept of its mandate too far in order to justify a major initiative or radical measure. Here it is worth noting the condition that accompanied Meighen's statement that each government measure should be tacitly assumed to be within its mandate, even if 98 percent of them had never been contemplated by the electorate, *provided* "it does not affect positive principle going to the root of our institutions."

Indeed, the real issue here is not the credibility of a particular government in relation to its chosen policies. Governments "of the day" come and go as the calendar changes, and loss of believability will simply hasten the day of its ending. The deeper problem arises from the fact that our entire system of government is based ultimately on the consent of the governed. Every government, whether in office for a brief flash or a long yawn, must never forget that exaggeration of a popular mandate beyond what seems reasonable or appropriate to the people will become like acid dissolving the very guy-wires of consent that hold our governing system in place. It is easier for us to recognize this truth, perhaps, when we see it carried to extremes elsewhere – such as communist governments that arbitrarily issue commands that are adverse to the interests of the people, but always doing so in the name of "the people" themselves.

Three recent issues that tested this legitimacy of a government's mandate in three different ways were those of Canadian participation during 1990–91 in the Gulf War, Canada's entry into a free trade treaty with the United States, and the government legislation to replace the manufacturers' sales tax with the goods and services tax. The war could not have been contemplated in the 1988 election; the trade treaty was at its centre (but had not even been proposed in the 1984 election after which the government began this major change); and the GST was in the Progressive Conservative Party's platform, had been debated in Parliament, but was largely obscured by other issues that were more dominant at the time. Each of these questions was fundamental to our country. They were also questions of a precise nature. The feelings Canadians have had about these three matters, and the political and parliamentary resolution of them, make more prominent the issue of distinguishing between a general mandate to govern and a specific mandate for major changes in policy direction.

British Concepts of an Electoral Mandate

Since Canadian democratic theory and parliamentary institutions are largely derived from the British experience, and since debate on these questions of popular mandate in Great Britain was closely followed in the nineteenth and early twentieth centuries by Canadian politicians, it will increase the understanding of our situation to look at several characteristics of and highlights from the British experience.

Some 200 years ago the theory of electoral mandates began to be developed in Great Britain. Those were simpler times, and election interpretation, like any interpretation, as H.D. Forbes has pointed out, "relied upon a mixture of simple rules and common sense." If a party stated a policy on a major public question, he says, and that policy was disputed by its opponents but the party still won a majority, then it must logically have been because the people supported the policy. "This loose rule of interpretation allowed commentators to work in their own opinions about what the government should do under the guise of explaining what the people had said it must do," suggests Forbes with a touch worthy of Stephen Leacock. This was long before pollsters were on hand, he concludes with impish truth, "to confuse commentators in their interpretation of elections."[57]

Of course, political institutions and practices in Canada today, whatever their origins, are significantly different from those in contemporary Britain. Although the British parliamentary system did provide our model and our constitution expressly imported British customs and practices as developed to 1867, there were important differences. The existence of a federal form of government, created by the constitution of 1867, itself "profoundly modifies the wholesale application of British constitutional theory," as Ronald Blair says.[58] In addition, there are major differences in our party systems, forms of cabinet, committees of Parliament, office of Speaker, and more. Yet Blair also observes, "the assumption remains that, except for a federal form of government, parliamentary government in Canada remains a close approximation of that in Britain" and that "with a blithe disregard for reality, academics (and journalists) accept uncritically the validity of analysis of British government for Canadian government also."[59]

To note the parallel developments in Canada and Britain, however, is to examine the joint evolution of both the colony and the imperial power, and even to see stages at which Canadians were ahead of the British in implementing direct voting to obtain a mandate from the people. Canadian politicians, for instance, seized on the idea of a popular mandate and the holding of direct votes through plebiscites well before the British. Canada's House of Commons echoed with debates about plebiscites and mandates in the mid-1890s, whereas the first such formal debate on a referendum never occurred inside the British Parliament until April 1911. Discussions about fitting plebiscites into the parliamentary system of representative government, however, had engaged leading British political thinkers before that date. The context in which the concept of "a mandate from the people" was first debated at Westminster was that of a general election.

By 1832 in Britain "the principle of the people's mandate was first genuinely operative," according to Cecil Emden.[60] Enactment of the great Reform Bill of that year demonstrated how "the election of a majority of representatives, pledged to a particular measure, could be interpreted as having imposed an obligation on the Government to introduce it." Politicians saw the advantage, notes Emden, in that it could mean securing a majority in Parliament and inviting the new electorate to exercise its judgment in public affairs. Each successive extension of the franchise made this advantage more obvious. The electors, Emden says, "were treated as capable, not merely of electing members, but of making decisions on vital political questions, such as the maintenance of free trade, or the disestablishment of the Irish Church."[61]

The introduction by Prime Minister Gladstone's government of the first Home Rule Bill in 1886 provoked debate in Britain about the need for the electorate to be consulted on matters involving constitutional change. Originally, the best form of consultation was felt to

111

be an election, which would produce a specific mandate, rather than a referendum. After 1890, however, the recognition that a general election was an inadequate means of producing a specific mandate led to advocacy for direct democracy in the form of plebiscites or referendums in Britain.

The Radicals in British politics, such as Joseph Chamberlain, felt that under the rule of democracy the control of government ought to pass from the Commons to the electorate. By appealing directly to the voters on specific programs, political parties would be limited in their actions once in government. The Radicals believed that MPs should be obligated to support all the items in their party program, and the electorate, in voting for a party, could be assumed to have endorsed them all. "In this way the voter would gain more influence over government policy, but the role of Parliament would be further diminished," observed Vernon Bogdanor in assessing the Radicals' view.[62]

Even those who rejected this extreme view, as did the Whig leader Lord Hartington, still insisted that the electorate had to be consulted on matters involving constitutional change. "Although no principle of a 'mandate' may exist," he said in the debate when the Gladstone government was roundly criticized for failing to consult the electorate, "I maintain that there are certain limits which Parliament is morally bound to observe, and beyond which Parliament has morally not the right to go in its relations with the constituents."[63] Hartington saw the constituencies of Great Britain as "the source of the power" of the House of Commons, and maintained that "in the absence of an emergency that could not be foreseen, the House of Commons has no more right to initiate legislation – of which the constituencies were not informed, and as to which if they had been so informed, there is, at all events, the very greatest doubt as to what their decision might be."[64]

Many Conservatives in British politics, meanwhile, also argued in favour of a popular mandate, but from a different perspective. They felt that greater popular participation would itself form a safeguard against the abuse of power, since they believed that the electorate was basically hostile to change. So, as Bogdanor notes, "they championed the referendum as a weapon against the unlimited sovereignty of a potentially tyrannical House of Commons."[65]

The deeply political debate in Britain over constitutional matters, which continued between 1867 and 1918, from the second to the fourth Reform Acts, centred on a twofold effort to define the place of political parties in the British constitution and limit the authority of party government. A Commons composed of shifting groups (the "loose fish," as Sir John A. Macdonald identified them in the Canadian Parliament) would be vigilant in watching the executive, while the House of Lords "could check a Commons majority whose pretensions outran its discretion," observes Bogdanor. Yet could these checks and balances be maintained under a system of party government in which the government controlled the Commons and limited the powers of the Lords? "Of what value was the sovereignty of Parliament," asks Bogdanor, posing the same question that galvanized the British constitutional debate about popular mandate, "if it turned out to be no more than the sovereignty of party?"[66]

Dicey and the Transformation of Popular Government

A.V. Dicey, the legendary constitutional lawyer, emerged as the first major advocate of referendums in Britain. This deeply conservative jurist inquired whether the people – by whom he meant the much larger British electorate that had recently been enfranchised – were to exercise their power only through representative institutions, or also through the machinery of direct democracy. Dicey, both doctrinally as a believer in the sovereignty of Parliament and philosophically as a conservative, had accurately discerned the trends that were under way in Britain. With the coming of popular government and the rise of political parties, the earlier power of the Commons was declining.

A government returned to office after a general election would naturally claim that it enjoyed a mandate from the electorate, Bogdanor writes, and one of the many consequences of an election was that the House of Lords would be enjoined not to interfere with its work. "The intensification of party loyalties," he says, "meant that the supremacy of the Commons would become merely a cloak for the authority of government: for power would lie not with MPs but with the party leadership and organization."[67] This situation was also arising in other countries, including our own, whose British-inspired parliaments were feeling the transforming effects of the rise of organized political parties.

In the British case this led Dicey to emerge, not hostile to so radical an innovation as the referendum (which some parliamentarians criticized as a technique to devalue the authority of Parliament), but rather as its champion, embracing the direct vote as a new and important part of British political institutions. The great advantage of the referendum for Dicey, notes Bogdanor, "lay in its being a *democratic* check upon the excesses of popular government [and] therefore an instrument which suited the spirit of the age."[68]

The referendum offered the electorate a veto over bills that had been passed by Parliament. In this way it could complete the symmetry in the transition from an absolute monarchy to a constitutional monarchy with a broad-based electorate. Until the eighteenth century the monarch had enjoyed just such a veto over laws passed by Parliament. So, in turn, this power should now pass to the electorate, reasoned Dicey, which would become in effect a third chamber, thus finishing the process by which "the prerogatives of the crown" would be transformed "into the privileges of the people."[69]

This is the historical context from which our "constitutional monarchy" of today has evolved. The real powers of the Crown have been reduced to important symbolic functions and are exercised by others (the government, the courts) in the Crown's name. This reality has produced the doctrine which necessarily holds that sovereignty has passed to the people. Another result is the rhetoric that expresses the concomitant theory that elected representatives are not the masters of the people but rather their "servants."

The dilemma posed by these early transformations in constitutional arrangements in Britain, so astutely understood by Dicey, remains a vital consideration, and is present even in the current Canadian debate about our Parliament. For example, in 1991 Government House Leader Harvie Andre spoke of how in other federal systems citizens are represented in three different ways: nationally, regionally, and individually. "Ideally in Canada," he said, "the national body would be the Monarchy or the Governor-General, the

regional body would be the Senate, and individuals would be represented by their MPs in the House of Commons. But because the roles
of Governor-General and Senate have been reduced to figure-head
and patronage posts, the Commons has to do all the representing."
Parliamentary reporter for *The Globe and Mail* Susan Delacourt indicated, in the same article in which Andre's remarks appeared, that the
House of Commons has become the one-stop, all-purpose institution
for every kind of government function in Canada. Pointing out how the
prime minister is supposed to be the national figure, and the cabinet
and other Commons committees are supposed to cut across all the
regions, while the MPs despite all the obstacles of party discipline are
supposed to represent individuals in their ridings, Andre was quoted as
saying, "We're trying to do a lot of things through one institution, and
you know, it doesn't work all that well."[70]

The rule changes regarding the internal operations of the
House of Commons that were being proposed by the government in
the autumn of 1991 were intended to address some of these problems, particularly party discipline and the possibility of free votes. So
far, though, any suggestion of giving further power to the people has
only taken the form of a proposal to elect yet another legislative
assembly (namely, a revamped Canadian Senate), rather than opt-
ing for the solutions contemplated in Britain in similar circumstances a century ago when Dicey asked, "Ought the Referendum to
be Introduced into England?" Modernization of the operations of
the Canadian House of Commons, while urgently required, will not
of itself be an adequate substitute for broader political changes, for
what Peter Dobell points out needs to be "a coherent approach to
enhance the role of Parliament in ways that will cause the public to
feel that their government is responsive to their concerns."[71]

Dicey discerned that a referendum, apart from its role of
balancing political power, could also be an important educative
motivator. Since it would encourage the elector "to decide public
issues upon the weight of the argument, and not on the basis of party
loyalties – it [would enable] him to distinguish men from measures."[72]

Dicey's advocacy of the referendum and popular participation was
specifically intended to secure constitutional protection. He did not
advocate the right of electors to initiate legislation themselves. The

people's role in a referendum on a specific bill would be to serve as a restraint on any ill-considered alterations in the fundamental institutions of the country put forward by the government. He saw this process supplying the best, perhaps even "the only check on the predominance of party which is at the same time democratic and conservative."[73]

Dicey also saw the referendum as "the one available check on the recklessness of Party leaders." Moreover, it could be the means for giving "formal acknowledgement of the doctrine which lies at the basis of English democracy – that a law depends at bottom for its enactment on the consent of the nation as represented by the electors." Vernon Bogdanor concludes from this that Dicey's motivation in advocating the referendum

> stemmed less from a theoretical belief in the sovereignty of the people than from distrust of representative institutions, and especially the party system. The referendum would be a powerful weapon against the wire-pullers in local constituencies, for it denied the fundamental premise of the Radicals that victory in a general election yielded a mandate for specific legislation.[74]

Disraeli and the Doctrine of the Specific Mandate

The flamboyant and forceful Conservative leader Benjamin Disraeli first advanced the claim that a government required a "specific mandate" for truly major change. In 1868 he objected to Gladstone's raising the issue of disestablishing the Irish Church in the House of Commons without having first brought it before the country. Disestablishment would have separated church and state, a profoundly significant development. Disraeli, who Bogdanor describes as having had a "romantic conception of an alliance between Crown and People against a predatory Whig Parliament," denied the "moral competence" of Parliament to disestablish the Irish Church without an appeal first to the nation. "You cannot come," he said,

> on a sudden, and without the country being the least informed of your intention, to a decision that will alter the character of England and her institutions . . . Technically, no doubt, Parliament has power to do so. But, Sir, there is a moral exercise of power as well as a technical, and when you touch the principles on which the most ancient and influential institutions are founded, it is most

wise that you should hold your hand unless you have assured yourselves of such an amount of popular sympathy and support as will make your legislation permanent and beneficial.[75]

Disraeli, of course, enjoyed the success which he did in British politics and as prime minister because of his instinctive understanding that in a democracy governments must proceed on major matters only with the consent of the governed. While there are many ways to obtain and discern consent, Disraeli was astute enough to recognize the centrality of the voting process as a means of clarifying the people's mandate.

Disraeli's doctrine of the specific mandate was subsequently picked up by other prominent British Conservatives, such as Lord Salisbury of the House of Lords. Salisbury held that

> there is a class of cases, small in number, and varying in kind, in which the nation must be called into counsel and must decide the policy of the Government. It may be that the House of Commons in determining the opinion of the nation is wrong; and if there are grounds for entertaining that belief, it is always open to this House, and indeed it is the duty of this House, to insist that the nation shall be consulted.[76]

This doctrine formed the basis of the Conservative Party's defence of the constitutional role of the Lords until 1911. In Canada, it was also the basis for Arthur Meighen's position, articulated in 1937, that the Canadian Senate might on a few issues of transcending importance – even where the Canadian electorate had already pronounced on the issue – force reappraisal.

Some Conservatives in the House of Lords went even further. Lord Derby, for example, insisted that only the general principle of a bill may have been approved by the country in a general election, and that the specific bill encompassing the measure should itself again be submitted after its passage in Parliament for ratification by the people. Of course, Derby did not apply this view to routine or regular matters of government, but only to bills that would alter the "fundamental law" of the country. Debate naturally arose next as to just what constituted such a law.

In any event, it was in this form that the doctrine of the specific mandate came to be advocated by a number of British Conservatives.

The same idea, about the imperative nature of a mandate from the people for a specific change to fundamental arrangements, spread elsewhere among parliamentary democracies. Australians incorporated it in their constitution in 1900, by requiring a direct vote of the people to ratify any amendment to the country's constitution. Today in Canada it is the approach adopted by democratic conservatives like me who believe that constitutional amendments must be ratified by direct popular vote in a referendum.

Where to Draw the Line

The doctrine of the specific mandate has many problems, but the one that must be solved first is, where do you draw the line? The answer to this question cannot be given for all time by preparing two definitive lists that strictly define all those issues that must, and all the others that need not, be submitted to the people in a direct vote. Instead, several criteria or guidelines can be stated to help us make the decision in specific cases. A half-dozen or more criteria, for example, can easily be drawn from the historical experiences described in this chapter alone.

- The first one could be Arthur Meighen's rule, articulated in 1937: does the proposed change "affect positive principle going to the root of our institutions"?
- Next, one might add the 1886 stipulation of Lord Hartington that says, in "the absence of an emergency which could not be foreseen" legislation cannot be introduced when the public at the time of an election were not informed of it and there is "the very gravest doubt" as to what their decision might be if they were informed.
- Third, following Dicey's observation in 1890 about the educational role of a referendum: is the proposed measure one where the public must be well-informed, and where for the good of the country the electors should consider the issue on "the weight of the argument and not on the basis of party loyalties"?
- A fourth criterion could be based on Dicey's concern about abuse of power and could use this question: is the referendum needed as a check on the recklessness of party leaders?

118

- Fifth, one might adapt another concern of Dicey's in this way: is the proposed law or change one which "depends at bottom for its enactment on the consent of the nation as represented by the electors"?
- As a sixth criterion, one might use a point made by *The Economist* magazine, which is discussed later in this chapter, to ask: will a referendum mandate help make the government stronger or more credible in international negotiations on a specific issue?
- Finally, a seventh test: is the issue one that needs for the sake of the national interest to be resolved separately from the personalities of the country's politicians? Can the holding of a direct vote help the government or the country find a way out of an impasse?

Specific Mandates and the Canadian Electorate

The concept of seeking a specific mandate from the Canadian electorate is not alien to our country. As discussed earlier, Prime Minister Mackenzie King, for example, had campaigned in the 1940 general election on the basis that there would be no conscription for overseas military service. Having won that general election and concluding that he had a mandate from the people in favour of that policy, King felt, in conscience as well as in terms of Canadian political realities, that he could not, when circumstances later changed, reverse the mandate from the people without their specific consent. Accordingly, direct consultation with the Canadian electorate took place in 1942, on the narrow and specific question of whether the government could be released by the electorate from its previous pledge.

On an earlier occasion of Canada's being at war, Liberal leader Wilfrid Laurier was one of a number of people who believed a specific mandate was required to send Canadian troops overseas in World War I. In this case it is especially significant to understand the background of the situation because even the government's "general mandate" to govern comes into question.

By the time the Borden government began proceeding with its Military Service Act in 1917, more than the normal five years had

119

passed since the government's mandate had been conferred in the general election of October 7, 1911. This 12th Parliament should have been dissolved by October 6, 1916, but was not because by that time the country had found itself in the midst of war. So Prime Minister Borden proposed an amendment to the constitution to extend the 12th Parliament's life a further year to October 7, 1917, but in doing so declared the motion would not be pressed if the Opposition objected as a party. Borden observed at the time that while it would have been constitutionally proper to seek a new mandate from the electorate after the redistribution of constituencies in 1914, this had not happened and a wartime election was undesirable.

Opposition leader Laurier, in reply, emphasized the unfortunate conditions that would arise from an electoral contest during time of war, and said that the extension of the parliamentary term would implicitly involve a pledge by the government that no election would take place before the autumn of 1917. The resolution passed the Commons, and the British Parliament duly enacted the amendment to the Canadian constitution, the British North America Act, to extend the life of the Parliament by a year.

This postponement of a constitutionally required election and the mandate that it would confer was a significant precedent in Canada. Parliament – the people's elected representatives – rather than the people themselves, had extended the government's mandate. The extraordinary nature of the circumstances, however, and the approach taken by both leaders, must both be emphasized. It must also be pointed out that Parliament would not extend the time for a new election by more than one year. The 12th Parliament was dissolved on October 6, 1917, and the election was held on December 17. So, for all this, the general election did take place during the war.[77]

It was in this period of an extraordinarily extended parliamentary mandate that the conscription issue and the Military Service Act arose. Laurier opposed conscription, unless the measure was approved by a majority of the voters. He said that a Parliament elected in 1911 on entirely different issues was now moribund and had no right to involve the people in so serious a matter unless their mandate was renewed by a general election.[78] Laurier stressed that the clear authority of a specific mandate on conscription from the people was required because a principle of long-standing had been that Canadians not be conscripted for overseas military conflict. Following weeks of intense debate, however, Laurier's amendment calling for a referendum to seek direct authority from the people for the fundamental change of imposing military conscription was voted down in the summer of 1917 by 111 to 62, a majority of 49 for the government.

A third illustration of the Canadian approach to a specific mandate involved the Canada-wide plebiscite in 1898 on prohibition. The vote came about as the direct consequence of a campaign promise made by the Liberal Party under Prime Minister Wilfrid Laurier to hold a popular vote in order to obtain a specific mandate on the matter. The election promise had been based on the Liberal Party platform of 1896 adopted at the party's convention at Ottawa in June of 1893. It declared, "That whereas public attention is at present much directed to the consideration of the admittedly great evils of intemperance, it is desirable that the mind of the people should be clearly ascertained on the question of Prohibition by means of a Dominion Plebiscite."[79] Having won the election, Laurier and the Liberals considered themselves under a mandate from the people to proceed, and although the measure was delayed by a year, ground-breaking legislation did come before Parliament in 1898 to authorize the holding of Canada's first plebiscite.

The relationship between the general and the specific mandate, incidentally, involves more than abstract considerations. It also has immediate practical consequences for politicians who have taken public positions on a given matter. The tug of war between the various elements of an electoral mandate and the additional cross-currents between an MP's personal position and that officially required by government policy and party discipline is exemplified in the case of George Elliot Casey. The MP for Elgin West constituency was speaking during the debate of May 3, 1898, on the government's Prohibition Plebiscite Bill. Casey, who for years had declared his opposition to the principle of plebiscites, now faced the dilemma most troublesome to all government backbenchers. Giving vent to his problem, he told how he felt "compelled to support the Bill," since the government itself was "compelled to keep their promises and I, as a supporter of theirs and one who shared in their pledges," could do nothing other. Casey then explained with tortured logic how the bill had "my hearty support in its general features ... though in opposition to my judgement in its principle." The bill was presented "in consequence of a promise given and arrangements made over which I had no control," he protested. How much simpler it would have been for the anguished MP just to accept that in a democracy this quest for a specific mandate on a policy so profound as prohibition is how things should normally work, given the vague general nature of the electoral mandate.

On the matter of the prohibition plebiscite itself, however, Casey aspired to the intellectual company of Benjamin Disraeli and Lord Salisbury. He said,

> The people should not be asked to vote for an abstract proposition, but they should be asked to say whether some particular scheme of prohibition which is laid before them suits them or not. Anybody who knows anything of the popular vote knows that it is easy to get people to vote for an abstract proposition like Free Trade, or Protection, or Prohibition, or anything else, while you could not get them to agree, by the smallest majority, upon some particular plan of carrying out the principle that might be adopted.

Casey therefore urged the government to adopt the referendum rather than the plebiscite, and then to pass a bill through Parliament with the condition that it should not become law until it was carried by a certain specified majority of the people of the country.

Referendums and plebiscites "are both foreign to our constitution," he said, "but of two foreign experiences, I would adopt the more reasonable and logical one. Therefore, I should prefer the submission of a bill rather than the submission of an abstract proposition."[80] That would be about as specific a mandate as one could get, and to submit a bill for a direct vote in a referendum that would be legally binding would be the most explicit form possible of law making by the people.

The Paradox of Strong or Weak Mandates

Germane to any appraisal of an electoral mandate from the people is the frequency of general elections. If general elections occur only every five years, for example, the legitimacy of a government's general mandate to govern is running to the very end of its tether. This is one of the important reasons governments in Canada generally seek a dissolution of the elected legislature and a new election a year or so before the five-year term is up. Frequent elections suggest that the government's mandate is fresher and stronger for having been renewed. This characteristic of flexibility has a drawback, however, in that under our parliamentary system elections can occur at virtually any time short of five years, which can mean an undesirable frequency in elections that is most likely to happen with minority governments.

Yet, as we saw in the earlier discussion of the Diefenbaker government's popular mandate following its re-election as a minority government in 1962, the legitimacy and extent of such a new mandate is then challenged by political opponents of the government. These opponents claim that because the party forming the government only received a minority of seats in the Commons, the people had not entrusted it with a real mandate to govern. In other words, frequent renewal of mandates is most likely when there are minority governments, but minority governments are themselves an indication that the public is unwilling to give any party a strong mandate. Conversely, the stronger the mandate, the less frequent will be its renewal.

There is clearly a paradox in the doctrine of a mandate as it has been uncritically accepted in Canadian political thought. This problem is further complicated by taking into account the level of popular vote which parties receive. Since the demise of Canada's two-party system, majority governments have normally been formed – even with a "landslide" victory as far as the number of seats is concerned – on the basis of a minority of popular support. Some majority governments are formed nowadays in Canada with only one-third of the electorate having voted for the "victorious" party.

Specific Mandates within General Elections

Sometimes, as was discussed in Chapter 4, a plebiscite question is included with the ballot at the same time that citizens go to the polls to elect representatives in a general election. This approach can serve to separate a contentious or fundamental issue from the particular party platforms and personalities involved in an election campaign.

Where particular measures are submitted directly to the country in this way and the people have given a specific mandate by their approval, the newly elected legislature and government, whatever its stripe and composition, ought then to directly carry the measure through into law. The October 17, 1991, results of British Columbia's two election-time referendum questions are a recent example of this: because of the approval of both propositions, by a ratio of about four to one, NDP leader Michael Harcourt, who formed a majority government as a result of that election, said he would respect the outcome of the referendum.

This discussion about a specific mandate would perhaps be entirely theoretical, or at least rhetorical, if there were no instrument at hand to give it meaning. For the British Conservatives who developed the doctrine there was such an instrument, the House of Lords. This body could ensure the reference of fundamental changes to the electorate. As Bogdanor writes, the doctrine of the specific mandate could thus be used "to justify the pretensions of the Lords in forcing a dissolution of parliament." This was exactly the justification of the action of the House of Lords in 1893 in rejecting the second Home Rule Bill. Since the lords believed there was no majority in the country for Home Rule, they "challenged Gladstone to dissolve parliament and prove them wrong."[81]

For Canadians, the corresponding instrument is the Senate, and the British situation is comparable to ours when one considers the similar position of Opposition Leader John Turner to that of the British Conservatives in the House of Lords, in urging the Canadian Liberal senators, who likewise willingly obliged, to oppose the government's legislation on free trade with the United States. The Liberal senators challenged the government of Prime Minister Mulroney to dissolve Parliament and prove them wrong.

A problem raised by the traditional Canadian doctrine of mandate stems from the inclusion of specific measures in the election-time program or platform of a political party. In the form in which the specific mandate concept was adopted by most of the British Conservatives, the unanswerable question was: how do you distinguish what really goes on in an election? For example, even if a government accepts a challenge and dissolves Parliament to secure an election victory, that party, suggests Bogdanor, "could never be justified in claiming that they had won the election *because of,* rather than *in spite of* the contentious legislation in question."[82] Conversely, the Opposition cannot readily say that the government failed to achieve a mandate from the people. We all saw how the credibility of such a claim was strained when some Liberal and New Democratic parliamentarians sought to argue that the Progressive Conservative government had no mandate to implement the free trade treaty with the U.S. because some 57 percent of the electorate voted for parties other than the Progressive Conservative Party in the 1988 general election. At the same time, many people believed the PCs won much support in spite of the party's free trade policy and, therefore, doubted that the people's mandate had been given on this specific issue.

Another problem with the accepted concept of mandate, be it general or specific, was illustrated in the 1988 general election also. The Mulroney government campaigned on the very specific proposal to acquire nuclear-propelled submarines for the Canadian Armed Forces, outlining the role of such vessels and their estimated cost. During the election, Mulroney as party leader explicitly reiterated, in response to specific questions from the news media, that their acquisition remained a policy of his Progressive Conservative government. Since it was re-elected, one could reasonably claim that the Mulroney government then had a mandate to proceed with this program. In fact, it cancelled its plans shortly after the election.

Such reversals seem to happen after most Canadian general elections. In 1974, for example, the election commitment by Liberal leader Pierre Trudeau to "double track" the railroad from the prairies to the west coast in order to accommodate faster transportation of wheat to the sea ports was a popular proposal. It was, however, dropped after the Liberals were re-elected; Finance Minister John Turner quietly announced that funds for the project were not available. The railroad plan was cancelled even though, according to our election doctrines, it had been mandated by the people.

Another reversal occurred after the 1974 election, in which PC leader Robert Stanfield pledged that if elected he would impose price and wage controls to curb inflation. Liberal leader Trudeau ridiculed the idea ("Zap – you're frozen!"), and it was clearly *not* Liberal policy. When the Liberals won the election and received their mandate to govern, however, Prime Minister Trudeau proceeded to impose the controls that, arguably, the electorate had expressly rejected.

A decade earlier, Liberal leader Lester Pearson's promise to build a causeway to Prince Edward Island met the identical post-election fate of Prime Minister's Trudeau's second track of rails. Trudeau in earlier days had himself been outraged by Prime Minister Pearson and the Liberal Party's breathtaking flip-flop on nuclear weapons for the Bomarc missiles that led to a major national debate about nuclear arms and Canadian independence from American political control in 1963.

Even the New Democratic Party, which has sometimes sounded rather sanctimonious in describing itself as a "party of principle," has shown in office that, just like the other brokerage political parties, it too could autonomously change its electoral mandate. A recent example is the Ontario NDP government under Bob Rae. The NDP had campaigned vigorously for a state-operated automobile insurance plan as a matter of party principle, but announced a year after the election that this fundamental commitment would have to be "postponed."

In short, if one subscribes to the theory of an electoral mandate, one must admit that governments of all political stripes in Canada frequently repudiate specific mandates received from the people. No leading politician has actually questioned the principle of mandates in the longest time, although human nature and the pressure of circumstances have, suggests Cecil Emden, "caused party leaders to take divergent views in varying circumstances on the extent to which it is applicable."[83] Not only have questions of expedience given rise to differences of opinion regarding the applicability of the principle of mandate, but also, he says, "problems regarding the nature and the extent of the authority to be obtained have puzzled those who are anxious to see that the people's newly acquired political capacity has a fair chance of being exercised."[84]

This behaviour by parties of contradicting and reversing themselves shows why the constitutional fiction that an electoral mandate settles specific issues becomes a dangerous doctrine in the context of Canadian brokerage party politics. It also helps account for the levels of public anger with politicians, the public's mistrust of the intentions of government, and the significant decline in the number of Canadians with fixed allegiances to political parties.

A general election simply cannot be restricted to one issue. Moreover, under our electoral law the distribution of MPs following a general election does not bear a precise relationship to the distribution of votes, and therefore it is possible for a minority of voters to elect a majority of MPs. For these two reasons, a general election could not be said to provide a mandate for any particular line of policy. That, to many people, in fact becomes the whole case for the referendum.

Elections for People, Referendums for Issues

Elections are mostly about people, while plebiscites and referendums are about issues. This simple distinction can perhaps help clear away some of the confusion about where and how our governments get their mandates. With all the misinformed "experts" around, however, Canadians should not be judged too harshly if their thinking about the roles of elections and plebiscites is a little fuzzy. When a public issue boils up, people are often heard to exclaim, "Let the people decide!" This instinct is good, yet often these intuitive democrats err by not choosing the most refined or appropriate method for achieving their purpose, like a painter who uses a roller rather than a small brush for the precision work.

Our political leaders themselves often contribute to this confusion over elections and plebiscites. In his 1987 bid to scuttle the proposed free trade treaty between Canada and the United States, for example, New Democratic Party leader Ed Broadbent solemnly called for a chance to "let the people decide" – but then urged a general election. The New Democrats had two excellent reasons for wanting a vote on free trade: they fundamentally opposed the initiative, and they were then receiving very high levels of support in the public opinion polls. "Even so," I said of them at the time, "they have selected the wrong democratic instrument. If Canadians are summoned to the ballot box on free trade, it should not be to vote in a general election, but in a plebiscite."[85] Only by passing judgment on a single issue can voters offer an accurate, democratic expression of their will. A general election is, by its very nature, an event in which various personalities, programs, and policies are rolled into a single phenomenon from which it is impossible to extract a clear mandate on a specific issue.

Had a general election been called then on the issue of the trade treaty, as Ed Broadbent was urging, it would have included, along with free trade, such issues as the Meech Lake Accord, tax reform (including the GST), the new defence policy (including nuclear-powered submarines), patronage and conflict-of-interest matters, privatization of Crown corporations, the deficit, and the personalities of the party leaders. A general election cannot be restricted to a single issue any more than a person can approach an appetizing smorgasbord and help him- or herself from just one dish. "If anyone genuinely wants to take the free-trade issue to the Canadian people," I countered at the time, "the only way to do it is in a national plebiscite."

Ed Broadbent was not the only Canadian political leader to seek an appeal to the electorate. In a mid-1988 bid to scuttle the same trade treaty between Canada and the United States, Liberal leader John Turner, for his part, declared "let the people decide" – then looked for co-operation from the Senate. By proposing that the Liberal senators use their majority in the upper house to block passage of the legislation until an election had been held to resolve the issue, the former prime minister set off a new round of dialogue on democracy in the barbershops and editorial rooms of the country. Turner was trying, by other and additional means, to force the same result – a general election – that Ed Broadbent had argued for the year before.

Turner's tactics and the role of the Senate in forcing a direct vote have already been considered in this chapter. Debate about the Senate's function in this was, of course, secondary to the matter of having the people decide on free trade. The real challenge – if one was sincerely concerned about the trade deal with the Americans – was to get a specific verdict on it in a national plebiscite.

On July 21, 1988, I rose in the House of Commons to introduce a private member's bill, the Canada Referendum and Plebiscite Act. "On a morning when there is controversy in Parliament and the country over whether a specific question such as free trade ought to be submitted to a general election or to [the Senate]," I said, "I am happy to be able to introduce for first reading a Bill that would point to a third way."[86] Others at the time were urging this common sense alternative, too, including several newspaper editorialists and columnists.[87]

The controversy in 1988 about how best to proceed could have produced a sense of *déjà vu* in older Canadians, or those who know their history. In 1911, as in 1988, Canadians elected their representatives to Parliament, having been told by their leaders in both those years that in doing so they would be approving or rejecting the government's policy on trade with the United States. Many leaders, in the name of democracy and in the process of serving their political ends, proclaimed these elections to be "plebiscites" or "referendums," as did a number of commentators. Since that claim touches the central issue here, both of these elections warrant closer scrutiny.

The General Election of 1911: A Plebiscite on Reciprocity?

On September 21, 1911, Canadians defeated the government led by Liberal Prime Minister Wilfrid Laurier, which by then had been in office for fifteen years. Fifty-seven years later, the scholar J. Murray Beck, still finding of interest the question of whether this election constituted a plebiscite, wrote, "The election appeared to be a referendum on a specific issue or its implications: in Quebec the naval question and in the rest of Canada reciprocity."[88]

A more detailed analysis of the bitter and tumultuous campaign of 1911 shows, however, that like all general elections – even those where one or two seminal issues dominate – much more was moving in the political subterrain. The Laurier government, after one and a half decades in office, had gained many opponents, from those who disagreed with the government's farm and immigration policies to those who had been overlooked for appointments. The government was labouring under countless charges of maladministration, and the public had begun to find it arrogant. In British Columbia, the Liberal government's immigration policies provoked strong animosity, especially over the charge that the province's federal minister William Templeman had relaxed immigration laws in favour of Orientals – a charge that Beck notes was "certain to win votes in British Columbia" for those opposing the government. In other parts of the country, especially the Maritimes, the election results were not what one reasonably would have expected, given correlations between economic interests, patriotic loyalties, and trade reciprocity with the U.S. This surprise could mostly be attributed to "an election of individual contests in which local factors often dominated,"[89] including the election of individuals who were personally "strong vote-getters." Such factors as these were not part of a national referendum, but they were certainly part of the election.

Instead of describing the 1911 general election as a "referendum" (if one takes this position), however, it should more properly be called two referendums. While the reciprocity question on Canada-U.S. trade formed the core of the campaign in the rest of the country, the dominant issue in Quebec was the controversial Naval Bill. Two rather separate worlds were spinning together under the umbrella of a single general election.[90]

Examination of the 1911 Canadian election, therefore, shows once again why in a multi-dimensional political campaign it is wrong to suggest that people focus on a single issue as they would have to in a referendum. Canada did *not* have a referendum on reciprocity in 1911.

The General Election of 1988 – A Plebiscite on Free Trade?

Our November 21, 1988, general election was fought extensively on the issue of the Canada-U.S. trade treaty. Yet this election, in so many ways echoing the earlier one, constituted no more of a plebiscite than did the 1911 vote.

As any political scientist or pollster will attest (and as I can vouch from personal experience as a candidate in that 1988 campaign), Canadians once again decided how to vote based on a complex response to many elements, including the personalities and performances of the respective party leaders, Brian Mulroney, John Turner, and Ed Broadbent; the past record and current promises of each of the parties; the varying qualities of the local candidates; the effectiveness of the national campaigns; and the skills of the local vote-getting organization.[91]

The trade treaty was the hook on which much discussion fastened, to be sure, but this single issue itself embraced many others. Canadian sovereignty, Canada-U.S. relations, environmental concerns, the continuance and quality of social programs, economic growth, de-industrialization, the nature of Canada and its future, and world trading patterns were some of them. All of these "free trade issues" were quite apart from debate over tariff schedules, countervail provisions, and dispute-settlement mechanisms. These many concerns were stirred up further by the major campaign interventions from business and labour organizations, which served to heighten interest in the trade treaty as an election feature.

Beyond free trade and the diverse matters related to it, however, the following issues also affected specific voter decisions in the 1988 election: tax reform (including the GST), child care, nuclear-propelled submarines, abortion, the deficit, patronage and conflict-of-interest questions, newly authorized spending programs, western Canadian alienation, forestry programs, unemployment insurance abuse, housing, fishing quotas, young offenders, capital punishment, parole and the criminal justice system, pensions, the disabled, and a vast range of serious environmental concerns. Anyone, therefore, who contends the election was based on a single, specific issue is either politically mischievous or was not canvassing door to door!

As to what the people actually did decide, two political scientists who were involved in a 1988 survey tried to shed light on the question. The survey, called the Canadian National Election Study, was financed by the Social Sciences and Humanities Research Council of Canada and conducted by the Institute for Social Research at York University. It involved interviews with about 80 Canadians a day during the 1988 election campaign – some 3,600 in all. In the final analysis, 80 percent of the Canadians polled had a definite opinion on the free trade agreement, and of these, 90 percent voted in accordance with that opinion.

"For all that," the researchers, Richard Johnston and André Blais, explained, "a majority for or against the agreement simply could not be found because a significant minority could not make up its mind." Moreover, many with apparently fixed views on the agreement could be made to have "second thoughts" by supplementary challenge questions included in the survey. "In the end, the government's mandate is the traditional one," they concluded, "a reflection of the fact that in our system seats are the real currency of the parliamentary game. Neither government nor opposition seems to be entitled to claim otherwise."[92]

An election is not a referendum; a referendum is not an election. Nor indeed are all elections alike, as the campaigns of 1911 and 1988 demonstrate when contrasted with some of the more lacklustre contests over the years.

"Something Different Kept Trying to Happen"

Rick Salutin, writing in *Toronto Life* in February 1989, pronounced: "At the best and most joyous, the electoral campaign of 1988 exploded into a kind of democratic chaos with only a tenuous relationship to the political processes we are used to."[93] Salutin, no friend of the free trade treaty, found the fact that the two sides campaigned so arduously for their preference gave him the hope that our democratic process either was changing or was about to undergo a revolution of some sort.

What was unusual about the campaign, it seemed to Salutin, was that "something different kept trying to happen":

> Sometimes, [the campaign] seemed like a referendum on an issue
> – free trade – attempting to break out of the framework of an
> election. People were trying to marry the one with the other and
> finding it difficult. Other times, it seemed like something more
> radical was trying to get out . . . a radical participatory democracy,
> in place of the usual shallow choice between similar candidates
> who are then left to do as they wish for another four years . . . It
> seemed many people would have preferred to disconnect from the
> party and electoral systems and have an all-in, all-out debate on the
> kind of society we want.

When the election confirmed the Progressive Conservatives in office and ostensibly gave the go-ahead to the free trade agreement, Salutin predictably found the results of the election saddening. "Yet,

I felt not just gloom; I also felt, though I know it sounds strange, a sense of exhilaration. So did many other people. It was the oddest mix," he said, adding, "I know the source of the gloom; it's that wretched deal our government has now signed. But the exhilaration? I'm still not sure, but it has something to do with having had a foretaste of a whole different kind of public life."

Motives for Choosing an Election or Referendum

For the purpose of "letting the people decide" about free trade, Ed Broadbent and John Turner by November 1988 got the election they had wanted. As for Prime Minister Mulroney, who alone had the power to make the decision on when to call an election, he had not wanted a plebiscite on free trade. Like the two other leaders, the prime minister also wanted a general election, but only when the time was ripe for his party. For that, the choice was his alone.

That the time was ripe was apparent from the basic calculation: if, on a major issue like the trade treaty, the Tories supported it while both Liberals and New Democrats were opposed, one party would collect all the positive votes and the other two would split the remainder between them. The result, because the country almost equally divided on the issue: a majority Tory government. One cannot quibble with this mixture of prescience and logic, especially since events subsequently proved it correct.

Motives are therefore quite relevant in choosing one particular democratic instrument – such as an election – over another – such as a plebiscite. It is not only how the issue will play out, but the anticipated result, which will clearly influence the choice. This was obviously the case with the three party leaders, but the same logic also seems to motivate many other people in our country, too. I became well aware of this sitting in the Montreal studios of the CBC on Sunday afternoon, November 27, 1987, as guest on the "Cross-Country Check-up" radio program, hearing callers from coast to coast explain their reasons for wanting or opposing a plebiscite on free trade. Some callers reflected a fairly objective view of the pros and cons of direct democracy versus representative democracy. Yet a great many people agitated for an election, rather than a plebiscite, because they clearly believed this was a way to defeat the Mulroney

133

government, which for them seemed a more important goal than the settlement of the trade issue on its own merits.

This was further evidence for the idea that if one wants a clear verdict from the people on a specific issue, there is no satisfactory or genuine alternative to a plebiscite. To pretend otherwise is to hide deeper motives, or it may reflect muddled thinking and poor learning about our political system. It may even betray a deep-seated distrust of actually letting the people decide for themselves.

Three Reasons for a Referendum over an Election

The November 10, 1990, editorial entitled "Let's Vote on It" in *The Economist* magazine neatly outlined three reasons a referendum may be preferable to an election on a specific question. Margaret Thatcher, then prime minister of the United Kingdom, had been claiming that her opposition to a single currency for Europe reflected the views of the British people. "Very well: Let her prove it," said the editors, adding, "On an issue as singular and far-reaching as currency union, the people should vote, in a referendum."[94]

Three points from the piece are worth repeating, and it is worth remembering, as they are repeated, that the editors of *The Economist* are hardly reckless radicals, nor are they unmindful of a British political tradition (which carries such weight with many Canadians) that is cool to referendums.

They argued, first, that a referendum campaign would be "a refreshing change from the stale, party-disciplined rituals that too often pass for political debate." Freed of their party whips and less intent on gaining a party advantage, MPs would have to confront and debate an issue on its merits. Furthermore, said *The Economist*, "Those who say that 'ordinary voters' would not understand the single-currency issue show a remarkable lack of confidence in their own ability to explain things in a debate, and a remarkable contempt for ordinary voters." To Mrs. Thatcher, who had claimed that Parliament is sovereign, the editors said, "Wrong: on a subject as important as currency union, the people should take precedence over Parliament."[95]

Second, the confusion surrounding the single-currency issue, evident from the results in late 1990 of one opinion poll showing a majority in favour and another indicating a majority opposing, was inevitable. The confusion, the editors wrote, "will remain, so long as the issue is bound into other questions, like whether Mrs. Thatcher is a winner or a loser, a saint or a witch. Only by lifting the single-currency debate out of that maelstrom will it be given the undivided, intelligent attention that, for Britain's sake, it deserves."

Finally, the proposal for a referendum on single currency incorporated a number of practical political considerations. These are noteworthy, because essentially the same points or problems arise each time someone contemplates putting an issue directly to the people. Prime Minister Thatcher, said *The Economist*, "ought to view a referendum not as a threat, but as a way out of an impasse." If she had a mandate on the precise issue of currency union, she would be a far stronger figure at the European Community summit meetings. Also, in contrast to a leadership struggle or a general election, "she would not be risking her premiership by calling a referendum." Turning a referendum into a vote of confidence would, it was implied, be to misunderstand the significance of the single-currency question. The question, the editors said, "does not deserve to be kept in Britain's constitutional straightjacket. It requires a specific popular mandate, not the back-me-or-sack-me histrionics of general political debate."[96]

The Virtue of Using All the Techniques of Democratic Decision Making

The suggestion that on transcending national issues a specific popular mandate ought to be obtained may startle those who are comfortable with the doctrine that an election gives a general mandate to govern and that this authorization is sufficient for all that may pass until the next election in several years' time. General elections tend, however, to be about popular mandates of the most all-encompassing kind, as we have seen in this chapter, whereas direct democracy is precise about specific popular mandates.

To "let the people decide" is more than a noble virtue: it is the essence of a democracy. However, an election is not the only instrument available in the arsenal of techniques of a robust and mature democracy.

As befits a parliamentary democracy, our constitution requires that mandates be conferred by the people upon those who govern. The main evidence that a mandate exists has been a parliamentary majority, but as this chapter has demonstrated, our operating theory and our conventional wisdom about parliamentary mandates contain serious flaws. In practice the effort to stretch the constitutional fiction of a mandate beyond reason has understandably contributed to doubt and distrust on the part of many Canadians about our system of government.

The ideas and beliefs that originally formed the basis of the mandate doctrine have, in reality, been shouldered aside by other developments in Parliament. It was not referendums that posed any threat to the mandate theory, but rather the rise of partyism in Parliament. Indeed, the referendum is a device by which the people could renew or particularize their mandate during the life of a parliament, thus reinforcing rather than undermining the general mandate given at the previous election.

A direct democracy could complement or enhance the operation of representative democracy by bringing about a continuous working relationship between the people and their MPs, rather than just an infrequently granted mandate at election time. Knowledge that the electorate would have its say on a bill of major national importance might encourage members of Parliament to seek improvements in the legislation that would make it more acceptable to the electorate; such efforts, in turn, would lead to an increase in the influence and importance of the MP and of Parliament.

In the practice of Canadian democracy, a proper and much-needed role exists for the intelligently employed use of the referendum device. It could help us move to substantive issues in a mature way, and pass beyond the parliamentary posturing game of "Mandate, Mandate – Who's Got the Mandate?"

6

Referendums Initiated by the People

How do we, then, in contemporary Canada, view the "initiative," which is the petition by which citizens themselves initiate through popular demand a process to place questions about new laws or constitutional changes on a referendum ballot? The answer begins with recognition that the initiative cannot be isolated from the political context in which it is used, and then the acceptance that in a world of imperfections, the initiative is an imperfect but useful procedure.

Canada's Changing Political Culture

Disdain for the democratic excesses and republicanism of the Americans, an enduring theme in Canadian political culture, is particularly vocal in central and eastern Canada. An anti-American attitude was passed down through generations in the British colonies, which were excluded from the American War of Independence. Thirteen other Atlantic seaboard colonies fought from 1775 to 1781 to separate themselves forever from the mother country and the British Crown. These remaining loyalist colonies would eventually form the Atlantic provinces of Canada. The original Tory touch in these regions – stronger than in western Canada where, consequently, direct democracy flourished more readily – has reinforced a hierarchical and orderly view of society that holds, for example, that judges ought to be appointed rather than elected as many are in the United States. For the many Canadians who adhere to the tradition of the sovereignty of the Crown, disdain for the American concept of sovereignty of the people and criticism of that country's overly democratic practices is the national consequence. What Canadian has not ridiculed an American about "electing the local dogcatcher"?

In a Canadian political culture and intellectual climate such as this, a negative attitude readily developed towards the "citizens' initiatives" for the local and statewide referendums that have been a staple of American politics for many years.

Some Canadians view with alarm, for instance, the excesses to which they consider U.S. initiative practices have gone, so that on a given election day, voters who have just chosen their representatives may additionally be asked to vote "yes" or "no" on several dozen citizen-initiated plebiscites. Other Canadians suggest the initiative device has become just a tool of special interests and pressure groups. This criticism was made, recently and forcefully, for example, by Richard Cashin, one of the commissioners of the 1991 Citizens' Forum. Concern is similarly expressed about the expense of the campaigns involved, as both sides seek voters' attention and endeavour to persuade them.

Canadian experience with initiative legislation has, not surprisingly, been quite limited. Early in this century several statutory mechanisms were developed in western Canada for initiatives, but these have become part of our history rather than part of our functioning democratic system.

Yet recent signs in Canada suggest that traditional attitudes on this subject are in flux. Constitutional experts and political researchers appearing before the joint Senate-House Committee on the Constitution early in 1991, for example, advocated referendums as a part of the constitution-ratification process, and did so in a number and to a degree one could not have imagined even five years earlier. Their reasoned and scholarly arguments helped give greater respectability to the role of direct democracy.

At a more populist level, meanwhile, the National Citizens' Coalition (NCC) launched a campaign on February 13, 1991, to promote the use of citizen-initiated referendums at both the provincial and federal levels of government. The NCC began its campaign in Alberta, a province most receptive to direct democracy, and formed "Albertans for Responsible Government" to run a grass-roots campaign aimed at convincing the provincial government of Premier Don Getty to introduce legislation allowing citizen-initiated referendums.

In Saskatchewan recently enacted legislation allows non-binding initiatives. The Referendum and Plebiscite Act, which became law in 1991, provides that upon petition of 15 percent of the voters, the government is obligated to hold a plebiscite on the issue in question. In the October 17, 1991, British Columbia referendum, one of the two questions on the ballot asked, "Should voters be given the right, by legislation, to propose questions that the Government of British Columbia must submit to voters by referendum?" Eighty-two percent of those casting ballots answered "yes," clearly indicating the popularity of the initiative concept.

At the national level, the bill I have been repeatedly introducing in the House of Commons since July 1988, the Canada Referendum and Plebiscite Act, includes a provision for citizen-initiated votes. Judging from letters I have received, news media interest, and comments from fellow politicians and members of the public, such a provision is no longer seen as an aberration, although many have questions about such points as frequency, restrictions on ballot topics, abuse by special interests, and the need for rules.

Pros and Cons of Initiatives

On October 21, 1991, the British Columbia Referendum Office distributed background information to help provincial voters make up their minds on the "initiative question" on the ballot. Initiatives in British Columbia would work in conjunction with the province's Referendum Act, the background paper explained, and the initiative process "would represent a significant change to British Columbia's system of government." While the legislative role of elected representatives would be preserved, the paper also said that the initiative "would provide an additional method of passing legislation" and that "this could have a major effect on the traditional functions and responsibilities of elected officials." The Referendum Office also provided information on jurisdictions that use initiatives, "for comparison purposes," but at the same time advised, "As with other direct democratic procedures, British Columbia may, or may not, be suited to measures that are in place in other countries."

The Referendum Office publication, ever balanced in its approach, then cited five strengths and five weaknesses of initiatives, as perceived "by others who have examined the issue." The five strengths were: initiatives potentially involve all citizens in public decision making; the threat of an initiative may put pressure on representatives to reflect the views of citizens in legislation; the initiative may serve to educate voters about important issues; initiatives may allow citizens or groups with little political power to affect the government process; and initiatives may allow consideration of controversial issues that might otherwise be avoided by elected officials.

The five weaknesses listed were: contradictory and complex initiative ballots may discourage voter participation; elected officials may be able to avoid responsibility for matters affected by initiatives; initiatives may oversimplify complex issues and reduce chances for legislative compromise; initiative advertising campaigns may be one-sided, misleading, or unequally funded; and minorities and low-income groups may be adversely affected by initiatives.

The background paper also informed voters of the effect of initiatives on parliamentary government. The initiative, instead of addressing political concerns through the delegated powers of the electoral process, places issues directly before the voters, and this, the paper said, "is a significant departure from traditional methods of governing [that] requires a broad, thoughtful examination of the way a democratic government should function."[1]

A "Democratization" – Not an "Americanization"

Before examining more closely the pros and cons of the citizen initiative process for local and statewide referendums south of the border, it is important to differentiate between what some might rightly fear as the "Americanization" of Canadian politics versus its "democratization." At the same time, it is important to see, as we shall, that the "initiative" also operates in western democracies, other than the U.S., including Italy, France, Sweden, the United Kingdom, and Denmark.

Twenty-five American states and the District of Columbia permit either initiatives or referendums statewide. Still more states allow them at the local government level. This is similar to the practice in many Canadian provinces where, at the municipal level, electors can petition to bring on a ballot question. Since the passage in California in 1978 of the Jarvis Property Tax Initiative – the famous "Proposition 13" – an increasing number of initiatives have resulted in questions being placed on state ballots.

These ballot propositions, or referendums, might seem an assault on the carefully constructed system of checks and balances that the American Founding Fathers put in place to restrain the "tyranny of democracy." Yet many of those checks, including the electoral college for presidential elections, have grown increasingly anomalous in a society committed to thoroughgoing democracy, as has the Canadian Senate in our context. Moreover, in a complete contradiction of the fears of both those Founding Fathers and others of an aristocratic bent who similarly believed in institutionalizing the hierarchical society, the results of direct popular voting on specific issues have shown broadly that the people can be trusted and that they tend rarely to be won over by demagogic measures. Indeed, as a system of "checks and balances," the power of popular initiative is an important element in a dynamic political process that can both constrain and inspire action by powerful legislatures.

Prudence by the people was equally evident in nineteenth-century Britain, when the franchise was made universal and the popular "revolution" that the aristocratic Tory elements feared never materialized. One important reason for a successful transition to full popular government in Britain, of course, was the visionary leadership of Randolph Churchill in his fusing of both the elements of social order and mass public participation into the vital new force of "Tory Democracy." The conditions and programs for a democratic society do not simply appear like the morning dew, and as is always true of individuals working with the characters and circumstances of history, they must seize the opportunity, as did the determined Randolph Churchill. Ultimately the collective wisdom of the people showed itself to be sound, as the events of British modern history have on balance demonstrated.

This same prudence was displayed in ballot propositions in Nov-

141

ember 1990 in the United States. For instance, pollsters frequently report that Americans are highly sensitive to taxation issues, yet citizen initiatives in 1990 that would have required drastic tax cuts or limits on government spending were defeated in Massachusetts, Nebraska, Colorado, and Utah. Likewise radical environmental reforms may seem to have become a primary motivation of the electorate, yet far-reaching land-use and pollution measures were turned down by voters in California, Washington, Oregon, Michigan, and New York. The contention, moreover, that voters will seldom support what seems an unpopular measure is hard to sustain in light of the November 1990 decision of voters in Arizona to deny themselves a 20 percent reduction in automobile insurance premiums, or the decision rendered by Oregon voters to make wearing seatbelts mandatory in cars.

Some Attributes of Initiatives: From California's Experience to British Political Theory

California, Oregon, and Washington are the three most active states as far as citizen-initiated plebiscites are concerned, and the Oregon and Washington numbers are far more moderate than California's. The excesses which are sometimes associated with California in other areas of life, from movies to politics and from health fads to religious cults, extend to some degree to plebiscites. Speaking in Canada at a conference in October 1990, two Californian direct-vote consultants warned that initiative provisions could become a vast and costly growth industry here. Pointing out that the referendum process in California is "no longer a mom and pop . . . spontaneous reaction to legislative inactivity," but a sophisticated, expensive, and lengthy process that involves polling, fundraising, coalition-building, and advertising, Kelly Kimball, the founder of Kimball Petition Management, then outlined to the British Columbia Social Credit Party convention the methods used by the high-powered industry and special interest coalitions that now direct the state's "people power" process.

A service industry has developed in California to initiate referendums around the concept of "people power," a fact to which the existence of firms like Kimball Petition Management, a California law firm specializing in state initiatives and referendums, pays clear

142

testimony. Kimball and partner Barry Fadem, all the same, endorse the referendum process as an effective instrument for the public. "By hook or by crook, California voters thus seemed to have the initiative to figure these things out," Fadem told the B.C. Social Credit Party audience, adding that "voters are more concerned about the state initiatives than about voting for political candidates."[2] The two California experts predicted the creation of a multi-million-dollar industry to promote special interests.

The comments of Kelly Kimball in her speech were prominently reported at the time in the press and quoted by those prone to being alarmed about direct democracy. Yet Kimball and Fadem failed to take into account the reality of Canadian political culture. Being "outside experts," they spoke only from their experience in California, an exuberantly enterprising state with a unique political culture – unique even in the United States, let alone in contrast to Canada. The phlegmatic attitudes of Canadians, together with our demonstrated willingness to enact laws that govern campaign spending and rules to regulate campaign advertising and broadcasting, would all serve no doubt to contain and constrain the direct-voting process. The California fixation is understandable, but conditions in that state are not particularly relevant to our Canadian situation as we contemplate the greater use of initiatives.

Recently the producers of CTV's program "W5," sparked by interest in the British Columbia referendum on "initiatives," decided to do a story on the topic. Their press clipping file, of course, brought to hand articles about Kimball and Fadem and the alarming spectre they had raised of a multi-million-dollar petition and initiative lobbying business for special interest groups springing up in Canada. This "angle" naturally drew the "W5" reporters like a magnet draws iron fragments.

When Susan Ormiston, a producer and reporter for "W5" spoke with me for background information, I stressed that a more authentic story would be one about our own Canadian experience to date with initiatives and gave her several illustrations. I also explained the interesting consequences of these examples. However, nothing I said had quite the appeal of going to California to prepare for Canadian audiences a story on propositions and initiatives. The resulting program was broadcast October 27, 1991. On her return from interviewing the Californian experts, Ormiston said, "the advice from 'down south' was to take note of the excesses of propositions/initiatives and avoid them, but not necessarily throw the baby out with the bathwater."[3]

California's experience should not, in any case, be too quickly dismissed as excessive. The state's well-educated voters, noted Charles M. Price, seem far more able to cope with intricate initiatives than had been presumed by political scientists. Moreover, he wrote, "The easy assertions about the apathy, indifference, and susceptible nature of voters can at least be questioned by the California experience."[4] At the same time, California has a responsive political system. The concerns expressed about over-use of the initiative process in the state, which included 264 initiatives during the 1980s (double the number proposed during the 1970s and far more than the number submitted during the previous decades) and some thirteen questions on the November 1990 ballot, have registered. California has been re-examining its initiative process,[5] and a January 1991 report by the Senate Office of Research suggested five steps for reform.

First, the report suggested, a pre-ballot review should be conducted. A review by the attorney general of the petition prior to its circulation could identify legal defects, unconstitutionality, or violation of the constitutional rule limiting initiatives to a single subject. Proponents would not be required to incorporate suggested changes, but the analysis would have to be printed on each petition.

Second, a single subject test should apply. Stronger constitutional language could require that all provisions be reasonably germane to the central purpose of the initiative, as described in the title of the measure.

Third, disclosure should be required, in the sense that paid signature-gatherers would be required to identify themselves as such by a button. Since the initiative is often described as "the people's law," the report noted that Californians "deserve to know if signatures are being gathered by volunteers who believe in the measure or by individuals who are being paid to do this and who may or may not be devoted to the cause of the measure." Major contributors and major beneficiaries of initiatives should also be identified, the report suggests in the legislative analyst's summary that is included in the ballot pamphlet.

Fourth, the number of signatures and paid circulators should be increased to a higher threshold. The report suggested raising the number of signatures required to qualify measures for the ballot to 10 percent of the total votes cast in the last gubernatorial election when paid circulators are used by the proponents. (Currently, in California, an initiative statute requires signatures equalling 5 percent of the last gubernatorial vote. Initiatives to change the state constitution require signatures equalling 8 percent.)

Finally, a multiple-county requirement was proposed. No more than 10 percent of the signatures necessary to qualify a measure for the ballot, it was suggested, should come from a single county.

Like any device of direct democracy, the initiative can be used, or it can be abused. So it is important to become more familiar with some basic aspects of referendums initiated by the people, in order to better understand their potential value in making Canada a more democratic society.

In the abstract, one can see the initiative, in Vernon Bogdanor's words, as "a weapon of direct democracy whereby the electorate itself can trigger off a referendum."[6] One form of the initiative, for instance, involves a certain number of electors petitioning for a referendum on legislation already enacted by parliament. This form of initiative, found in Italy and Switzerland, is a form of what is commonly known as "popular veto."

A second variant allows a specified number of electors to secure a referendum on whether a legislative proposal of their own ought to come into effect through a direct vote of the people. This is found in Switzerland and is called a "popular initiative" since it permits unelected citizens to initiate proceedings themselves that could lead to a law.

Experience in a number of democracies shows that acceptance and use of the referendum does not necessarily also lead to the introduction of the initiative. There is, observes Bogdanor, "no necessary political connection" between the two.[7] Those who have sought wider use of the referendum have sometimes even been opposed to the initiative. A.V. Dicey, the British constitutional expert, for example, was in this category, as was J. St. Loe Strachey, who, in his 1924 book *The Referendum*, claimed that the initiative was "an encouragement to crude legislative schemes."[8] As Bogdanor sums it up, Strachey simply doubted that the initiative process could work in a complex modern community because of the vast number of laws already on the statutes book that would have to be brought into harmony with initiative proposals.[9]

In 1980, Professor S.E. Finer, discussing the British party and parliamentary system, argued powerfully for the initiative. In his view, a referendum that is held only at the discretion of Parliament – which he calls an "optional referendum" – "would not help the people to set their own agenda or to express their own view on what they themselves regard as impertinently unrepresentative measures. On the contrary, it would reinforce the two-party system, confirm its closed nature, merely calling in the public as an ancillary."[10] Finer proposes instead that Britain adopt the popular veto, with a half-million signatures being required to secure a referendum on government legislation, while the popular initiative would require one million signatures to secure a referendum on a legislative proposal deriving from the electorate.[11]

Transforming Canada's Top-Down Government

An interesting prospect comes from contemplating the role of initiatives in relation to the operation of our existing political system, and the ways they can help transform Canada into a more democratic society.

Too much analysis of Canadian politics and government proceeds from a top-down view, which is understandable given the dominant position of the Canadian political élite to determine the issues, set the agenda, and conduct the dialogue. Our approach to the study of politics "focuses disproportionately on the problems posed for governments by the transformation of society," notes political scholar Alan Cairns astutely, "and too little on the problems posed for society by the escalating demands of government."[12]

Yet looking "upwards," which is how most MPs close to their constituents find themselves looking, gives a perspective that ought to make a reflective person both more conservative and more democratic. To see the men and women in Canadian society, "constantly challenged by new public policies ranging from education, economy, and welfare to the basic questions of life, death, and human meaning"[13] is to see how they must devote ever more of their resources to the task of responding to government. The frustrated Canadian taxpayer who must continuously foot the bill for "the numerous ill-conceived government ventures that litter the contemporary landscape of public choice"[14] is also the one who sees too little government financial assistance available for needs that he or she considers far more basic.

To contemplate a greater measure of popular sovereignty in this context, the initiative presents several interesting possibilities. First, it can help loosen the near strangle-hold that a fairly small group of people in the upper echelons of our political parties, civil service, and news media have on the public agenda. It would loosen this control only in the sense of supplementing the public agenda with ideas or concerns that are important to a significant enough portion of the Canadian population to be addressed.

An example from Italy, where the right of initiative exists, illustrates the point. In 1978, the Italian Parliament "rapidly approved an abortion law so as to pre-empt a threat by the Radical Party to collect signatures for a referendum on the issue."[15] It is fair to say that without this initiative no such legislation would have been passed, according to S.E. Finer, given the opposition of the Roman Catholic Church. "The incident provides," he says, "an instance of how the device can break the parties' monopoly on issue definition."[16] In Canada the abortion issue was kept on the public agenda, and Parliament spent considerable time debating a broad range of proposed solutions. In a substantially "free vote," however, it failed to enact any new law in 1990. The momentum from grass-roots organizations and from churches ensured that the abortion issue would not be ignored.

The Italian example, of course, pertains to *process* more than to a specific issue. In Canada, after all, we had no trouble getting the abortion question on Parliament's agenda. Yet there are other issues that have not, for long decades, broken through onto the public and parliamentary agenda – and for these the initiative process could have served us well, just as it served the Italians on abortion. For

147

instance, the initiative power might have been used years ago to force our political parties to deal with questions affecting Canada's aboriginal people and Canadians with disabilities. The initiative can be an important instrument for the empowerment of sections of Canadian society whose members want responsibly to bring matters of genuine importance forward for democratic resolution.

Second, as a corollary to responsible empowerment, the initiative device can help place items on the public agenda. By concentrating on political *issues* rather than on parties or personalities, the initiative process can contribute, just as it does in those countries and states where it is used, much more to the education of the electorate than does a general election. Experience in the state of Washington, for example, demonstrates how those in power can have called to their attention "the wishes of certain people who may not have as effective access to the legislature as some others who have effective legislators to introduce and support their bills. In short, the process is an additional method for getting problems on the public agenda."[17] The Coastal Conservation Act in California in 1976, to cite another example, drew its major provisions from a citizen-initiated ballot proposition, and the action of the California legislature in passing this important law "was clearly the result of the prior initiative."[18]

A third positive change possible as a result of the initiative device is related to the current practices of lobbyists and special interest groups. Rigid party discipline controls the proceedings in our legislatures, while special interest groups seek to press their own advantage meanwhile by "working" the Canadian federal system, exploiting their optimum relationship with its double layer of governments. The insidious way many of these organizations have thus been able to ingratiate themselves and integrate their operations into the current workings of Canadian government and public decision making has become a major challenge to Canadian democracy.

While some critics of the initiative claim that the process is vulnerable to being taken over and manipulated by interest groups, most of the evidence simply does not bear this out. The rate of failure of initiative proposals in jurisdictions where they exist clearly indicates that no interest group can be sure of achieving its goal as a result of an initiative.[19]

What is noteworthy is the fact that those who criticize the initiative technique tend to be those who fear others might use it better than they can. A fine example of self-interest parading as concern for the public has arisen in the United States. Many "liberals" are today opposed to the initiative, the petition referendum, and the recall,observes Joseph Zimmerman, because these "weapons of direct democracy" have been employed by "fiscally conservative" groups. "The weapons, of course," he says, "are available to all groups and successful use of the weapons by one group is an inadequate ground for their abolition." Interestingly, "these devices originally were advocated and employed by 'liberal' reformers," he says.[20]

Fears regarding special interest groups' manipulation of the initiative process can be best allayed, however, by calling attention to the fact that any interest group that "seeks to get its proposals on the statute book through the initiative process must succeed in convincing the public through open debate when its proposals will be critically scrutinized by voters and by the media," says Bogdanor, who feels that persuading the public through argument may be harder than tricking the legislature or the government.[21] In short, private interest lobbying efforts on a number of major issues could be forced into broad daylight by the full public scrutiny of a plebiscite campaign, and lobbyists and special interest groups could consequently forfeit their overly cosy relationship with decision makers.

The Progressives early in this century advocated the initiative as a means of neutralizing special interest groups. Perhaps theirs was an idea whose time has finally come. We have seen the emergence recently of many groups whose special interest can be said to be the furtherance of good public policy, but even these worthwhile organizations can benefit from having their proposals considered more fully on the hard anvil of public scrutiny and debate. In California, for example, where "special interests in the state are as active and powerful as anywhere," their numbers include, as Eugene Lee points out, "effective grass-roots environmental protection and civic reform groups as well as dominant economic forces."[22] Since 1911, when the right of initiative was achieved by Californians, these contending groups have faced one another and interacted with the general public, which after all is directly affected by the outcome, in having open decisions openly arrived at.

A fourth improvement that could come about through the initiative process is that behaviour might be modified and remedial action taken simply as a voluntary by-product of this direct democracy process. For instance, in the most recent round of initiative votes in the state of Oregon, one ballot proposition would, in furtherance of basic environmental goals, have imposed far more strenuous requirements on packagers than had existed to reduce packaging and eliminate unnecessary product wrapping. In face of this "threat" to their established way of doing things, the organization representing the packaging industry mounted a vigorous campaign, which included spending a large amount of money to defeat this ballot proposition. Although the packaging industry "won" in that the proposition was defeated, its leaders realized that the same issue would come up again in the next elections through a further initiative. Rather than spend additional energy and money to defeat such a packaging reduction proposition once more, and suffer poor public relations in the process, the industry moved on its own to implement most of the initiative proposals on a voluntary basis. Enlightened self-interest is still an operative force. It is genuinely encouraging to those of us who believe in the intrinsic value of a thoroughgoing democratic society to see remedial action taken in response to an initiative – rather than from a government top-down threat to industry – originating with the consumers themselves. A healthier democracy exists in a society where government itself need not do everything.

A fifth point in favour of the altered dynamic that the initiative process might achieve is that it is likely legislatures will take greater care to ensure their legislation is as good as it can be, as happens in countries where the device is available. In Italy, for example, the initiative exists in the form of a "popular veto" and although it has been used only three times, the very threat of its use has persuaded governments to alter the law "so as to forestall humiliation at the hands of the electorate."[23]

Protection for State Interests and Minority Rights

Whether it is necessary to limit the issues for which the initiative would be available is a point worth some debate. In Switzerland, the initiative cannot be used in relation to international treaties or budget matters. In the United States, a number of states restrict use of the initiative to certain subjects, and specifically exclude such topics as the government's financial appropriations, the judiciary, emergency measures, and the support of the government. Individuals of a more libertarian bent argue that there is "no compelling reason to restrict the subject matter of any initiative," unless the system is established as a delegated law-making power, and given some requirement as well for a review to ensure the constitutionality of the initiative in question.[24]

A legitimate cause for concern, for instance, would be an initiative that infringed on minority rights. Rather than having an initiative proceed and only after its conclusion at the polls be declared unconstitutional by the Supreme Court,[25] it would be preferable to have the initiative's constitutionality clarified in advance. This would eliminate any humiliation or embarrassment that minority groups might otherwise suffer as a result of discussion of certain extreme proposals that could come forward in an initiative.

Provisions for Canada-Wide Initiatives

The Canada Referendum and Plebiscite Act, which I introduced in the Canadian House of Commons in 1988, includes the possibility of initiatives. Under Section 14 of the bill, which deals with a "petition for public consultation," 10 percent of the electors who voted in the last general election and who believe that a question of national and public importance within the jurisdiction of Parliament should be submitted to a direct vote by the electors, may petition the prime minister for this purpose. Ten percent of the electors would, based on the voters' lists in the general election of 1988, mean some 1,800,000 people, which is a significantly high threshold. A two-stage process could, however, be even better. The one followed under the Florida Initiative statute, for example, requires an initial qualifying petition whereby far fewer signatures may be needed and, upon establishing constitutional and procedural compliance, stipulates a second and final step of obtaining the larger percentage of signatures.

A petition under the proposed Canada Referendum and Plebiscite Act would be accompanied by a declaration signed by petition-

151

ers, stating their names and addresses, and setting out concisely the question that it is proposing should be submitted to the electors. The Governor in Council (the federal cabinet) would, after receiving the petition, issue a proclamation directing that a referendum or plebiscite be held on the question submitted by the petitioners.

While the subject matter of an initiative is not delimited in the proposed act, the topic must be one which, in the opinion of the petitioners, is "a question of national and public importance within the jurisdiction of parliament" and the petitioners would be required to state concisely the question that would be submitted to the electors. The petition to the prime minister is, moreover, not binding, so in the course of taking the initiative petition under advisement, the cabinet could obtain an interpretation or legal opinion from the minister of justice as to the constitutional validity of the question proposed by the petitioners, in advance of submitting the question to the country in a plebiscite. I consider this a common-sense approach to the provision for an initiative device with appropriate safeguards.

On the topic of constitutional protection, it is helpful to observe how the state of Florida has pioneered its two-tier approach, which is both practical for government officials and respectful of citizens' constitutionally protected rights. A petition with a relatively small number of signatures is sufficient to trigger the process. The attorney general of the state then reviews the ballot proposition the petitioners are seeking, and subsequently renders a legal opinion as to whether it passes constitutional and other tests. If it does not, that is the end of the road for the petition – a far more sensible approach than letting the entire plebiscite process run its full course before a court challenge is made over its constitutionality. If the proposition sought by the petition poses no constitutional problems, on the other hand, the Florida Initiative law then permits it to proceed to the second phase, where a higher number of signatures must be obtained and, this done, the question can then appear on the next statewide ballot. A staged approach similar to this one has been advocated for Canada by Duff Conacher, a University of Toronto law student.[26]

The timidity with which we have embraced democratic measures in Canada has been a reflection of the political establishment's fear of a process that is not entirely predictable as to outcome. While prudence is an admirable quality, cowardice is not. As we enter the 1990s, a mood of anger with our political system has grown as the cumulative result of the Canadian people having been left on the sidelines – spectators to an unending cycle of major changes in our country, changes on which they had never been directly consulted and for which they had given no mandate. The prospect that Canadians outside the governing political class could have an opportunity to bring major national issues forward by means of an initiative would be one more element of the many needed to redress the current imbalances in the operation of our political system.

7

Ratifying Constitutional Changes by Referendum

The extent to which the general public ought to be involved in the constitution-making process is indeed a current Canadian preoccupation, but it is neither a question exclusive to us nor new to these times.

The People's Involvement in Constitution Making

A "remonstrance," or protest, by a great many members of the legislature urging that general elections be held as a means of providing broad popular consultation on the proposed new constitution arose in Canada prior to Confederation in 1867. The four New England colonies of Connecticut, Massachusetts, New Hampshire, and Rhode Island, following their Declaration of Independence from Britain in 1776, decided to replace the old colonial charters with new constitutions *and* to require that "those constitutions should take effect only after they had been considered, voted upon, and approved by the States' voters."[1] Many paths can be followed in constitution making, but along each one the same double-headed question is soon encountered: ought the people to be involved, and if so, to what extent and by what procedure?

In 1991, the Soviet Union, coming to grips with democratic reform after decades of totalitarian structures and single-party control, held a referendum on the basic constitutional future of the U.S.S.R. Canadians could spot flaws in the referendum, but we could hardly be smug as we ourselves inhabit a still-timid democracy when it comes to public participation in anything but general elections. For the Soviet Union, such a democratic exercise constituted a remarkable about-face through its involvement of the people in the process of reform and constitution making.

In every country, sooner or later, the public must in some way participate in the constitutional process. Some nations have had particular difficulty with this. Pakistan was created, for instance, out of religious conflict, and only after the failure of its democratic institutions did it get a viable constitution, one created by the edict of a semi-dictatorial president. The West Indies collapsed as a federation, primarily because its constitution, designed to placate dissident local elements, was too weak to support a federal government, particularly on the financial and commercial levels. Malaysia, troubled by deep conflicts between Malays and Chinese, lost Singapore as a member state in 1965.[2] "The dustbin of recent history," as Canadian political scientist Alan C. Cairns has observed, "is littered with discarded constitutions cast aside after brief and withering exposure to reality."[3]

Such failures, however, are not the rule. The United States, Australia, and India all achieved constitutional success, though in each case serious conflicts of a fundamental constitutional nature threatened the country for a time. Public participation was accommodated in different ways and to different degrees in each of the countries. In America and Australia, citizen participation either in referendums or in electing constitutional conventions formed part of the story, while in India a combination of colonial conferences and direction by Britain with local election of a constituent assembly proved to be a workable formula. In the least developed colonies, Alex Mesbur writes, participation has been less intimate, but has been assured by having local leaders, not only politicians, shape their own destinies as far as possible through conferences and committees, often touching popular feeling outside the scope of any conference. "Thus in some way the people help to create their own governing instrument," observes Mesbur, "a result which, for the democratically inclined, is surely the only reasonable one."[4]

Constitutional Talks and Our Political Agenda

We Canadians now find ourselves at an interesting juncture along this pathway of constitution making, since we have already, as

Cairns notes, "one of the most durable and successful constitutions in the world," although we remain curiously preoccupied with changing it. The now defunct Meech Lake Accord even incorporated a breathtaking provision whereby the "first ministers" would gather *annually* to review constitutional provisions. There can be no greater evidence than that of our instinctive Canadian desire to adapt and change. Change is a prerequisite to growth, and our historic evolution in a peaceful and orderly fashion has been a model for other countries.

Yet Canadians have become fatigued by constitutional discussion. Many media reporters are approaching burnout at covering the endless rounds of constitutional negotiations, and on many of the issues now being discussed we seem to have advanced hardly at all from where we began decades ago. For instance, major elements in the 1991 recommendations from the Beaudoin-Edwards Report on constitutional amendment go back to the same approach adopted by the first ministers in the Victoria Charter of 1971.[5] Similarly, in reading the twenty-eight constitutional proposals presented by the Mulroney government in September 1991, and then rereading the Quebec Liberal Party's "beige paper" of 1979, one finds many common elements. No matter how long we play the game, it seems there are only so many chess pieces on the board, and a limited number of squares on which to move them. This view is only fortified the more one looks at Canadian history.

We have parlayed the process of constitutional talks into a major enterprise – a modest "cottage industry" that has become an elevated "palace industry" – with attributes such as the unending rounds of high-level constitutional discussion employing the time, energy, and financial resources of our country; intellectual efforts by countless dozens of experts from the academic and professional worlds; many organizations and associations constantly on hand to submit briefs and appear as witnesses before an endless parade of parliamentary committee hearings; and editorial writers, columnists, and broadcast commentators who must express their suggestions and verdicts at every turn along the way.

Despite our fatigue with the constitutional process, we ought not to lose sight of two of its fundamental features. First, we are at least *talking* about our constitution and the changes needed in it, a stark contrast to countries where no dialogue has been possible and fighting and civil war have been the result. This is no small achievement, and Canadians can be proud that we are a nation of talkers. Canada has been transformed several times over as a result of our willingness to treat our constitution as an organic and evolving document. Canadians' willingness to discuss and be adaptable when required is not only the genesis of the Meech Lake provision requiring annual talks by the executives of our federal state on the constitution, but throughout our history it has also been an important attribute for making Canada what one historian has called "the peaceable kingdom." The point here is that dialogue forms the basis for democratic processes at all levels in Canadian society, and we ought to be sure we are doing all that is possible so that this valuable Canadian quality is given fullest scope.

Secondly, we ought not to be misdirected by the thought that the "constitution" concerns only esoteric institutional arrangements and arcane legal questions. The debate on our constitution is also a deeply political debate. Behind the "constitutional" issue lies the crux of political conflict within our country. Deep political antagonisms shape what could seem purely constitutional matters to some. In coming to grips with these so-called constitutional questions, we are in truth dealing with the most serious parts of Canada's political agenda.

Nevertheless, the fact that these profound concerns find their primary expression in endless rounds of constitutional meetings ought finally to be recognized for what it really is: a further indictment of how irrelevant our existing legislative assemblies have become. Rendered virtually impotent by executive dominance and rigid party control, our elected legislative bodies have generally failed to resolve these issues in an authoritative way – nor have they, in the main, even had the opportunity to do so.

Public Participation in Constitution Making

The biggest challenge in this process of Canadian constitution making, on both an institutional and political level, is to find a radically more effective way for the public to participate. This is fundamental to a democracy, since its constitutional arrangements must be agreed upon and supported by the majority of its people if these arrangements are to succeed. Indeed, they must be understood by Canadians, and it is through participation that understanding can best be generated.

When we ask about the meaning of democracy, we do well to note, together with C.B. Macpherson, that "the answer depends, ultimately, on whether you consider democracy to be a system of government only, or whether you take it to be a kind of society."[6]

There is a widespread view in the upper echelons of government that once some hearings have taken place the public has been consulted. This is definitely not the perception, however, with my constituents. The public meetings are usually held on a tight timetable, at a place and time of day inconvenient for most people to attend. In a country of twenty-six million people it is preposterous to assume that even one hundred well-attended meetings across Canada counts as public involvement in the process. Meetings can be helpful for generating ideas and comments, and should continue to be used in this role for helping to define and clarify issues. Yet they should not be used, when it comes to something so major as the constitution, as a substitute for total public involvement through a referendum to ratify the proposal for amendment. A "democratic society" means a great deal, including structures and procedures that accommodate the interests of all Canadians and inspire their effective participation. It certainly means an attitude that welcomes total public involvement in the final stage of constitution making.

In countries that seek to make their society more democratic and that find ways for the public to participate in constitution making, the use of a referendum or plebiscite has been a common device. Sometimes direct voting is employed to ratify a constitution; in other cases, it is used to obtain general popular approval before a constitution is framed. As a pre-constitutional device, for instance, the referendum was used in India, Pakistan, and Malaysia. In the area of ratification, Australia provides a noteworthy example of referendum use both for its original constitution and subsequently for amendments. In the United States democratic participation marked all constitutional development, and the ratification procedure followed in each state was one in which citizens elected delegates to conventions to consider and ratify the constitution. Ratification by state legislatures was avoided, among other reasons, to prevent subsequent legislation being passed to withdraw consent. This problem is one Canadians clearly understand from the example of the Newfoundland Legislative Assembly, which voted to ratify the Meech Lake Accord, but later voted to rescind its earlier ratification.

In the United States, the framers of the constitution, who accepted the sovereignty of the people and began their charter document with the words "We the People . . . ," felt that seeking ratification of the constitution by the people was a resort to the ultimate source of authority in the nation. The constitution drafted at Philadelphia from May to September of 1787 contained a provision requiring that the new constitution be presented for ratification to specially elected conventions in the various states rather than, as mentioned, to their legislatures. Thus, the constitution – when so ratified in at least nine states – would take effect, and have as its basis the solemn will of the people. Eleven states ratified by the summer of 1788, and the new federal government of the United States of America came into being in the spring of 1789. In the twentieth century, academics have debated just how democratic this constitution-making exercise really was, and in 1913 Charles A. Beard, an American revisionist historian, suggested the constitution was opposed by a majority of the voters in several states and that it was probably not favoured by a majority of the American people. In his book, *An Economic Interpretation of the Constitution,* Beard contended that the making and the ratification of the constitution had been the work of merchants, lawyers, manufacturers, and capitalists, all dominated by personal interests in property, and that the constitution's adoption had thus been "undemocratic." However, this criticism has itself been answered by other historians who more recently challenged Beard's assertions. For instance, Robert E. Brown and Forrest McDonald have both shown that conclusive evidence is lacking that one's economic status in general dictated allegiance or opposition to the constitution. Certainly the process of adoption was as "democratic" as any used in that era for the ratification of state constitutions.[7] The contrast with the Canadian approach shows a much stronger desire on the part of American political leaders to consistently include the people in constitutional formation.

Australians began their robust democratic experience by using a referendum to ratify their constitutional arrangements. Under the enabling legislation that established the constituent assembly that drew up Australia's constitution, the document had to be submitted to the electors in order to be accepted or rejected by means of their direct vote. If accepted by the voters of three or more colonies, it was agreed in advance, the constitution could be submitted to Britain with a request for the requisite legislation, as Alex Mesbur notes. In the first referendum, held in 1898, New South Wales refused to approve the constitution. Since New South Wales was a key state, the constitution was not sent on to Britain. Although three other states had approved, an Australia without New South Wales was not politically feasible. After conciliatory amendments were made at a premiers' conference, the document was again submitted to a referendum. This time the constitutional proposal was passed by all five states and sent to Britain where legislation brought it into being.[8] "Thus ratification in Australia did not have the legal effect of bringing the Constitution into effect," observes Mesbur, "but merely of opening the door for the final legislative step which would occur outside Australia."[9]

Canada got off to a shakier start in its public involvement in constitution making and has yet to find its balance. While Australia used referendums to obtain initial authority for its confederation constitution, the early petitions here for pre-confederation elections – which would have served as a form of public consultation, at least, on the proposed new Canadian constitutional arrangements – were ignored.

Ratification of Constitutional Changes in Australia

Australia is a valuable country to compare and contrast with Canada, like the "experiment" and "control" examples in a laboratory of democracy. The countries have many similarities: both are large land masses originally inhabited by aboriginal peoples and subsequently occupied and colonized by European settlers; both were parts of the British Empire and evolved from colonial status to full self-government; the populations of both mainly occupy only a small portion of the countries' peripheries;[10] both are constitutional monarchies that have parliamentary systems of government with a fairly stable party system; and, finally, both are federal states with similar histories of struggle between their central governments and the state or provincial governments over jurisdiction and power. With so many points of similarity, it is revealing to note that the Australians have used the referendum procedure while Canadians have been more reluctant to do so. Australia's frequent use helps account, I believe, for the more certain self-identity that they enjoy.

When Australia became a federal state in 1901, the makers of its constitution formally adopted the referendum for popular ratification as an integral part of the means by which their constitution was to be amended. The first national referendum took place five years later.

Under article 128 of the constitution of Australia, only the federal Parliament, which has both a lower and an upper house, can initiate a constitutional amendment. Any amendment must be adopted by an absolute majority of both houses of Parliament. Should one of the houses withhold its consent or propose changes, the house in which the process began may either adopt the changes or reject them. In any event, the proposed amendment must subsequently be adopted once more and receive an absolute majority. Following adoption by Parliament, the amendment must then be put to the people in a referendum.

In this direct voting by all Australians on a proposed constitutional amendment, the majority required varies according to the nature of the amendment. For example, special majorities are required for proposed amendments to reduce either the proportionate number of representatives any state has in the Senate or House of Representatives or the minimum number of elected representatives of a state in the House of Representatives. Special majorities are also required for amendments that would alter the borders of a state or affect the provisions of the constitution in relation to a state. In any of these cases, a majority of voters in the nation as a whole is required for approval, as well as a majority of voters in a majority of states, and a majority of voters in the state affected by the amendments.

About forty times to date referendums have been held at the nationwide level in Australia, some pertaining to constitutional matters and others on questions of national politics. For example, in

1916 and 1917 referendums were held to ascertain public opinion about whether Australian men should be conscripted. In 1977 a referendum was held to select the country's national song.

Most Australian referendums are, Don Aitkin writes, "understandable only in the context of the politics of the constitution."[11] This becomes clear when one looks at the subject-matter of the nationwide referendums. The wide range of topics has, in addition to those mentioned so far, included Senate elections, finance, state debts, legislative powers, monopolies, trade and commerce, corporations, industrial matters, railway disputes, trusts, nationalization of monopolies, essential services, aviation, marketing, postwar reconstruction and democratic rights, social services, organized marketing of primary products, rents and prices, powers to deal with communists and communism, Parliament, aboriginals, prices, incomes, simultaneous elections, mode of altering the constitution, democratic elections, local government bodies, Senate vacancies, and the retiring age for judges.[12]

The procedural hurdles listed in the requirements of article 128 of the constitution that relate to obtaining approval for a proposed amendment in Parliament, as well as the combination of majority votes required for an amendment's approval, have proven more problematic than the framers of the Australian constitution likely wanted. Of more than eighty proposals raised in Parliament, only half have gone to the people in a referendum; of those only eight have been approved by the electors.

The Australian experience with referendums has been mixed, and much attention has been paid to ways of improving referendums in that country. Like Canadians, Australians have progressed, with minimal results, through a series of constitutional conventions or meetings, notably in 1934 and 1942, then again in Sydney in 1973, in Melbourne in 1975, and in Hobart in 1976. The conventions in Melbourne and Hobart paid particular attention to the question of referendums. In 1959 a joint committee on constitutional review of the Australian Parliament proposed changes, including altering the amendment requirements to reduce the number of approving states from a majority to one-half in order to lower the procedural hurdles, but nothing came of that proposal. So, in this respect as well Australians are similar to Canadians: we spend much energy discussing our constitution, but in the end it is about the same as when we started. An interesting difference, however, is that among the issues with which Australians grapple, while Canadians have not – at least at the senior political levels – is the question of how to improve their existing mechanism for public participation in the process of changing their constitution.

Democratizing Constitution Making in Canada

In Canada democratizing the process of constitution making has at last become a contemporary cause, and we may finally follow the Australian lead. This new imperative reflects three realities all at once: first, our national preoccupation with constitutional debate; second, an indictment of the failures of the "executive federalism" amending formula embodied in the 1982 Constitution Act, developed only after a dozen constitutional conferences from 1927 to 1981; and third, the rising strength of democratic values favouring participation, inclusion, and popular consent.

This stage in our evolution as a mature democratic country has been a long time in coming. The British government wanted to decolonize us in the 1920s and give Canada full constitutional powers. Canadians liked the idea but were unable to agree on an amending formula, and so we continued in our humiliation and to their annoyance by having to go to Westminster for important categories of amendments. There was no point having our constitution, the British North America Act of 1867, patriated here if we had no way of changing it by amendments that would be needed from time to time with our growth and evolution. Our constitution, being a statute of the British Parliament, could really only be amended by further acts of that Parliament. We were a self-governing country with a colonial problem. At the height of the turmoil, Prime Minister Trudeau sought to patriate the constitution by a "unilateral" initiative of the Parliament of Canada, but the Supreme Court ruled it would be unconstitutional in a broad sense to do so without the involvement of the provinces. British MP Enoch Powell suggested to Canadians at the time that instead of going to Britain to have a new constitution made, we should make our own, as the Americans had done in 1787.

By the time we had patriated our constitution, together with its new amending formula and its newly entrenched Charter of Rights, we were among the last guard of the former British colonies to gain total constitutional independence.[13]

Now that we have our constitution to ourselves, we have witnessed the bizarre spectacle of trying to amend it according to the 1982 formula. The creation and attempted ratification of the Meech Lake Accord is a testament to the difficulties this formula involves.

Apart from countless discussions on the constitution and the degree of failure to produce results, the country keeps operating, and the reality of Canada is constantly being remade.[14] These new realities find expression in various ways and through diverse networks that cover the country as a whole: ministerial summits; civil service meetings; and gatherings of groups of professionals, women, consumers, natives, workers, academics, and business people. Many groups share similar viewpoints and goals despite their ethnic or regional differences. Their inability to unite in a common front, however, limits the impact of their demands and the weight of their opinions. It also weakens the democratic process and the quality of the debate within Confederation.

"The essence of our debate in the last few years has been the political organization of the country and its constitutional basis," said Jean-Louis Roy in an editorial in *Le Devoir*, commenting on this phenomenon of our diverse networks and how fragmentation actually weakens the democratic process. He observed, furthermore, that "our inability to resolve the constitutional crisis has deeply shaken the consensus without which a federation is nothing more than an arbitrary, contentious structure." How would Canada best be described? The honest answer, Roy suggested, is: "A confused entity, a divided federation, a political system heavily taxed by suspicion, confrontation and failure." It is a sobering fact that Roy wrote this assessment more than a decade ago, on July 1, 1981.

Such dramatic statements have been made at regular intervals throughout our history, and in 1791, 1841, and 1867 new constitutional arrangements have actually come into effect. In 1981, one of our countless "years of decision," to borrow George Woodcock's phrase, the country stood on the brink of getting a new constitution, a culmination of the on-again, off-again process which had been under way since the 1920s. Yet this new constitution, even if judged legal or constitutional by the Supreme Court of Canada, already stood condemned by some of the major partners in Confederation.

"The new constitution perhaps may soon become a reality," Jean-Louis Roy wrote, at the same time cautioning, "We will then have to live under an imposed structure perceived by the majority of the provinces as a forced union . . . We will one day have to reopen the political discussion and negotiations in the light of another constitutional model and another way of reaching consensus. We will then be able to celebrate Confederation with more spontaneity and ease."[15]

How prophetic that assessment now appears, as today we have indeed reopened the political discussion and negotiations in the light of another constitutional model. Yet Roy also spoke with equal emphasis of "another way of reaching consensus," a quest "for the more democratic method that will involve the Canadian people in the re-making of our Constitution."

The rise – and fall – of a movement for broader public participation, not only in constitutional issues but in governmental processes generally, has gone through two cycles in the past quarter-century. The similarity of the pattern, first under Prime Minister Trudeau and more recently under Prime Minister Mulroney, leads one to conclude that there are a limited number of forces and issues at work in Canada that mould the policies and the responses of whoever the occupant of the prime minister's chair may be into the same general contours and conclusions.

Trudeaumania and "Participatory Democracy"

In 1968, the words "Come work with me," the rhetoric of "participatory democracy" that Pierre Trudeau used in his first electoral campaign as prime minister, engendered a climate of active accommodation that seemed to surround all issues, including constitutional change. The mood set by that campaign and the concomitant "Trudeaumania" created public expectations of widespread participation in discovering new directions for Canada and for Canadian government, all propelled by the optimism generated by Expo '67 and the centennial celebrations of a year earlier.

Just a few years later, in 1971, rejection of the "Victoria Charter" by Premier Bourassa's Liberal government was, for its part, the consequence of a parallel tide of rising expectations within Quebec. Quebec nationalists used the desire for public input to mobilize popular opinion against Ottawa, with the result that the new prime minister's first constitution-amending attempt failed.[16]

From that setback, it took some six years for Prime Minister Trudeau's faith in participatory democracy, it seemed, to be restored. In July 1977, the prime minister dispatched the Pépin-Robarts Task Force on Canadian Unity across the country to solicit support for federalism and find new ways to achieve national unity. Jean-Luc Pépin, who had been a Liberal cabinet minister, was the effervescent spirit of the task force, always talking enthusiastically about imaginative ideas. John P. Robarts, a former Progressive Conservative premier of Ontario whose stolid approach, experience, and sound judgment were a valuable counterbalance, brought partisan balance and clout. The two men, exquisitely personifying the Quebec and Ontario political cultures that had created them, were a good mix, like pepper and salt, as co-chairmen of this task force. Although numerous briefs were heard, the entire exercise in retrospect turned out to have been a public relations show; recommendations from the Task Force Report did not translate into any of the constitutional changes subsequently promoted by the government. For instance, the ill-fated attempt by the Trudeau government to change the status of the Senate in 1978 contravened the spirit of co-operation that the task force was advocating. Another example was the Pépin-Robarts recommendation to create a special category of MPs in the Commons to be allocated on the basis of representation which would be proportional to a party's popular vote. This suggestion aimed at getting Liberals from the west and Conservatives from Quebec into the House of Commons, thereby overcoming by institutional change a political problem of imbalanced party representation. This idea was ignored, too.

All of this presaged the cycle that would be repeated by Prime

Minister Mulroney: the failed attempts at constitutional amend-ments and the frustrations born of that failure; the cross-Canada tour by a task force (in the 1990–91 version it would be chaired by Keith Spicer); and the effort at Senate reform, which began with a gener-ous offer to the provinces in the Meech Lake Accord, proceeded with invoking for the first time an extraordinary constitutional provision to appoint eight extra senators, then next involved proposals for an elected and more effective Senate. These are just three of the half-dozen or more ways Brian Mulroney would come to resemble Pierre Trudeau, but we are getting ahead of the story.

In 1980 the combination of Trudeau's federal election victory and the Parti Québécois's referendum defeat set the stage for a second major round of constitutional amendments. This time public input would play a much greater role in the substance of constitu-tional change, and in the process itself. The initial negotiations and various court challenges were conducted entirely by federal and provincial officials, a sign that it might just be "business-as-usual." However, on October 6 of that year the Trudeau government tabled its unilateral proposal in the House, and on December 6, public hearings of a Special Joint Committee of the Senate and House of Commons got under way. The public response was enthusiastic, and it supported strengthening Trudeau's proposal for a Charter of Rights and Freedoms. Many analysts and provincial officials felt Ottawa was using the hearings to win public support for the federal position, and to undermine enthusiasm for the provincial positions.[17]

Soon the process of public participation grew beyond what Ottawa had intended, and the business-as-usual methods were no longer adequate. Public pressure forced a resumption of negotia-tions once the Supreme Court ruled that constitutional "conven-tion," if not the express words of the constitution itself, required both federal *and* provincial involvement in constitutional change. Groups – from aboriginals to feminists, from people with disabilities to civil libertarians – demanded and secured a strengthening of the Charter of Rights and Freedoms. Public expectations of a resolution of the federal-provincial impasse necessitated a compromise between the governments that would give rise to "a further try politically" at the first ministers' conference of November 1981.

Trudeau's Proposal for a Constitutional Referendum

On October 19, 1977, Prime Minister Pierre Trudeau had proposed a national Referendum Act, initially as part of an arsenal of legal procedures whereby a referendum in Quebec might be countered by a federally conducted vote on the same question. He stated that draft legislation setting out the conditions for a national referendum had been prepared by the national unity group in the Privy Council Office, along with an analysis of what the federal government considered unacceptable aspects of the Quebec government's White Paper on referendums.

Prime Minister Trudeau explained to the Commons the following day that the government's intention to enact enabling legislation for referendums "would not be intended to change in any sense our parliamentary system." The prime minister continued to believe that "the responsibility for legislation and policies should rest in Parliament." Accepting that Canadians live under a form of representative democracy, and not intending to change that, the prime minister clarified that his government "would not want enabling legislation which would permit any government at any time to come forward with referendums to solve problems that the House of Commons or the Government find too hot to handle." Rather, he explained, the direct voting "would be a tool used perhaps only for a limited number of years to permit us to deal with constitutional questions of national unity."[18]

The following spring, on April 3, 1978, the Trudeau government introduced "An Act Respecting Public Referendums in Canada on Questions Relating to the Constitution of Canada"; the short title of the bill was the Canada Referendum Act. Although this legislation was not enacted, the concept was subsequently revised by the prime minister when he sought to establish a means for public ratification of the new constitutional provisions his government was developing in 1980 and 1981.

The constitutional accord, finally signed on November 5, 1981, by Prime Minister Trudeau and the premiers of nine of the ten provinces, unfortunately ruled out the use of referendums as a formal part of a constitution-amending procedure. It was to the prime minister's "everlasting regret," he said, that he had been forced to drop his proposal for a referendum.[19]

At the first ministers' conference in Ottawa in November 1981 at which a reluctant Prime Minister Trudeau made a final effort at political negotiations with the premiers, who, except for Bill Davis of Ontario and Richard Hatfield of New Brunswick, were generally hostile and intractable towards his constitutional patriation plan, the referendum option had been scuttled. On the morning of November 4, Trudeau, firm as ever in pursuing his course, "unexpectedly challenged René Lévesque to resolve their constitutional differences through another referendum," political observers Stephen Clarkson and Christina McCall wrote, adding,"To the dismay of William Davis and the anglophone members of the so-called Gang of Eight, Lévesque – who was confident Quebec opinion was solidly on his side – accepted Trudeau's dare."[20]

That gambit set in train a series of events which, while ultimately helpful to Trudeau because it led to a patriated constitution that incorporated his long-sought Charter of Rights, also generated a compromise from which the opponents of direct democracy emerged victorious over the prime minister's proposal for a referendum. "By so imprudently accepting Trudeau's referendum idea," said Clarkson and McCall, "Lévesque had liberated his sometime allies to make their own compromise with the federalist devil. The emotional solidarity of the Gang of Eight was broken."[21]

The pressure on Trudeau to drop the idea of a referendum came from two fronts: a group of premiers who never much liked the idea, led by Hatfield and Davis, usually his two staunchest allies; and his own closest political supporters, Intergovernmental Affairs Minister Marc Lalonde and Justice Minister Jean Chrétien. Neither Chrétien, Trudeau's chief constitutional negotiator, nor Lalonde, his strongest minister and Quebec lieutenant, liked the idea of institutionalizing a referendum in the constitution, having just battled through the "no" campaign on the sovereignty-association referendum in Quebec in 1980. (A decade later, as Liberal Party leader, Chrétien would reverse himself and call for a national referendum on the constitution, having subsequently become convinced of the overall efficacy of such a democratic process.)

Trudeau took Chrétien and Lalonde's advice seriously; doing so was reasonable, moreover, because of the opposition he was confronting from his strongest supporters among the premiers. Hatfield spoke against Trudeau's idea of a tie-breaking referendum at the Ottawa Conference Centre, after the prime minister had insisted on holding one. The premier had never liked direct democracy and represented the only province in Confederation never to have held a provincial plebiscite.

Late on the evening of November 4, Trudeau and Davis spoke at length by telephone, as the premiers were pressing ahead to work out a compromise based on the "Kitchen Accord," which had been developed by Ontario Attorney General Roy McMurtry, Saskatchewan Attorney General Roy Romanow, and Jean Chrétien when the three shared an intense and direct discussion about how to solve the impasse. Like many good discussions, this had taken place informally as they were standing in a small kitchen at the conference centre.

Davis calmly conveyed the ultimatum that he would be unable to continue supporting Trudeau if the prime minister did not agree with the deal that was being worked out. Trudeau knew that if there was to be any hope of success he needed Ontario's support. "Trudeau realized," according to Clarkson and McCall, that "Davis's dictum on the telephone meant giving up the idea of the referendum."[22]

The substantial consent achieved on November 5, 1981, with respect to the amending formula, and the fact that the Supreme Court of Canada had ruled on September 28 of that year that substantial consent (rather than unanimity) was all that was required to amend the constitution, together suggested that the prime minister no longer would need a popular direct vote to ratify the steps taken to patriate the BNA Act.

Resort to a referendum, however, had been a distinct possibility throughout most of 1981. With the premiers of eight provinces opposing the prime minister's constitutional proposal, extraordinary steps may have been called for in an effort to demonstrate some other basis of support for the Trudeau government's action. At various times prior to the November accord, a number of senior government officials and politicians had publicly suggested that a referendum would be appropriate in the circumstances. In his statement at the time of the accord, the prime minister formally placed on record his regret "that we have not kept in the amending formula a reference to the ultimate sovereignty of the people as could be tested in a referendum."

The package thus arrived at was subsequently enacted by the British Parliament, and signed by Queen Elizabeth in Ottawa on April 17, 1982. The Quebec government never did agree to the package of amendments. The irony was that the only three Canadian signatures on the document that the Queen signed were those of Pierre Trudeau, Justice Minister Jean Chrétien, and Registrar General André Ouellet – all of whom were from Quebec.

This "explicit denial of any referendum role for the people" in amending the constitution, as political scientist Alan Cairns of the University of British Columbia put it,[23] meant that the 1982 formula was "governmental." "The formula," Cairns said,

> reflected the traditional assumption that the constitution was about federalism, that federalism was about governments, and that accordingly it was necessary and appropriate for the formal amending process to be dominated by governments. After all, they dominated the intergovernmental arena by means of executive federalism, and the practice of responsible government sustained by party discipline meant that premiers and cabinets were considered to be in effective control on their home turf, and thus capable of delivering the goods.

In retrospect, Cairns concluded, "it is evident that the assumptions on which the formula was based were backward looking."

All the same, the possibility of a plebiscite was not ruled out by the new amending formula. It requires for most amendments the consent of Parliament and the consent of the legislative assemblies of at least two-thirds of the provinces that have, in the aggregate, at least 50 percent of the population of all the provinces. For some amendments, all provinces would have to consent. If a proposed amendment to the constitution appeared to be short of the required level of provincial consent, a federal government that sought the amendment could always hold a nationwide plebiscite on the subject of the amendment in the hope of being able to demonstrate to the reluctant provinces the existence of deep popular support in the country for the proposed change. The plebiscite, of course, would not be binding, but it might be persuasive to those provincial legislatures that the federal government wished to convert to its own thinking, if a majority of the people voted for the proposal.

Nothing in the constitution would have prevented the government of Canada, for instance, from holding a plebiscite on the Meech Lake Accord. This was advisable at the early stage of the process, but inadvisable towards the end of the three-year ratification period, since by then the question had become too encumbered by extraneous matters for resolution by *any* process. As is its role, such a plebiscite would have been advisory to government and would have supplemented (not replaced) the other formal procedures required by the constitution's amending formula.

By the same token, a provincial government might hold a province-wide plebiscite on whether or not a particular constitutional amendment ought to be authorized by a resolution of that province's legislative assembly. (This step is in fact required by law in British Columbia.) The point, quite simply, is that we have the possibility of a popular consultation on constitutional matters in Canada, even under the existing arrangements.

The Flawed Amending Procedure

Alan Cairns has explained how the amending formula adopted in 1982, particularly as employed in the case of Meech Lake, is not a viable method for formal constitutional change because it offends the assumptions that the 1982 Charter inevitably engendered in many Canadians who had hoped to participate in the writing of future amendments – especially those élites who identified with particular constitutional clauses.[24]

The amending formula's inappropriateness for the constitutional future, Cairns argues, arose primarily out of the simultaneous insertion of the Charter of Rights in the constitution. This changed the constitutional order to which the amending formula would apply, and implicitly challenged the validity of the assumptions on which it was based. This was not, Cairns suggests, understood in the years 1980 to 1982 when the compromise of the 1982 Constitution Act was viewed as a reasonable compromise between the two groups of agreeing parties – the "Gang of Three" (the federal government playing the lead role, with its allies of Ontario and New Brunswick) and the "Gang of Seven" (the provincial governments remaining after Quebec refused to go along with its former partners in what had been the "Gang of Eight").[25]

(Incidentally, as much as some people not enamoured by democracy may fear "mob rule," I have never heard anyone refer to the Canadian people, who might have had a role in ratifying the constitutional amendments by referendum, as a "gang." The gang terminology says much about the executive-federalism process and people's perception of it.)

From the vantage point of Meech Lake, however, the compromise of 1982 can no longer be seen as only a minor incoherence, but must rather be judged as containing a serious contradiction. The Charter greatly increased the cast of constitutional actors. "It brought new groups into the constitutional order," observes Cairns. "They," he says, "and especially their elites, identify with particular clauses that they view as 'their own'; after all, they won them as the feminist movement indicates in *The Taking of Twenty-Eight*."[26]

These new constitutional actors dispute the hegemony of governments in formal constitutional change. They view as a serious constitutional flaw the fact that the constitution, via the Charter, gives citizens rights against governments and simultaneously excludes those rights-bearing citizens from any meaningful input into the formal amendment process that might erode, or eliminate, their rights.

The frustrations of these new constitutional actors over the Meech Lake attempt to treat them as no more than impotent onlookers, explains Cairns, were compounded by their distrust of the political élites who operated the system of executive federalism. To assert that aboriginals, women, multicultural groups, official language minorities, and others have no confidence that their concerns will be understood and attended to in closed first ministers' meetings is simply to sum up the basic thrust of their presentations in various legislative hearings. It appears, according to Cairns's assessment, "that the Meech Lake strategy of an attempted executive federalism coup is not a viable strategy for future amendments. It offends participant tendencies in our constitutional culture that the Charter has stimulated."[27] This lesson had to be learned also by

Prime Minister Mulroney and his cabinet ministers, whose frustration surrounding the failure of the Meech Lake Accord profoundly exceeded even that of these "new constitutional actors."

It is important to understand the historical weight against which this movement for popular participation has been struggling, and why the transition is proving so difficult. Most of Canada's experience both with constitution making and constitution amending has been predominantly élitist (or "governmental," using Cairns's term), to the exclusion of the wider public. The Quebec Act of 1774, the British North America Act of 1867, the Statute of Westminster of 1931, and the Privy Council amendments of the 1940s, were all arranged between British parliamentarians and Canadian officials. Our more recent experience of this enduring conflict began with the struggle, in the Trudeau-led round of constitutional negotiations in 1980 and 1981, between the traditional political élite approach and the more potent possibility of popular participation.

In the wake of the failure to ratify the Meech Lake Accord by the deadline of June 23, 1990 – after three years and the anti-climactic and emotional national drama of late-night and last-minute marathon talks by the first ministers – Canadians had grown tired of constitutional issues, disliked the process that led to the negotiation and final failure of the Meech Lake Accord, and overwhelmingly preferred to have future changes dealt with by referendum.

A July 1990 *Globe and Mail*–CBC News poll showed that, unlike their attitudes towards many other facets of language and constitutional questions, respondents from Quebec and from the rest of the country had virtually identical views about the constitution-making process. The survey found a clear desire to have a more open process, with 54 percent of respondents saying they believed constitutional talks should be held in public. A mixture of some private and some public discussions was endorsed by 32 percent, and only 10 percent of those surveyed said the talks should all be in private. Also, while 27 percent were prepared to leave changes to elected federal and provincial leaders, fully two-thirds said future changes to the constitution should be submitted to a referendum.[28]

If that was the broad public view, it was also one increasingly shared by Canada's intellectual and academic community. The late

Eugene Forsey, a constitutional expert, commenting in his determined way on the process even before ratification of the Meech Lake Accord failed, spoke with prescience of how Meech Lake "has shown that the present process is dangerous, and may be ruinous," adding that it put "the whole thing at the mercy of provincial politicians who, in most cases, were elected on purely provincial issues. Often, the election that put them in office may [have been] several years back, and the electors may well have changed their minds."[29]

Forsey urged that we "take the power to change the constitution away from the politicians and give it to the people. The constitution belongs to the people, not the politicians," he said, asserting that "the people, not the politicians, should decide what goes in or out, and what does not."[30]

Former Supreme Court Justice Willard Estey, for his part, opined how "the process that they followed just inflamed anybody with a sense of democracy," and elaborated on the problem, saying, "You can't have a parliamentary system and then have the chief executive officers of 11 units in the parliamentary federal system turn around and present their legislative branches with a fait accompli. You then would have a constitutional process which is never carried to the people."[31] Describing the inadequacies of a procedure that would only allow the general public to play a role years later, and then only in a general election when many other issues would be involved, Estey concluded that "the process is what killed Meech Lake. I don't think the content did as much to bring it down as the process."[32]

Howard McConnell of the University of Saskatchewan has suggested a formalized constitutional mechanism be put in place by which Canadians in every part of the country could advance their views more readily on the merits of initiatives like the Meech Lake Accord. Such a mechanism would serve not only a needed constitutional purpose, he said, but could also educate the public on the character and effect of new constitutional provisions in a political order where "constitutionalism" has not always played a leading role in the past. New constitutional norms must have "legal legitimacy" in the sense that they are accepted and used in practice not only by the main political actors in the country, McConnell concluded, but also by a majority of people in a majority of our regions.[33]

176

The Beaudoin-Edwards Report and the Referendum Possibility

On December 13, 1990, Prime Minister Brian Mulroney, following further the pattern of former Prime Minister Trudeau, tabled a discussion paper in Parliament on amending the constitution and established a joint Senate-Commons committee to make recommendations by July 1991. The prime minister's paper asked the committee to look at various methods of breaking Canada's political impasse on amending the constitution. Incorporating a referendum in the ratification process was one of the methods.

The Beaudoin-Edwards Committee had been asked to consider the so-far nebulous possibility of a relevant but non-binding plebiscite as a solution. It was a start in looking for a fresh approach. This committee's new mandate included an attempt to resuscitate the idea Pierre Trudeau had advanced, then reluctantly dropped, a decade earlier.

As the Beaudoin-Edwards Committee hearings progressed through the winter and spring of 1991, the case for a referendum was powerfully made. Jennifer Smith, a constitutional expert from Dalhousie University, told committee members that a referendum would be a natural tool to use if Canada decided to do a complete overhaul of Confederation. In fact, she said, it might be the only way to ratify major changes of that nature because "our amending formula, as it now stands, cannot withstand that kind of change."[34] Vincent Lemieux, a political science professor at Laval University, held similar views and came before the committee with a virtual how-to program for designing and holding referendums, arguing that they were inevitable.[35]

Use of the referendum in this constitutional amending process was one of the recommendations from the Beaudoin-Edwards Committee. In its report of June 1991, the committee, noting that the existing Canadian constitution is silent on the subject of referendums, concluded that "since it is neither explicitly authorized nor explicitly forbidden, recourse to a referendum is thus left to the preference of our political leaders: it is optional."[36] A great number of witnesses who appeared before the Beaudoin-Edwards Committee took the position that the constitution belongs to the people and the people must be enabled to pronounce on it. "From the perspective of those witnesses," observed the committee, "a referendum is one of the best means of giving the citizens the feeling that the Constitution does indeed belong to them and of allowing them the last word on approving or amending it."[37]

Some witnesses expressed the view that Canada's experience with referendums was, in the committee's words, "such that the prospect of holding another one, and even more, of using the procedure regularly, was not particularly appealing." Before resorting to this mechanism, the committee therefore observed, "the precise goal would have to be made very clear."[38]

The committee considered that an obligatory referendum could replace ratification of constitutional amendments by Parliament and the provincial legislatures. "At this point in our history," however, the committee did not believe "that a ratification referendum should be entrenched in the constitution," but rather that it should remain optional, as is currently the case. For the federal or provincial governments to resort to this mechanism, all that would be needed, suggested the committee, "would be for the federal Parliament or the provincial legislatures to bring in simple legislation in keeping with the legislative power-sharing structure. This has been the situation since 1867," the committee said, rather ambiguously, "and we could easily continue in this manner."[39]

In the committee's opinion, furthermore, the "federal authorities would be well advised to table draft referendum legislation before Parliament." Noting that "authorities could resort to this mechanism when they deem it necessary," they also said that, "given the heterogeneous nature of the country, the draft legislation should stipulate a double majority: a national majority and a majority in each of the four regions (the Atlantic region, Quebec, Ontario, and the West)."[40] It is interesting to compare this position with the earlier view expressed in a written paper by Senator Gérald A. Beaudoin, one of the committee's co-chairmen, which was presented at a conference on constitution making held on April 29, 1990, at the University of Ottawa. He declared at that time, "Notre proposition était la suivante: la Constitution du Canada serait amendée par un vote à la Chambre des communes et au Conseil de la fédération (qui remplaçerait le Sénat), vote qui par la suite devait être ratifié par un référendum canadien recueillant une majorité dans les provinces de l'Atlantique, au Québec, en Ontario et dans les provinces de l'Ouest."[41] Although referendums would not amend the constitution of Canada, in the committee's view, "the results would carry some political but no legal weight. The results would not be binding on the two levels of government, but would constitute an eloquent message."[42]

In formally recommending that a federal law be enacted "to enable the federal government, at its discretion, to hold a consultative referendum on a constitutional proposal, either to confirm the existence of a national consensus or to facilitate the adoption of the required amending resolutions,"[43] the Beaudoin-Edwards Committee had suggested that the Mulroney government do what the Trudeau government had attempted to do in 1978, when it drafted the Canada Referendum Act and tabled it in Parliament.[44] A bill enabling referendums and plebiscites, such as the one that I introduced in 1988 and have kept before Parliament continuously since then, the committee was suggesting, ought to be enacted.

In addition to recommending that the referendum require a national majority and a majority in each of the four regions, the committee stipulated that the territories should participate in the referendum and that they do so "after having selected the region in which they would be included for the purpose of calculating regional majorities."

Concerns about referendums raised by witnesses who appeared before the Beaudoin-Edwards Committee ought not to be ignored, since these points continue to be debated as we Canadians ease ourselves into a new mode of democratic operation with a constitutional referendum. The four most serious of these concerns pertain to referendums and minority rights, political responsibility on the part of governments and politicians, the nature of popular participation, and the risk of division.

Referendums and Minorities

Given the heterogeneity of Canada's population, some witnesses appearing before the Beaudoin-Edwards Committee questioned the appropriateness of holding referendums within such a society. The idea of direct popular voting sparked opposition from groups representing minorities, several of whom feared "the dictatorship of the majority" might deprive them of their rights. In their view, making decisions by referendum is not at all suited to a pluralistic society. They feared that doing so carried the risk of stirring up prejudice and accentuating differences.

On a theoretical level, this concern seems groundless. The rights of minorities are fully entrenched in the Canadian Charter of Rights and Freedoms, and can only be removed with further constitutional amendment or by temporary legislation passed by a legislature invoking the "notwithstanding" clause that could set aside some of the Charter's protection. We all know what the existing formula for amendment requires, and the apparent impossibility of achieving the required unanimous consent is a solid practical guarantee that these entrenched rights will continue. If we move to a referendum phase for amendments, the Charter of Rights could not be changed without our heterogeneous society itself voting to repeal the Charter's protection of minority rights. That would, on all evidence, be an even greater barrier to change than the current amending formula in practice affords. Moreover, the wording of any question in a national referendum or plebiscite would have to be approved first by Parliament.

The experience elsewhere with referendums on constitutional matters is that they generally tend to be conservative, that is, wary of change. The much more probable risk to minority groups comes, not from all the people voting in a referendum, but from a legislature invoking the "notwithstanding" clause to set aside some Charter-protected right in the course of passing a new law.

Although some speak of the "dictatorship of the majority," Canada does not really have a majority; rather, it is made up of countless minorities who share a common Canadian citizenship. The problem in the past with minority rights has not been so much a threat from the general population as from governments and legislators. Some of the worst expressions of discrimination have been enacted in earlier statutes. Indeed, the people themselves could be a bulwark of support and protection against measures that would diminish the position of racial or religious minorities. As

Chief Justice Rinfret observed in 1951, "The constitution of Canada does not belong either to Parliament, or to the Legislatures; it belongs to the country and it is there that the citizens of the country will find the protection of the rights to which they are entitled."[45]

On a practical level, nevertheless, it is understandable that some minority groups would be wary of referendums, given the bad experience of Manitoba's French-speaking minority in a series of municipal plebiscites in October 1983. However, on this issue, as indeed on all others involving the direct participation of Canadians, the ultimate question is whether one trusts the collective judgment of well-informed people. The reason that prejudice has been stirred up and differences accentuated is that small vocal groups who do not represent the broad cross-current of mainstream Canadian opinion have had their views publicized and amplified, while the tolerant majority, busy with its daily pursuit of making the country run and lacking any ready forum for expressing its views, has remained silent. Nothing is risk-free in an open society, but minority groups, secure with the protection of the Charter, ought to find more, on balance, to favour than to fear in measures – including direct popular voting – that will make Canada even more democratic than it is.

Political Responsibility

Some witnesses before the Beaudoin-Edwards parliamentary committee criticized the use of referendums on the grounds that by resorting to them, Canada's political leaders would be abdicating their responsibility, leaving decisions up to the public instead. These witnesses felt politicians would thereby be evading the consequences of difficult decisions. Similarly, some witnesses pointed out that politicians are not elected to act only as popular opinion demands, but that they must, as leaders of the community, display judgment and make far-sighted decisions.

One could counter, however, with even greater force that politicians have too often avoided the political responsibility of finding proper channels for popular participation by Canadians in the government processes of our country. It is also part of our responsibility as politicians to educate people about public issues.

The referendum, used in special cases, is a way of fulfilling that obligation, not shirking it.

There are ways we can significantly improve our present governmental institutions and procedures, and we politicians must fulfil our responsibility by opening up the processes in a way that permits Canadians to share more completely in both understanding the issues and accepting the consequences of decisions collectively arrived at. This is hardly the approach of a timid politician seeking to avoid political responsibility. As leaders of the community, we, its elected representatives, can help our country evolve beyond its existing pattern of political decision making.

As Finance Minister J.L. Isley said in the House of Commons during the February 1942 debate for a national plebiscite, "Surely the cowardly Government or Parliament is the one which fears to ascertain the views of the people."

Popular Participation

Witnesses before the Beaudoin-Edwards Committee expected the public would turn out for a referendum in fairly large numbers where there was a crisis or when feelings ran high, but that if the subject was not one of national interest, or if there was no particular link with people's concerns, a high level of participation would be unlikely. An example was made of Switzerland, where frequent use of referendums has tended to diminish voter turnout at the polls. Some witnesses concluded that referendums, therefore, ought to be held infrequently, and only on important issues. Others argued that the effect of using referendums might be to make people more aware of the workings of government and more eager to participate.

I agree with each of these observations on participation. Canadian referendums should be held on major constitutional amendments and on issues of transcending national importance only. Like any other democratic instrument, the referendum and plebiscite process should not be trivialized, nor used when it is unwarranted. Direct votes should not be held too frequently, nor on routine matters of government. In other countries, most referendums are on constitutional matters, on various aspects of sovereignty, or on issues that are clearly moral and, therefore, outside party politics – such as

182

prohibition and divorce. In Denmark and Sweden there have been national referendums dealing with pragmatic questions of government like pension plans and land laws.[46] Our own history suggests that we already do lean towards infrequent use and respect the important nature of the ballot question as an instrument of popular participation.

Divisiveness

The concern that a referendum would be divisive and the conclusion that it should therefore be avoided is one of the silliest arguments anyone in a democracy could advance. Of course it is divisive. It divides us into two camps – those who favour and those who oppose a particular measure. It then enables everyone to see, without speculation and without intense reliance on opinion polling, which is currently a far more insidious, nearly *daily* source of division in Canada, exactly how many Canadians are for and how many against. Then the country can move forward from there.

As in a dialectic process, it may only be possible at the stage following a referendum vote to approach some synthesis. Or, no synthesis may even be needed: the outcome may be clear enough that everyone – even those whose viewpoint did not prevail – will accept the verdict because it was an open decision, openly arrived at. *Everyone* had a chance to have their say; *everyone* had a chance to cast their ballot. No one, furthermore, should be surprised that in a democracy the result will not be unanimous. What it will be is valid, and it will probably be more persuasive and positive in its impact than any other approach. Our own history affords good evidence of that.

Divisions within Canada exist; to avoid debating and confronting them publicly has, generally, been the preferred approach in the past. How successful has that course been? Isn't the cathartic experience of dealing with some of these problems precisely what many Canadians are currently yearning for?

The 1942 plebiscite on conscription – with significantly different results in Quebec from the rest of Canada – did not create that division, it merely recorded it. By having the breadth of the chasm recorded for all to see, the government of Prime Minister Mackenzie King was able to use that result in a successful prosecution of the war effort and kept the country united in the process.

The Necessity of a Fresh Approach

In the months ahead, it appears we Canadians will have our say, through a direct vote, on what we think of the new package of constitutional proposals. The campaign period for a direct vote by *all* Canadians to ratify amendments to our constitution could last for perhaps six or eight weeks, during which time both the "pro" and "con" sides could fully outline their views. Enabling legislation under which such a referendum would occur could provide for two umbrella organizations, representing each side of the question, through which broadcasting time, fundraising, public speaking, paid advertising and all other matters related to a contemporary campaign would be channelled.

Quite apart from the number and results of ballots added up at the conclusion of voting, such a campaign process is itself of incomparable importance as an educational exercise. A referendum campaign can be an important force for our self-definition as Canadians. When constitution making is a process for the political élite only (with, at most, some public committee hearings as a sop to the people), we suffer the malaise of Canadian democratic life: most people are left as spectators to the process.

Participation and involvement, on the other hand, give citizens a role in the process, a sense of being part of a major decision affecting the future of our country, and, through learning about the issue prior to voting on it, an education in the nature of our country. An amendment ratified by a free vote of the people will have a measure of support and acceptance that could never be achieved in any other way.

Many leading Canadians have held back their support for the idea of a referendum on the constitution, but the failure of other older ways ought to make them more confident of the democratic prospect that awaits us. I think it is significant that Jean Chrétien, for example, has changed his mind on this since talking Trudeau out of it in the 1981 constitutional talks. Chrétien's feelings then were very strong: "I'm telling you now," he said to Trudeau, "if at the end of this meeting you decide on a referendum, I won't be putting on my running shoes again for you. I've had enough of families divided, villages divided, French divided against English. A national referendum will be worse. You'll get East divided against West, Protestants divided against Catholics – everything."[47]

Yet today his policy is that there must be a national referendum to ratify constitutional amendments. In this change, he joins other notable political leaders. Woodrow Wilson, a United States president, for instance, said in 1911, "For 20 years I preached to the students of Princeton that the referendum and recall was bosh . . . I have since investigated and I want to apologize to those students. It is the safeguard of politics. It takes power from the boss and places it in the hands of the people."[48] Canadian prime ministers Wilfrid Laurier, Robert Borden, Arthur Meighen, and W.L. Mackenzie King all had misgivings that they set aside upon recognizing the appropriateness of an occasional direct mandate from the people on fundamental questions.

Constitutional change in Canada must seem, to those who try to practise it, a no-win situation. With the public appetite whetted for participation in constitution making, "executive federalism" arrangements become increasingly hard to arrive at and then to legitimate. Yet previous Canadian experience has demonstrated how new circumstances and fresh ideas can give life to a further round of constitutional negotiations. Methods of fuller public participation could be among the fresh ideas that will lead to better success and greater legitimacy.

8

The Quest for a Canadian
Direct-Vote Statute

I t would be anomalous to discover that a Canadian general election was being planned if no Canada Elections Act existed and that the vote could not in fact take place. The people would rightly conclude that their legislators had been negligent in failing to enact the requisite legal framework for an election. By the same token, enabling legislation for a referendum or plebiscite must be on the statute books before the process of direct voting on a law or question can ever occur.

Six provinces and both territories have such acts governing plebiscites and referendums, but Canada itself does not. A call for a ratifying vote on the constitution, or on any other subject, rings hollow in the absence of a legal means to make the vote happen. Those who glibly assume that such an act could quickly and easily be passed by Parliament are, it is safe to assume, unaware of the difficulties that have surrounded the long quest for a Canadian direct-vote statute.

Prime Ministers and Plebiscites

In the late 1970s while Quebec Premier René Lévesque prepared for the referendum on sovereignty-association, Prime Minister Pierre Trudeau considered holding a federally sponsored referendum within Quebec on the question of Quebec sovereignty, a populist reply to Lévesque's political strategy. Realizing that Lévesque had a Referendum Act in place under which to hold such a vote, while the federal government did not, Trudeau accepted that he, too, would have to have a Canadian direct-vote statute enacted. Otherwise, all his talk about holding a Canada-sponsored vote would be mere rhetoric.

The Canada Referendum Act was accordingly introduced in the House of Commons by Justice Minister Marc Lalonde on April 3, 1978. The same bill was reintroduced in a new session of Parliament that autumn. Although it proceeded to second reading on January 2, 1979, and was debated, the legislation never became law. It died on the order paper when the Thirtieth Parliament was dissolved for a general election on May 22, 1979. That election was won by the Progressive Conservatives, and the new government under Prime Minister Joe Clark, lasting a scant forty-nine sitting days of Parliament, neither produced a bill to enable direct voting by the people, nor appears to have even contemplated doing so.

Still, the activity of the late 1970s by the Trudeau government at least represented some progress. A few years earlier, when the Pépin-Robarts Commission spoke of the value of a double-majority plebiscite, nobody had even bothered to start the legislative mill turning. By 1979, the enabling legislation for such direct voting had at least seen the light of day, and significantly, it had been introduced as government legislation.

Getting such a statute enacted by Parliament is a major hurdle, since some MPs and cabinet ministers see direct votes as a threat to their positions and a challenge to the nature of a representative democracy, rather than as a useful complementary procedure. Conversions, including important ones such as that of Jean Chrétien, discussed in the previous chapter, are today taking place, and this represents some further progress in the quest for a Canadian direct-vote statute. As with any legislation, it is valuable to understand both its "legislative history" and the political context which gives it birth.

By the spring of 1991 and release of the Bélanger-Campeau Commission's report on Quebec's future relations with Canada, talk of another referendum in Quebec on the subject of either independence or revised constitutional arrangements with Canada was heard once again, and history appeared to be repeating itself. The Quebec

National Assembly duly enacted a law requiring that a referendum on Quebec's future in Canada be held no later than October 1992. At the same time, Prime Minister Mulroney, echoing Trudeau, began alluding to the possibility of a federal government referendum within Quebec, or possibly across the entire country, on the same issue.

Mulroney's position on direct voting had been gradually, if just perceptibly, shifting. Fundamentally opposed to the idea of referendums, he had earlier preferred the party system in Parliament which, not coincidentally, he substantially controlled. In the summer of 1986, facing questions about capital punishment from reporters in western Canada, Mulroney speculated, for the first time, that perhaps a referendum would be one way to deal with the contentious issue. Yet he was not advocating the idea. "I'm not big on the idea of referenda generally," Mulroney told reporters. "I think that the British parliamentary system provides for our elected MPs to make up their mind."[1] Of course, with rigid party discipline in the Canadian parliamentary system, MPs do not so much make up their own minds as follow their leader. Certainly nothing came of that speculative thought about a direct popular vote on capital punishment, and the matter was resolved instead by a free vote in the House of Commons two years later.

"In the midst of the Meech Lake crisis, Mulroney had rejected Premier Clyde Wells' suggestion of a referendum," columnist Michel Gratton observed, "saying he would never put Québecers through another painful conscription debate."[2] Yet after the collapse of the Meech Lake Accord in June 1990, as the political box in which Mulroney found himself grew smaller, options and alternatives previously rejected began to look interesting. In December 1990 many people were pleasantly surprised to hear the prime minister mention in the Commons the possibility of a referendum – among other options – to help extricate Canada from the post–Meech Lake constitutional mess.

When visiting his constituency of Charlevoix in mid-March 1991, the prime minister answered a question from a Baie Comeau radio interviewer in a way that hinted at a nationwide referendum on Quebec and the constitution. "If ever we have to ask questions," he said, "we will do it with great precision. There will be no flim-flam in it!"[3]

In the Mulroney government's Throne Speech on May 13, 1991, moreover, Parliament was explicitly told, "You will be asked to approve enabling legislation to provide for greater participation of Canadian men and women in constitutional change." This signaled the clear intentions of the government, for the Throne Speech had been by approved by cabinet and certainly by the prime minister.

Shortly after this, former Prime Minister Trudeau revealed, in a speech in Montreal, how he too had considered his way out of a tight box on constitutional matters. When the provinces continued to balk at his plans in the early 1980s for repatriating the constitution, he said he had considered a unilateral declaration of independence, coupled with a general election to win a mandate from the people of Canada for a complete break with the United Kingdom.[4] Although Trudeau considered the use of a general election rather than a referendum, no doubt at all existed in his mind that such a fundamental change could only proceed on the basis of a clearly expressed mandate from the people.

Is it not a significant commentary on the nature and operation of the existing political system of Canada that our prime ministers, when faced with profound dilemmas, are driven to consider seeking direct support from the people, in spite of their initial misgivings about doing so? We can also think of Prime Minister Robert Borden, who, pressed by turbulent political pressures that almost defied endurance, resolved to deal with at least one of his central problems by making plans to hold a national plebiscite to settle the issue of Senate reform in 1914. Yet it was not to be.

Just as Prime Minister Borden came to the realization (which forced him to curtail his plan), and as Prime Minister Trudeau discovered, so Prime Minister Mulroney also realized that in the quest for a direct verdict from the people, one needs a direct-vote statute to provide the legal basis and establish the rules for the process. Recommendations have sprouted from every side on the subject of referendums. From the royal commission on Canadian election law and financing, from the Beaudoin-Edwards Committee on the amending formula, from the Spicer Commission on the views of Canadians about the future workings of our country, and from other sources, including legislative committees set up in some of the provinces, the country is busy with the idea of direct voting by all the people. Yet now, as in the past, the same preliminary hurdle must first be cleared: a Canadian direct-vote statute must be enacted by Parliament in order for such votes to be held.

The Significance of Direct-Vote Enabling Legislation

Prime Minister Mulroney, in retracing this path previously walked by Prime Minister Trudeau, also seemed to face the same division of opinion that confronted the Liberal prime minister on the issue. *Maclean's* reported on January 7, 1991, for example, that "senior Tories are split on the issue of holding nationwide plebiscites on major issues."[5]

The article also reported results of the seventh annual *Maclean's/* Decima poll, which showed that a high number of Canadians want the government to consult the public before making major decisions. Those favouring popular consultation on major issues reached 67 percent in British Columbia, 76 percent in the Prairies, 80 percent in Ontario, 75 percent in Quebec, and 84 percent in Atlantic Canada. Although widespread support clearly persists among voters for the idea, the article said, "senior Conservatives argue that such a plan would carry enormous potential for divisiveness between different regions and language and ethnic groups." This report simply shows, once again, the presence of a benevolent élitist attitude that favours protecting Canadians from being exposed to who and what we really are, and from the unproven notion that such exposure would be harmful rather than therapeutic.

The prerequisite of enacting enabling legislation for a Canadian referendum or plebiscite, apparently viewed as a mere technicality by some politicians and political commentators, is in fact a significant step, one not as routinely taken as might appear. The recorded debate in the Canadian House of Commons, whenever the subject has arisen, is ample evidence of that. Yet until such enabling legislation is in place, commentary that assumes that referendums can be held in Canada seems somewhat superficial. For example, on the Meech Lake Accord issue, *The Toronto Star's* generally thoughtful

Ottawa columnist Carol Goar, writing on June 20, 1990, suggested that Prime Minister Mulroney could breathe life into the near-dead accord by removing himself from the equation. "One way to accomplish this would be to call a national referendum on the constitutional agreement," wrote Goar, "then announce that – whatever the result – he was stepping down as Prime Minister at the end of his current term."[6] While recommending such selfless acts of statesmanship may come easily to those who offer suggestions about how the country's problems can be resolved, it would be helpful if they took account of the reality that currently no national referendum can be held.

The same dilemma arose with the appeals heard in 1987 and 1988 to "let the people decide" about the free trade treaty Canada had negotiated with the United States, and the discussion about whether a general election or a national referendum would in fact have produced the more authentic verdict. Prime Minister Mulroney clearly preferred an election to a referendum, which in the end determined the matter, first within the electoral arena and then within the parliamentary context. Yet even if he had wanted a plebiscite, the absence of enabling legislation under which a national direct vote could have been held would have prevented it.

At the federal level, we also lack any legislation under which citizens can initiate a vote on a public policy or a law. The sole exception had been the provisions in the Canada Temperance Act, which could give rise to a local plebiscite on prohibition as a result of petitions, but this statute was quietly repealed by Parliament by an innocuous provision contained in the omnibus bill consolidating statutes in 1990.

The Canada Elections Act, for its part, deals exclusively with the election of representatives to Parliament, and is thus silent on the subject of referendums and plebiscites. A number of provinces – for example, Alberta and New Brunswick – deal with both elections of representatives and direct popular voting in plebiscites in their election acts. The gap in our federal law is a direct result of the fact that generally Canadian governments and parliamentarians have not been disposed to share their law-making authority with the voters at large, nor even to permit Canadians a non-binding say on vital questions of the day in a national plebiscite.

While Canada has no nationwide legislation in place, the majority of our provinces do. Some even have very comprehensive statutes. The Referendum Act of Quebec, for instance, under which the 1980 vote on sovereignty-association and a regional referendum in northern Quebec have taken place, deals with raising and spending funds, creating umbrella organizations for "yes" and "no" sides, advertising, publicity, voter registration, and all other attributes of contemporary electoral campaigns. Other provinces have simpler plebiscite acts. In Prince Edward Island, for example, the statute runs to only six sections. Under it, Premier Joe Ghiz held the 1988 plebiscite on a fixed-link crossing from the island to the mainland.

A British Referendum Scenario with Canadian Application

Most other democracies, too, have statutes in place to enable the holding of referendums and plebiscites. One which does not is the United Kingdom. The situation in Britain is instructive for Canada. Both countries have roughly similar democratic institutions and procedures, our differences being due to Canada's written constitution, a federal system, and an entrenched charter of rights. Both have held national plebiscites (on prohibition and military service in our case, on membership in the European Community in Britain's). Also, both have looming issues of far-reaching consequences that could fundamentally alter their nature.

We know about the strong public feeling in Canada favouring direct voting. If public opinion clamoured for a referendum in Britain on the issue of, for example, a single European currency, how might it happen? "No one knows," said a 1990 editorial in *The Economist*, a publication that champions the wise and selective use of referendums for the U.K., "because there are no established rules."[7] There is only one true precedent – the national referendum steered through by a Labour government in 1975 over Britain's continued membership in the European Community – and, as was done then, *The Economist* speculated, "the politicians would have to set the pace, leaving lawyers to jump up and down on the sidelines if it looked as though constitutional conventions were under threat."

In an interesting and valuable exercise, *The Economist*, in the same issue, presented precisely how one might go about carrying out a referendum on the issue of a single European currency for the U.K. It is worth repeating this publication's six-step referendum scenario, both for the insights it provides into our own system and for the fears about direct voting it may help assuage among devoted Canadian followers of the Westminster parliamentary model.

First, the government is advised that no existing law provides for a referendum-by-decree, and that a fresh bill is therefore needed. The Tory whips assure the cabinet that there is enough parliamentary support to avoid the disaster of a defeated bill. Mrs. Thatcher, who was still prime minister when *The Economist* presented this plan, appoints a special unit of the Cabinet Office (as in 1975) to draw up a bill, on the basis of two months of talks with both sides of the Commons.

Second, a cross-bench committee of MPs assembles under the chairmanship of the Speaker, to approve the bill's wording of a referendum motion. Polling experts tell the committee that voters take little notice of the wording of a referendum motion and tick "yes" or "no" in the light of the preceding campaign. After three months of wrangling, a draft bill is approved.

Third, the bill is presented to the Commons, proposing a referendum on the question: "Other members of the European Community envisage a move towards economic and monetary union in which all countries in the Community will eventually use a single European currency: do you approve of Britain following this path?" Despite the discouraging precedent of Labour's devolution bills of 1978, when clauses providing for local referendums in Scotland and Wales were amended at the last minute by critics opposed to them in principle, pressure from the media and constituency parties chivvies MPs into passing the three readings of the bill in a matter of days (as in 1975). A date is fixed for voting in May 1991, allowing for a three-week campaign.

Fourth, Mrs. Thatcher announces that Tory MPs (ministers included) are free to campaign according to their own views. The legal status of the referendum is advisory rather than mandatory, but she says that her government will be guided by its outcome. The Labour leadership agrees.

Fifth, those for and against the motion set up temporary organizations to promote their causes – and to help the media devote an equitable share of broadcasting time to the two sides. Both sides receive equal campaign grants from the Treasury.

Sixth, voting is run by the electoral registration officers within parliamentary constituencies. Completed ballot papers are collected by counties and boroughs, however, to avoid any count being identified directly with a parliamentary seat. The results are declared as a simple percentage of the total votes cast.[8]

This scenario is British, but it could very well be used in Canada, especially where the enabling legislation has to be prepared in the midst of intense focus on a specific referendum issue.

The Canada Referendum and Plebiscite Act – Attempts . . . and More Attempts

Sometimes a plebiscite act gets passed only after a government has decided to hold a direct vote, as in *The Economist'*s scenario for the U.K., when it realizes that enabling legislation is required. This, essentially, is what happened in 1982 with the plebiscite ordinance enacted by the Northwest Territories Assembly for the vote on the question of dividing the N.W.T. into two parts.

The problem with creating enabling legislation at the same time that a government is contemplating a specific vote on a particular topic is that the question to be submitted to the people invariably gets mixed up with the procedures for taking the vote itself. This was the Canadian experience with the 1942 national plebiscite on conscription for overseas military service. Likewise, special statutory provisions had to be developed for the earlier 1898 national plebiscite on the prohibition of liquor. There is value in avoiding the blending of the problem and the process, the substance and the form.

It was to avoid these earlier Canadian and Northwest Territories experiences and actually learn a lesson from history that I hoped we could enact the legal prerequisites in a relatively calm and deliberative atmosphere. Referendum-enabling legislation should proceed through Parliament in response to a need that is known but at a time when no looming crisis or controversy would distort people's judgment or produce a poor law because subjective considerations had gained the upper hand. For this reason I introduced the Canada Referendum and Plebiscite Act (Bill C-311) in the Thirty-third Parliament on July 21, 1988.

Described by the clerk of the House of Commons as the largest private member's bill ever introduced in the House of Commons, Bill C-311 is for direct votes what the Canada Elections Act is for parliamentary elections: a complete set of legal rules. It explains how referendums and plebiscites are initiated, and provides rules governing the campaign and voting, fundraising, advertising and broadcasting, voters' lists, conduct of the voting, officials involved, spending limits, registration of the "yes" and "no" committees, along with all the other elements and safeguards of modern campaigns and voting. It is lengthy because it is detailed legislation. It addresses all the questions and procedures one would need for an election of MPs, and is about the same length, therefore, as the Canada Elections Act.

The late Eugene Forsey came with me to the press conference following the tabling of Bill C-311 on the morning of July 21. Forsey told the reporters in his crisp and emphatic way, "I am here to express my support for this Bill . . . Plebiscites would allow voters to have their say when all three parties take the same stand on a major issue."[9]

I was certainly not the first member of Parliament to have proposed referendums and plebiscites. From a 1930s proposal for a national referendum on the issue of unemployment insurance, down to suggestions in the last decade or two for direct votes on abortion, capital punishment, Quebec separation, metrification, and other issues, many parliamentarians have sought to obtain a mandate directly from the people on fundamental questions.

Yet previous motions and private member's bills, while favouring the principle of direct democracy, focused primarily on a controversial issue of substance rather than on the actual process to be followed for voting. For those voting procedures, these MPs simply stated, if they addressed the procedural aspect at all, that the Canada Elections Act should be followed *mutatis mutandis* (a lawyerly Latin phrase, meaning with the necessary changes in points of detail). Having written five books on Canadian election law,[10] I am aware that the current Canada Elections Act is cumbersome even for running a general election, let alone a plebiscite. I came to believe it was vital to draft a complete statute with all requisite provisions for a direct vote, rather than sloughing off the work to harried election officials, operating under the pressure cooker atmosphere of a national direct-vote campaign.

For some years I have been convinced that national plebiscites will again take place in Canada, and that indeed on some questions they *must* be held. I have remained determined as a federal legislator, therefore, to see legislation in place to permit this to happen. So, after Bill C-311 died on the order paper as Parliament was dissolved for the 1988 general election, I reintroduced the same legislation in the First Session of the Thirty-fourth Parliament on December 14, 1988, as Bill C-2. It never had a chance to be debated then, so in the Second Session on September 26, 1989, I introduced it a third time as Bill C-257.

In the spring of 1990, it seemed persistence would pay off. My name was drawn, along with those of nine other MPs, under the new "lottery" system for private member's bills. The rules require each MP to select a bill from among the several he or she may currently have before the House as the one they want called for debate. Obviously I felt the referendum bill should come before the House, but the timing was awkward. The country was just then reaching "high noon" in the Meech Lake showdown.

In Newfoundland Premier Clyde Wells was musing, with his clear-eyed gaze seemingly fixed somewhere beyond the horizon, about having a nationwide direct vote on the constitutional amendment contained in the Meech Lake Accord. The idea was right; the timing was not. The issue, by June 1990, was already long past the point where it could be submitted to the people in a referendum. Had it been put to a vote in the early months following the accord's signing by the prime minister and the ten premiers, the issue could have been carefully considered by Canadians in a deliberate ratification vote. So much had taken place over the subsequent three years, however, that the Meech Lake Accord had become just a little wagon carrying an overloaded burden of Canadian concerns and resentments. In other words, even if a constitutional amendment were submitted to the people for their verdict on it, it would no longer have been possible to find a "panel of jurors" who could be objective about the accord itself. Canadians from the Atlantic to the Arctic to the Pacific had been bombarded with arguments about all sorts of other issues that legitimately form part of our country's serious national political agenda. These issues, which had been gradually piled onto "Meech Lake" over three years, were quite irrelevant to the contents of the Meech Lake Accord itself. Is this an argument against referendums? I don't think so, because no one in their right mind would ever suggest a three-year campaign period for a referendum, any more than they would suggest one for an election. Yet that is what we had gone through when Wells began tossing out the idea of a direct vote.

I then sought advice from the powers that be about designating my Canada Referendum and Plebiscite Act for the vote in the House, and was adamantly told "no." Although given no reason, I accepted that instruction, believing that, because of the delicacy of the further Meech Lake discussions with the premiers, the prime minister did not need one more element that might destabilize the situation – as debate in the House of Commons over the possibilities of a national referendum about Meech Lake could possibly have done. That, of course, was before the prime minister himself gave his beyond-the-record interview to *The Globe and Mail*, disclosing an apparent strategy of getting the premiers together in a highly pressurized session of executive federalism, and in a single moment "rolling all the dice." From then on I decided I would give more weight to what I personally believe to be important for the national agenda.

In the quest for a Canadian direct-vote statute, the next opportunity to advance the cause presented itself in May 1991. To keep the direct-voting matter before Parliament, I again introduced the Canada Referendum and Plebiscite Act for first reading in the Commons on May 15, 1991, and this time it was assigned the number C-201. Once again my name was drawn through the lottery system, along with those of nineteen other MPs, for consideration of our various private member's bills and resolutions. Each of us next had to appear in turn before a subcommittee of the Management Committee to explain our particular bill or motion and the reasons we believed it should be called for debate and made votable. Three bills and three motions are chosen by this process from each lottery selection to be debated and voted on. The remaining seven bills are simply debated for one hour each, which gives some parliamentary attention to the issues they address, after which they go "to the bottom of the order paper," effectively not to see the light of day again, at least in that session of Parliament.

The subcommittee members duly interviewed all the MPs involved, and we each diligently made our presentations. This was a parliamentary committee, and not a government body, deciding on the private members' business of the Canadian House of Commons, weighing each bill to decide which had the greatest urgency and public importance to proceed. This vastly improved process embodied the parliamentary reforms made in 1985.

I made my pitch to the subcommittee, and did some discreet lobbying, enough to discover there was "no problem," that committee members agreed that Bill C-201, the Canada Referendum and Plebiscite Act, should be made votable. This time, happily, the bill also seemed to fit with the government's declared purpose, expressed in the Throne Speech on May 13, of having legislation to "provide for greater participation" of Canadians in constitutional change, which could only mean a plebiscite or referendum. Bill C-201, I reasoned, could even serve as a stalking horse for the government, some of whose members (as *Maclean's* had reported) still harboured doubts about direct democracy. If the bill passed, the requisite enabling legislation would be in place. If it got into trouble, or attracted inordinate flak, the problem would be mine, not the government's. Besides, Bill C-201 incorporated substantially the previous Canada Referendum Bill of the Trudeau government from 1979, which represented the best efforts of the Department of Justice lawyers and the Privy Council Office at the time. In addition, it had been strengthened by further provisions contained in the Mulroney government's own legislation, such as Bill C-79, which had proposed important revisions to the Canada Elections Act. For these reasons, it was clear that any legislation the government itself would introduce could not help but be virtually the same as Bill C-201. The extra benefit was that Bill C-201 was already before the House, so a great deal of time, effort, money, and even some political risk could all be saved by the government if my bill proceeded. As *The Globe and Mail*'s national political columnist Hugh Windsor told me, "The time for your idea has finally come."

Given the statements of MPs involved in the Management Committee's work, it seemed the referendum bill would be made votable. After all, with so much discussion of the idea in the country and several political party leaders now calling for a referendum process, what committee of MPs would want to be responsible for deciding that a bill on referendums should not proceed to be debated and voted on in Parliament? Then, just hours before the committee made its decision, someone senior in the government interfered. The result? The committee decided at its in camera meeting that the Canada Referendum and Plebiscite Act would *not* be votable. It would get one hour's debate, then disappear. The hour's debate took place on June 18, 1991, and other MPs who spoke were Peter Milliken, Liberal MP for Kingston and the Islands; Brian Gardiner, NDP MP from Prince George-Bulkley Valley; Alan Redway, PC MP for Don Valley East; Jean-Robert Gauthier, Liberal MP for Ottawa-Vanier, who all favoured the bill; and Jean Lapierre, Bloc Québécois MP for Shefford, who opposed. By this time I had managed to get agreement from the PCs, Liberals, NDP, and independent members, including Deborah Grey of the Reform Party, for unanimous consent to vote on the bill and send it to a legislative committee. Yet consent of the House for this had to be unanimous, and the Bloc Québécois refused. Indeed, the Bloc was so intent to disrupt this that it forced a "quorum call" (a procedural delay tactic that includes ringing of the bells to call in the members to consume time of the sole hour's debate) – the first time this had happened in "private member's hour" in the living memory of parliamentary veterans.

Peter Milliken, lead-off speaker for the Liberals noted, "in the last few years there appears to have been some breakdown in Canadians' views about their elected representatives. I realize that there is a sense of unease, a sense perhaps of lack of representation of divergent views in this place."[11] Regretting that this was so, Milliken explained how "the arguments about referenda fit into this because the argument of those who believe that Parliament is not representative is that lack of representation can be cured by running to the people with Bills or with questions that can then be decided there." Milliken then stressed that while "occasionally resort must be had to such an unusual remedy," the usual practice must always be "that the elected representatives in Parliament make the decisions respecting the introduction and dealing with Bills." He also saw a peril in using referendums frequently, saying that this could "cause grave disorder in our country." Nevertheless, Milliken supported my bill as "a very good effort at providing for a means of conducting referenda quickly and efficiently in Canada. It is a start." Subject to the reservations he had mentioned, Milliken then confirmed the Liberal Party policy that had been announced by leader of the Official Opposition Jean Chrétien: "We support the principle of the Bill."[12]

Speaking next was Brian Gardiner of the NDP, who said he did not think "members of parliament or parliamentarians should necessarily be afraid of referenda and plebiscites," although he felt "there is room for caution." The position Gardiner endorsed is "to give people an opportunity through referenda or plebiscites to really have some citizens' democracy and make some decisions on major and significant issues in the country. I think that is particularly important in regard to constitutional matters." He did not wish to restrict the subject-matter of referendums, but simply stressed that they were especially important. Gardiner also expressed the view that if the decision on Meech Lake had been submitted to the people in a referendum, "it likely would have passed." Referring to the bill, all the work that had gone into it, and the learning experience for parliamentarians and citizens alike that could be associated with this referendum legislation, Gardiner hoped "that we can all become better in governing our country and give all Canadians that opportunity."[13]

The Honourable Alan Redway in supporting Bill C-201 stressed the provision in it that emphasized that referendums and plebiscites in Canada would be "on questions of public importance." A supporter of direct democracy, Redway did not want to see the process trivialized. Referring to the Citizens' Forum on Canada's Future, he pointed out "that the majority of the people who participated in that process feel that politicians lack awareness of their accountability to their constituents." As a consequence, one of the suggested solutions was the idea of a referendum, "not just on everything" but on constitutional and other major issues. Redway, turning to the topic of the Meech Lake Accord, said, "As time went on Canadians became quite disillusioned with the process of dealing with constitutional change behind closed doors. They wanted a process in which they could participate." He noted that it was not just the Canadian public that felt that way, but also "participants in the process itself, premiers and prime ministers [who all] had comments about the fact that we could never go through that kind of a process again. We had to do it differently." Then rhetorically asking, "How do you do it differently?" Redway answered that he had "not heard any better way suggested which involves all of the public of Canada than the referendum process." The problem, Redway said, "is that we do not have any legislation in place for a referendum," and this is why he supported the bill. He noted further that "there is nothing revolutionary about the concept. It is something we have done before. There is no reason why we should not have legislation in place to do it again and do it when we need to do it."[14]

Veteran parliamentarian Jean-Robert Gauthier of the Liberals then rose to say that Bill C-201 "comes at the right time in our history." Referring specifically to provisions in the bill, and reviewing the long course of Canadian history to emphasize his "serious concerns" for the position of minorities, Gauthier suggested that a referendum binding on the government "ought to be on a question worded with extreme caution, a short and clear question, a question without ambiguity of any kind." Where Parliament decided to "go to the people to ratify an Accord or a constitutional amendment," Gauthier considered it a prerequisite that the measure first be "carefully explained." Secondly, Gauthier said that the question being submitted to the Canadian people should "be endorsed by the political parties." He especially stressed that the ballot question "be such that it does not diminish existing rights and fundamental rights of Canadians, and in particular minority rights." Finally, he believed that a referendum or plebiscite "should require a double majority." By this he meant that the majority at the national level might prevail, but that when one of the four regions – Ontario, Quebec, the East, or the West – is involved, that part of the country would have a say. "This kind of double majority," he concluded, "along with the other conditions, might convince me that we could use a plebiscite or a referendum to get the view of the people of Canada on a given issue."[15]

The final speaker in the debate was Jean Lapierre, a former Liberal cabinet minister from the constituency of Shefford in Quebec who had now joined the Bloc Québécois. Lapierre, after congratulating me for the work I had done on the bill, suggested the government had chosen "a strange moment to table that proposal now before the House." I was amused by the irony in the fact that Lapierre believed this to be a government initiative. The government, he said, "should have the courage to take that responsibility on itself instead of trying to pass that legislation through the backdoor by way of a private member's bill." He explained that personally he was "not opposed to the concept of referenda and plebiscites" but was opposed "to the idea of using them as a means to create a diversion." Lapierre was "suspicious" of the idea that "a national referendum could carry regardless of the will of the Quebeckers!" He considered it "obvious" that such a measure "is designed to be used as a blackmailing tool now." He concluded by saying that "members of the Bloc Québécois will not put up obviously with a national referendum. We will, of course, fight that concept as of now."[16]

This subject, perhaps, was "too important" to have been handled by a private member's bill. From whatever source it comes, however, that overdue legislation will be welcome. The government's own legislation, urged at the recommendation of the Beaudoin-Edwards Committee, was anticipated at the time of this writing.

Meanwhile, I had reintroduced my private member's bill, this time numbered C-287, on September 23, 1991, in keeping with my efforts since July 1988 to keep the legislation continuously before Parliament in the hope it will be enacted. Intergovernmental Affairs Minister Joe Clark had said the government's enabling legislation for a national referendum limited to constitutional questions would be introduced in October 1991. Curiously, however, he discouraged its use in a statement as classic as Mackenzie King's "conscription if necessary, but not necessarily conscription." Clark said if we have a national consensus we don't need a referendum, and if we don't have consensus we wouldn't want a referendum. This attitude suggests one could divine whether a consensus exists without having the people express themselves – perhaps a nod in the direction of opinion pollsters. It also disregards the positive and educative aspects to be derived from a collective expression of the popular will. This attitude of distrusting the public is the reason for the halfway house of public committee hearings that cannot be attended by even one percent of our Canadian population. Clark, nevertheless, continued to delay, and even by March 1992 had not produced the enabling legislation for parliamentary consideration.

Simply telling Canadians in advance that everyone will be able to vote directly on whether to ratify the constitutional changes when the package has been refined through negotiations would do wonders to snap people's interest level to attention, and to remove much anxiety among the people about the process.

The legislation, be it a government bill or a private member's bill that is allowed to proceed, will have to address the same basic issues and procedures. For this reason it is worth highlighting in the next few pages some of the key elements of my private member's bill, the Canada Referendum and Plebiscite Act.

Basic Elements of a Canadian Referendum Act

The act is a single complete code for conducting nationwide referendums or plebiscites, and its ideas and provisions have been drawn essentially from six different sources: first, the British Referendum Act 1975,[17] which recognized the important concept of having two umbrella organizations, one for the "no" and another for the "yes" sides on the question; second, Quebec's Referendum Act, which is admirable for its simplicity and clarity of expression (similar to Quebec's Election Act and many other of the National Assembly's statutes in the past two or so decades) and which not only picked up the British idea for umbrella organizations, but also added important Canadian-context elements regarding financing and registration of referendum groups; third, the earlier bill introduced in the House of Commons in 1978 by the Honourable Marc Lalonde on behalf of the Trudeau government, the Canada Referendum Act, which dealt with many essentials for a nationwide vote in Canada, such as preparing voters' lists, conducting the vote, broadcasting rules, campaign financing, offenses, and time zone differences;

fourth, several ideas found in my 1982 book *Lawmaking by the People* have been added to the Canada Referendum and Plebiscite Act, such as legal provisions by which citizens themselves can initiate a direct vote; fifth, some provisions, such as those for "publicity pamphlets" from the 1912 Direct Legislation Act of Saskatchewan (by which both sides have equal opportunity to convey their arguments to the voters), have been incorporated in the bill and updated to include videotapes for the same purpose as well; and sixth, provisions from Bill C-79, by which the Mulroney government had proposed major amendments in 1986 to the Canada Elections Act, even though Bill C-79 itself regrettably was never passed by the House of Commons. These were measures incorporating equality provisions required by the Charter of Rights and Freedoms, including many recommendations from previous annual reports by Chief Electoral Officer Jean-Marc Hamel about matters ranging from level access to polling places for people with disabilities to the distinctions between urban and rural voters.

As with all draft legislation, I believe the Canada Referendum and Plebiscite Act could benefit from debate, detailed study, and amendment by a parliamentary committee. Even as it stands, Bill C-287 represents an effort to draw together and integrate contemporary procedures and experiences for holding such a direct vote. Here are nine of its key features.

The Subject of a Referendum or Plebiscite

The bill contemplates four possibilities under which direct voting may arise. First, a referendum could be held on a bill adopted by both houses of Parliament if the bill contains, at the time of its tabling in Parliament, a provision requiring that it not come into effect until it has been submitted to the electors by means of a referendum and the text of the question to be submitted is actually included in the bill. Second, a plebiscite could be held on a question approved by both houses of Parliament (with up to forty hours provided for debate on the motion in the House of Commons and up to forty hours' debate in the Senate). Third, a referendum could take place on a question relating to the constitution of Canada, or arising out of a proposed change in the constitution. Once again, the text to be submitted to the people would have to be debated in both houses of Parliament (with up to forty hours' debate in each). Fourth, a referendum or plebiscite could arise on a question submitted by electors. Since most procedures for a non-binding plebiscite and a legally binding referendum are identical, procedural parts of the Canada Referendum and Plebiscite Bill refer to both methods of direct voting by the generic term "public consultation."

This fourth possibility for a public consultation is in effect the "initiative" procedure. If 10 percent of the electors (using numbers from the last general election) believe that "a question of national and public importance within the jurisdiction of parliament" should be submitted to a direct vote of the electors, they may petition the prime minister to that effect. The petition must be accompanied by a solemn or statutory declaration signed by the required number of petitioners, their names and addresses, and a concise wording of the question that they propose be submitted to the electors.

There could not be more than one public consultation during a parliament on the same subject, or on a subject that is substantially similar to that of a previous public consultation held during the same parliament. The bill precludes the holding of a national plebiscite or referendum at the same time as a general election.

Public Consultation Council

A body called the Public Consultation Council would be established to function when a national vote is to be held. It would have exclusive jurisdiction to hear any judicial proceeding relating to a public consultation and questions about the application of the act.

The Public Consultation Council would consist of three federal court judges, one of whom would be the chairman appointed by the chief justice of the federal court. The council's decisions would be final and not appealable. It would give its opinion on any legal or technical question submitted to it by the Governor-in-Council respecting the holding of a public consultation, and others could have recourse to the council in specified circumstances.

Issuing the Writs for a Public Consultation

A referendum or plebiscite would be formally begun, like elections, by the Governor-in-Council issuing writs for this purpose to the chief electoral officer. The writ could direct that the question be put to the electors of Canada in all electoral districts, or in the electoral districts of the province or provinces specified (when a partial plebiscite was taking place, for instance, in the province of Quebec only, or in coastal provinces and territories only). The length of time from the day the writ is issued to polling day – that is, the duration of the campaign – could not exceed fifty-five days, but could be shorter.

Polling Divisions

The polling divisions of an electoral district would be those established for the previous general election, unless the chief electoral officer considers a revision of the boundaries necessary. Provisions are included in the bill for appointment of returning officers and election clerks, preparation of the voters' lists and their revision, and supplying all materials necessary for the public consultation.

The single largest cost associated with a general election in Canada is the preparation and revision of the voters' lists, and the same would be true for a referendum or plebiscite. For instance, the total cost in 1992 would be as much as $104.8 million if a referendum or plebiscite were held along the lines provided for in the existing Canada Elections Act (that is, with respect to salaries, fees, printing costs, and voters' list preparation). If modifications were made to the act, first to reduce the number of urban enumerators to one half and, secondly, to eliminate the mailing of the notice of enumeration card to electors registered during enumeration, a referendum or plebiscite held in 1992 under these conditions could be reduced to $85.5 million. The creation of a permanent voters' list for Canada, although costly, would not only help shorten the time of our general election campaigns significantly, but would also greatly ease the holding of referendums and plebiscites by removing the high cost of preparing voters' lists. The costs associated with the voters' lists is $34.3 million, a major part of the total.

Although the bill precludes a plebiscite's coinciding with a general election, it is worth noting (in case a future government bill would provide for such doubling-up) that a referendum or plebiscite held in conjunction with a general election would likely add little to the cost of that election. For instance, costs would be incurred only for additional printing of ballots with the "question" and for preparation of the extra ballot boxes needed for them.

Registered Consultation Committees

A procedure is provided in the bill for the formation of two "umbrella" organizations, one for each side of the referendum question.

When the proclamation is issued ordering a public consultation, the Speaker of the House of Commons must immediately send a notice to each MP and senator, advising them that they have seven days to register with the chief electoral officer as supporting one or other option of the public consultation. All those MPs and senators who so register establish the consultation committee supporting their side of the option. If not one MP or senator has registered as supporting a particular option by the end of the seven-day period, the chief electoral officer may invite at least three (but no more than twenty) electors to establish the consultation committee supporting that option. These electors must be selected from among persons publicly identified with the option for which there is as yet no registered supporter.

The chief electoral officer must promptly call a meeting of the members of each consultation committee. At this meeting the members enact the by-laws governing the committee and appoint one of their members to chair it. These by-laws may govern any matter relating to the committee's proper operation, including the name under which it is to be known and the manner in which it is to be established. The names of the two umbrella organizations in the British referendum of 1975, for instance, were "Britain in Europe" and "National Referendum Campaign." In the Quebec referendum of 1980, the two were simply named the "yes" and "no" committees. In Prince Edward Island in the 1988 plebiscite, although the act did not require umbrella organizations, they just naturally formed and were known as "Friends of the Island" and "Islandlers for a Better Tomorrow."

The by-laws may also provide for local branches of the committee to be set up in each electoral district, provided each is authorized by the chairman of the committee. The by-laws must provide for affiliation to the committee of groups that are favourable to the same option. Since there is only one organization for each side, it must be open and accessible to all who wish to actively support that option in the campaign. For this reason, the by-laws must establish norms, conditions, and formalities governing the affiliation and financing of these local groups.

Consultation Expenses

Raising and spending money in campaigns is of major importance and long-standing interest to Canadians, from the "Pacific Scandal" of the nineteenth century through to the 1974 Election Finances Act reforms to the present day. The effort to find balance and fairness has now taken statutory expression in a host of measures governing election financing, and the same approach is adopted for a public consultation campaign in the Canada Referendum and Plebiscite Bill.

All the expenses incurred, with eight specific exclusions, for the direct or indirect support or opposition of a submitted question during the fifty-five-day campaign period are "consultation expenses," meaning they are subject to regulation and control under the act. Consultation expenses are limited so as never to exceed, for a registered consultation committee during a campaign period, fifty cents per elector in the aggregate for all the electoral districts. This would mean, for example, using the 1988 general election total of 17,639,001 Canadian electors, a total budget ceiling of $8,819,500.50.

Agents and auditors must be appointed to ensure compliance with the financial contributions and expenses rules. Each consultation committee applying for registration must first appoint an official agent and an auditor. Both of these officials are assigned clear statutory duties to ensure compliance under the act.

Parliament would also be empowered by the bill to provide a

209

subsidy to help launch the two committees. When Parliament votes on the motion to adopt the wording of the question that will appear on the ballot, it may also include a direction to the minister of finance to send the official agent of each registered consultation committee, within three days of the writs being issued, a specified amount. If such a subsidy is decided on, the amount must be the same for each registered consultation committee.

Not all expenditures, as mentioned, would be included in the statutorily limited budget. The eight exclusions would be the following:

1. Publishing in a newspaper or other periodical of editorials, news, reports, or letters to the editor. For this exemption there are three provisos: that they be published in the same manner and under the same rules as would exist outside the campaign period, that is, without payment, reward, or promise of payment or reward; that the newspaper or other periodical is not established for the purposes of the public consultation or with a view to the public consultation; and that its circulation and frequency of publication do not differ from what obtains outside the campaign period.

2. The transmission by a radio or television station of a broadcast of news or comment, provided that such a broadcast be made in the same manner and under the same regulations as outside the campaign period, without payment, reward, or promise of payment or reward.

3. The reasonable expenses incurred by a person, out of his or her own money, for their lodging and food during a journey for the purposes of the public consultation, if such expenses are not reimbursed to that person.

4. The transportation costs of any person, again provided they are paid out of his or her own money, and only if such costs are not reimbursed to that person.

5. The reasonable expenses incurred for the publication of explanatory commentaries on the Canada Referendum and Plebiscite Act and the instructions issued under its authority, provided that such commentaries are strictly objective and contain no publicity of a nature to favour or oppose an option submitted to the public consultation.

6. The reasonable expenses usually incurred for the current opera-

tion of the permanent office of a political party registered under the Canada Elections Act, if the leader of that party gives, within the first week of the campaign, notice to the chief electoral officer of the existence of the office, and its address.

7. Interest accrued, from the day following the polling, on any loan lawfully granted to an official agent for expense purposes.

8. The expenditures, not greater than $300, incurred for holding a meeting, including the cost of renting a hall and the convening of participants, provided that the meeting is not directly or indirectly organized on behalf of a consultation committee.

Qualifications of Electors

Every man and woman who has attained the age of eighteen years and is a Canadian citizen is given the right to vote in the public consultation. Disqualified from voting are election officials, and anyone who has been disqualified from voting (pursuant to election law) as a result of a conviction for corrupt or illegal practices. Detailed provisions are given to determine residence of voters, to govern the enumeration process, and to prepare the lists of electors and their revision.

Information for Electors

The bill envisages two categories of information that must be provided to electors during the public consultation campaign.

First, the chief electoral officer (CEO) must tell citizens about the procedures for the consultation. As soon as possible after the campaign begins, the CEO is required to inform the public about the requirements for establishing the two consultation committees. Also, as soon as possible after the proclamation for the consultation has been issued, the CEO must inform the public by means of pamphlets, brochures, information kits, advertisements, and periodical publications or other appropriate means, about the purpose of the public consultation and how it will be conducted, including the manner and place of voting. Nothing in the bill, however, requires or authorizes the CEO to inform the public, or to answer inquiries, with respect to any argument in support of or opposition to the ballot question submitted to the voters.

Second, and apart from any paid advertising or publicity the two consultation committees may authorize, the bill would require the CEO to make available to the electors, at least ten days before polling day, a single booklet and a single audio-visual document explaining each option of the submitted question. The contents of the booklet and tape would be prepared by each registered consultation committee for their respective sides. Equal space, as determined by the CEO, must be given in the explanatory material for each option on the ballot question. Due to cost, it is not envisaged that the audio-visual tape would be made available to every voter, but would rather be used in public broadcasts, and for presentation at public meetings. The booklet would be distributed to each voter.

Political Broadcasts

A number of provisions would regulate the important matter of broadcasting during a campaign, including the question of free-time broadcasting, the allocation of paid-time advertising by radio and television, and a prohibition on broadcasts from outside Canada intended to influence the campaign. The bill authorizes the appointment of an independent broadcasting arbitrator to meet with the consultation committees and to allocate the free- and paid-time broadcasts according to the specified fairness formulas.

The Long Quest

In the welcome, growing crescendo about holding referendums, the absence of a Canadian statute to provide for actually holding one gives a comic dimension to all the serious talk. It is like a group of people arguing intently about whether one of them should apply for a driver's licence, without even bothering to see if they had a car to drive. The Canada Referendum and Plebiscite Act, or a government bill like it, is that vehicle. Having the vehicle in the garage does not mean, however, that you have to drive it – especially not to the corner store for a loaf of bread – but it is waiting there whenever it may be needed, especially for long and arduous journeys.

Those who assume it would be an easy matter, a mere technicality, to enact the enabling legislation for direct votes when the time is ripe perhaps have yet to ponder the lessons of the frustrating setbacks in our long quest for a Canadian direct-vote statute.

9

Reflections Upon the Trust of the People

H as the phrase "trust of the people" been so debased that today it is little more than rhetoric? In the theatre of politics, where does reality end and illusion begin? Indeed, are the ideals of democracy themselves mere illusion?

Illusion or Reality?

On the Monday afternoon of May 13, 1991, a new session of Canada's Parliament is just beginning. In the posh Senate Chamber of the Parliament Buildings, the stage is ready. Queen Elizabeth's representative has mounted to the Speaker's chair, and begins his script, the Speech from the Throne.

Spring is a good time for speeches from the Throne. A fresh beginning. A new start. Political life imitating nature. It is drama that uses the theatrical device of a sympathetic fallacy.

Governor General Ramon Hnatyshyn begins, informing us that to realize our "great promise" we must rebuild Canadian unity and "overcome the acrimony, apathy and incomprehension that currently undermine it."

This message does not imitate nature. It has absorbed the hard-focused sense of despair that has been fetished into the Great Canadian Problem.

Briefly pausing to glance down the red-carpeted Senate Chamber from where he sits ensconced on the elevated Speaker's dais,

Hnatyshyn sees privy councillors who at various times past were cabinet ministers. Also ranged before him sit the appointed senators, and the appointed Supreme Court justices in their splendid and colourful robes. Important people, formally attired and crowded together, all share this tradition-laden state occasion in a stuffy atmosphere now made even hotter by the unremitting glare of television lights. This is theatre where its audience is part of the cast.

The governor general even glimpses a few of the MPs crowding and straining for a view at the Senate entrance door. There is really no room for the elected members of Parliament at this ceremony. We are "outcasts," definitely not a part of the cast. So we have crammed ourselves into the unlit antechamber, standing on tiptoes, or perching on the great carved stone ledges, hearing little and seeing less, until, wearying of this peripheral role in a formalized pageant, we strike up conversations, some intensely serious, a few whimsically flippant, among ourselves. Others just wander off, perhaps to watch the proceedings on television. Ah, television!

Where does illusion begin?

In the 1950s, images of the great battles and historic events of the past half-century appear on the television screen. Walter Cronkite, host of "The Twentieth Century," is saying in his gravelly voice, "It was a day like any other day, only *you were there!*" I watch grainy black-and-white film footage of political leaders addressing vast city squares filled with cheering people. Whether these leaders were democrats or dictators, one thing seemed clear: those at the top got there because they enjoyed broad popular support from below.

I grew up in a household where discussion of history and current events was daily fare and where I absorbed this idea that political leaders needed to have strong popular support. The concept certainly did not come from Cronkite's televised history lessons alone, but they reinforced it. I even thought a person could not become a leader and do things unless most people agreed with his or her program and that this necessarily involved a long and painstaking process of persuasion to win over the support of hundreds of thousands of people in countless communities. It implied, of course, that someone who wanted to lead also had a program, indeed that he or she was imbued with it.

Because they could only emerge by succeeding in this daunting task, I was greatly impressed by those who became outstanding leaders. I read about the lives of people who made and transformed history – Mahatma Gandhi patiently teaching the people in India's villages to become economically self-reliant by spinning thread or producing salt, and to become politically invincible by practising non-violent protest. Gandhi did not lecture from on high, but imparted his lessons to people by working with them where they lived. Vladimir Lenin wrote, travelled, talked at meetings, agitated, and sacrificed friendships and himself to persuade others of his cause to establish communism. Mao Tse Tung made "the long march" with his people. I most certainly knew who the "bad" leaders were, the Hitlers whose evils of destruction were chronicled by Cronkite as the footage of bombardments and death camps held me in a fixation of dismay. No matter how these leaders would be judged on moral terms, though, I had a strong impression that they rose in their influence due to popular support, which they had assiduously earned. I assumed these same principles of leadership applied in Canada too, in a more muted way, and that is how I viewed the world around me. Before too long, though, I was disabused of these early, innocent ideas.

Participant Observer

By the time I was ten, my father was elected to the Ontario legislature in the provincial general election of 1955. For my fascination about how government worked, he provided an illuminating vantage point inside the political laboratory. By the time I was a teenager, vigorous and endless debates with friends about political philosophy and global causes formed a regular part of life in my home town of Bracebridge. We argued with intensity, over coffee and cigarettes, at the Thomas Company Café after school. Some of the topics we took seriously and kept returning to were the role of the United Nations and the relationship between minorities and majorities. Ideas about majorities – whether they really existed, and whether they could be manipulated by minorities – were the favourite subjects of Scott Sugden, who went on as associate editor to help launch *Canada Month* magazine in Montreal in 1961. By the time I moved through the education system and read many books, I had learned that history is not rich in happy endings, and that apparently harmonious broad-based political movements have their seamy sides and cabals. Although the illusion fell away, my idealism did not.

In these formative years, living with my family in our modest apartment above the newspaper office that became my second home, often attending the public events that preoccupied us after my father was elected MPP, I found it natural to both participate in events and be a close observer of them. I could not return home and write a good newspaper report of the meeting I had just attended without paying close attention to what had been really going on, but neither could I go to events as a member of our political family without participating actively as well. The fact that my father was both the newspaper editor *and* the district's elected representative, who could interpret what was taking place and describe it well in his editorials because he understood from direct participation what was intended, set for me an implicit model of the participant observer. I was sensitive enough, too, to the obvious conflict (or was it confluence?) of interest. As an answer to it, I often repeated what others said – that our family's newspaper was fair and balanced in its coverage. These comments even came from supporters of rival political parties in response to election-time coverage. Even then this reputation of our newspaper was important to me because I knew its role and the community's interests were somehow deeper and more enduring than politics.

I identified strongly with that newspaper. I was the fourth generation in the newspaper business in our family in Bracebridge. My great-grandfather's politics had not been Tory but Reform. In late nineteenth-century Ontario, that meant he was a progressive Liberal. While journalism and politics were family companions, politics was the less important of the two. In some respects, politics was simply a means to an end, which was that of being an active participant in deciding matters that had to be settled or creating programs that were needed for the community well-being. It also put us in a good position to observe the process, the personalities, and the events, which made us better able to write about them and make sense of it all in the newspaper.

As a sort of existential activist, a "participant observer" could have the best of both worlds. For me at least, it had developed as an automatic and natural process, like using two legs to walk. The two elements – participating and observing – simultaneously produced some obvious results: the newspaper columns I have regularly written since I was twelve as well as some forty articles and six books. When I see something happening, I automatically start writing an account of it. If I am not able at the moment to actually write it up, I begin doing so in my mind, and until the story has been physically written it is as if the event had not yet really taken place. Otherwise I still carry the memory of it, waiting for a chance to write about it. Words on paper form a reality. To write an interpretation and provide an account leaves behind a record that mere memory could never hope to hold.

On the other hand, another result of being a participant observer is that I mentally detach myself from an event I'm involved in to observe it as if I were the proverbial "fly on the wall." In public life this has the advantage of helping to keep one's perspective, as well as the disadvantage that one pulls back from battles where headlong, subjective combat seems expected. Two legs, perhaps, but only one body to be carried on them – so the participant cannot get far ahead of the observer, or vice versa.

At university in the mid-60s, Professor Frank Underhill urged me to do a careful reading of Alexis de Tocqueville's works, including *Democracy in America*. In that book de Tocqueville said,

> I have come across men of letters who have written history without taking part in public affairs, and politicians who have concerned themselves with producing events without thinking about them. The first are always inclined to find general causes, whereas the second, living in the midst of disconnected daily facts, are prone to imagine that everything is attributable to particular incidents, and that the wires they pull are the same as those that move the world.

He believed that "both are equally deceived."

At law school in the mid-70s, my friend Elliot Belkin always insisted on the importance of our subjecting ourselves to critical self-examination, constantly reappraising our ideas in light of our experiences, and indeed our old or accepted ideas in light of new ones.

The reason his quest for constant critical reappraisal struck such a responsive chord in me was, I now realize, that he was putting another name and a deeper meaning to the concept of the participant observer. It could be refreshing and creative, though unsettling.

Senator Keith Davey once asked me if I thought the then prime minister, Lester Pearson, was an intellectual. The senator argued that he was. Our discussion raised the issue of the relationship between a man of ideas and a man of action in politics, and whether the two are mutually exclusive or merely a rare combination.

As I reflected upon all this, I realized that the "delicate balance" we need in Canadian public affairs requires a measured blending of the approach of the pragmatist with the outlook and motivation of the intellectual.

A politician who is nothing but pragmatic bobs and weaves his way through issues, patching together a transaction here and a consensus there, employing individuals and institutions for today's purposes, knowing that if tomorrow will not exactly take care of itself, he will deal with tomorrow's problems tomorrow. A politician who is nothing but intellectual in his approach may, on the other hand, design a conceptually perfect universe, but then experience frustration trying to implement his neatly planned model in this imperfect world. Claude Ryan of Quebec once accurately remarked that a leader cannot devise a satisfactory plan for government by working alone in the splendid isolation and tranquillity of his library.

In July 1983, a year before I ran for Parliament myself, I wrote that "One's ideas of what can and should occur in the public life of our country must be worked out through the give and take of contending views, hardened on the anvil of experience, and, as befits a political democracy, must represent the collective wisdom of the people."

"Achievement of Canada's promise," I wrote at that time, presaging, it seems, Hnatyshyn and the 1991 Throne Speech, "requires clear thinking, plain talk, and direct action. It requires good feelings, tolerance and co-operation between our people, bolstered by a sense of optimistic realism. It requires, in our public life, a restoration of the delicate balance, a recognition of the importance of ideas in the actions of individuals and governments alike."[1]

218

A Society of Fractions and Fragments

After I had left small-town Ontario for university and studied political science, I increasingly recognized that those who are elected and rise to the top of our political system do so on the basis of fractions and fragments, a reality far different from my childish notion that those who led the people had broad, even unanimous, support. Leni Riefenstahl's movie *Triumph of the Will*, which dealt with the mass adulation of Adolf Hitler, had been propaganda.

A country does not speak with one voice, but is divided and then divided again into countless interest groups and types of constituencies. Within the formal electoral constituencies or ridings, those who are elected often assume office with only a plurality, not even a majority, of the votes cast by the people living there.

In the spring of 1966, working as a reporter for the *News-Optimist* in North Battleford, Saskatchewan, I watched the surprising election results coming in from Quebec, as the Union Nationale claimed victory. That night I saw how a party could form a government and its leader become a provincial premier even though they actually received fewer votes overall than another party.

In 1984, when, as I said, I first ran for Parliament, the early image I'd had as a boy about popular movements and the democratic system had been pretty well educated out of me.

To run for Parliament, I had only to win the nomination of my party. This meant intensively campaigning against six other aspirants, outlining my views on the issues of the day while canvassing door-to-door with my supporters, meeting neighbourhood groups, and seeking to sell more party memberships than the other candidates did. Although my team and I recruited 777 new party members, another candidate sold more than 1,000 memberships, and the crucial numerical advantage appeared to lie with him. Yet I had also learned about organization, and the importance of having delegates committed not only to coming to the nominating convention in the first place, but also to staying until the job was done. On the first ballot, of 1,153 votes cast, I received 457. The second-place candidate with 370 votes was the one who'd sold the most memberships. On the next ballot, I became, with 507 votes, the officially nominated candidate of the Progressive Conservative Party in Etobicoke-Lakeshore constituency. It was a very modest majority of the total 985 cast, although my father Robert Boyer was impressed: he'd won his first nomination in 1955 by just three votes on the fourth ballot!

Some four months later, on September 4, 1984, I was elected to the House of Commons by virtue of receiving 19,902 votes out of a total 44,856, a plurality representing just some 44.78 percent of all the ballots cast. In 1988, I was re-elected to the Commons on the basis of 20,405 votes out of a total 45,528, a plurality representing 44.81 percent of all valid votes.

So I hold office as a member of Parliament – one of a group of 295 elected representatives for all of Canada, a number of whom won considerably narrower electoral victories with even lower pluralities than mine – never having received absolute majority support from the people I represent.

To claim that our elected legislatures are "representative" institutions is true only in a qualified sense. Our political superstructure, along with the laws and institutions it brings into being, rests upon very slender supports. The mythology and rhetoric about our democratic system have certainly helped disguise this, just as a tablecloth stretching to the floor can hide the flimsy legs holding up a heavy table.

Visions from Our Subconscious

Part of me is now reconciled to this reality of our political system, and long ago I came to understand that differences of opinion and division of support are healthy and desirable in a democratic country such as ours. Yet the idealistic boy from Bracebridge is still in me, too. In William Blake's *Songs of Innocence*, the child is born believing that the world makes sense, but he grows up and discovers that the world isn't reasonable at all. So what happens to his childlike vision? As Northrop Frye explains, "Blake says it gets driven underground, what we would now call the subconscious."[2] My vision of a reality far different is not gone or dead, it is just waiting for a spark to bring it to the surface. My ears therefore perk up to listen even from a distance when our governor general says, as he did on behalf of the Canadian government on May 13, 1991:

> There is a need for change in the way Parliament does business and in the way governments conduct their affairs. The goal is to ensure that Canadians' agenda is Parliament's agenda.
>
> My government will propose further reforms so that all Members of Parliament can fulfil better their obligations to their constituents.
>
> The respect of the people for Parliament and parliamentarians is essential for a healthy democracy.

The idea is father to the deed. At last the powers that be seem to be onto the right idea here. Hnatyshyn continues,

> The appearance, and sometimes the reality, of excessive party discipline and over-zealous partisanship, of empty posturing and feigned outrage have eroded ... respect in Canada. Members will be asked, therefore, to consider new procedures for assessing legislation, for raising grievances on behalf of constituents and for questioning government. This will further enhance the role of individual members and afford them greater independence.

Such empowerment of the people's elected representative will actually require changing institutional relationships on a major scale. It will be an important part of the necessary reformation of Canadian democracy as we alter our institutions and practices to embrace the deep change that is already under way in Canada's political culture.

Another important and complementary advance must involve *empowerment of the people*. This phenomenon will take many forms, and will change the way our country works and the way we think about ourselves as Canadians, in many ways. The elements of direct democracy are a key part of this, but only a part. There is not going to be a single, magic-bullet solution to cooling Canadians' political distemper and channelling our energy constructively. The best approach will involve a mix of different measures. In broad terms, however, the solution to the problem of reconciling freedom with authority will be found in blending popular sovereignty with representative government.

So it is a real highlight of the Throne Speech message as

Hnatyshyn announces, from centre stage, that "parliamentarians will be called upon to enact enabling legislation to permit the men and women of Canada to play a more direct role in the process of constitutional change." That can only mean a plebiscite or a referendum.

Governments tend to turn to the referendum tactic when it seems the best way of resolving a particularly bitter issue without tearing apart the established political structure. Or sometimes, they suggest, in a rather cranky tone, that it should be used so the general public can share the burden of decision making and see the complexity of our problems. Prime Minister Trudeau spoke in September 1978 of "people grumbling that the Government is not doing things right" and suggested, in his taunting manner, "it might be time for the Government to throw a few hot potatoes back at them." I believe that governments ought to turn to direct voting, not as a desperate last resort or in a mood of hostile disdain towards the public, but rather with the positive idea that it is important as a principle of good government to involve the people, as one of the refreshing ways to implement the fine words and noble sentiments of the 1991 Throne Speech. Referendums can be an educational experience for the country, which, judging from polls and talk shows, has not yet come to grips with the tradeoffs that may be required to forge a new constitution.

Involving people more directly in our public business will only proceed, in a genuine way, if those in government believe they can trust the people to make hard choices and to make "the right" choices. In the end, it comes down to whether one is a democrat and, therefore, prepared to trust the people.

When I began studying Canadian elections, immersing myself in the experiences of our country with referendums and plebiscites in order to write my 1982 book *Lawmaking by the People: Referendums and Plebiscites in Canada,* I had been inspired by the instinct of a democrat, in me since childhood. In the course of the research, however, I became even more convinced about the importance of true democracy. Government errs when it veers away from the people; it is right when it goes to them.

I believe both in the importance of the process we have developed in Canada to provide for the accurate expression of the people's collective judgment, and in the appropriateness or correctness of that democratic verdict. I believe that, on balance, a well-informed group of diverse people can make the best decision when required to do so.

I disagree profoundly with those writers who contend that Canadian democracy is a sham and that it merely disguises class rule. I also dissent from the view that what passes for a system of government under Marxist regimes can be called democracy. In 1987 when the Soviet Empire was still very much intact, I wrote in my book on Canadian election law these words: "Marxism, a failed political theory, has served only as an intellectual veneer to mask totalitarian and repressive regimes, and to refer to those systems as 'democratic' is to sully the concept and misguide the ill-informed."[3]

Our democratic institutions in Canada are, in spite of the problems that afflict their operation, still our greatest resource for making our world what we collectively believe it ought to be – particularly if we use them to their fullest potential, and if we remain ever vigilant about finding ways to improve the laws and modernize the procedures.

For this way of life, too many Canadians before us have struggled through the pioneering days of democracy – to win the right to vote for women and natives and other groups who found themselves the butt of racial discrimination; to curb spending so that our politics is not just a rich man's game; and to ensure balance in political programming over the public air waves. For this way of life, many Canadians have also died in wars to protect us against totalitarian and militaristic states. So many have struggled and sacrificed that we can do no less today than vigorously exercise our democratic rights and obligations. Instead we keep devising ways to fragment ourselves and sap our energy, and these methods have become both the cause and effect of our lack of consensus about the purposes that bring us together as Canadians.

Harold Laski wrote that if all the criticisms of Parliament were added up, one might easily conclude that the institution ought to be abolished. A Newfoundland group participating in the Citizens' Forum on Canada's Future reported in 1991 that "it was the unanimous consensus that if we had to spend $27 million annually on the Forum as opposed to an annual $295 million on Parliament . . . and if the distillation of an annual Forum were by law imperative of implementation, we would opt for a permanent Forum."[4] That know-nothing attitude just about sums up the anger which many Canadians have come to feel about governments, politics, and Parliament.

The contemporary interest in referendums and plebiscites echoes the time a century ago when rural Canadians felt powerless in the face of deep change and became detached from the country's traditional political party process. In some cases the alienation causes people to turn away from the system altogether; but a large percentage of Canadians today still seem to want to find a solution *through* political action. If they dislike one party they turn to another, or create a new one. At the very heart of it all is still a drive to participate.

I have written this book because I am a democrat, and also because I am an elected representative who, like many other MPs, is exceedingly frustrated by our system. Like many Canadians, I have been smug about Canadian political ways compared with American practices. Yet after seven years of trying to function within the Canadian party and parliamentary system, that smugness has completely evaporated. The U.S. system is more transparent than ours, meaning everyone can see and understand when, where, and how public business is being transacted. Legislation introduced in Congress is not "government legislation" as it is here – and senators and congressmen go to work on it. There is more room for shifts and changes. Furthermore, there are many more entry points in the American legislature and governmental system.

In Canada, legislation, budgets, and other government programs are generally prepared in secret. The preconsultation is mostly secret. Bureaucrats behind closed doors fine-tune government measures, and in most cases by the time the measures are set and approved by the cabinet, virtually no change by a mere MP is possible. Despite my being an elected member of Parliament, I have virtually no scope in the legislative process to alter even a phrase in the wording of government legislation, and then the party line is imposed on voting in the Commons to make the measure law. We certainly lack a wide-open legislative process; we have one that is hardly open at all.

Although we call our parliamentary system democratic, we have witnessed on a profound level the institutionalization of some very anti-democratic processes. Is it not a curiosity of our country that we deeply embrace a collective concern rather than the ideology of rugged individualists, and yet so seldom seem prepared to entrust important issues to the collective wisdom of the people?

When the late Eugene Forsey wrote me a letter on December 14, 1987, to say he was "so glad" I had put forward my referendum bill in Parliament, he added, "Why Canadians are so scared of referenda I don't know, especially since we all whoop it up so incessantly about democracy."

Perhaps those in the Canadian political establishment would do well to consider the attitudes that led to the formation of their generally hostile position on referendums in the first place. Perhaps they could honestly assess whether they ever considered the positive and constructive role of direct popular participation, or whether instead they more or less uncritically accepted the conventional wisdom of the political élite that essentially holds that the people cannot be trusted.

When I was twelve I decided I wanted to be a member of Parliament. The "decision," in retrospect, was almost fated by the strong influences of church (including the social gospel), newspaper (our family's weekly was the hub of community activity and local "progress"), family milieu (community-service oriented; lovers of literature, history, music, and theatre; and active in promoting worthy public and private causes), and politics itself (propelled by my father's election to the Ontario legislature in 1955 when I was ten).

I then spent twenty-seven years preparing myself for the role of MP – by what I did, where I lived and worked, what I studied, and in many of my personal choices. In 1984 I became a member of Parliament – and walking to the Hill on a clear autumn morning, the sun shining and the air brisk, to begin my long-cherished dream, I felt a surge of excitement about the possibilities ahead. I plunged with energy into many issues and projects that had interested me for years, but was soon, for all this, described as "overly ambitious." I had heard many critics of the parliamentary system say that MPs were "nobodies," that they did not count in the system. Jim Gillies had been a highly regarded MP in the 1970s before returning to the faculty of York University. He told me at the time, "You just don't count as an MP." Yet still believing in what I had set my life towards since youth, I denied such assertions. I said a position in Parliament is what you make of it. The notion that a backbencher is powerless is just spread around by the frontbench, I argued, to inculcate a sense of passive non-resistance.

After seven years, I have serious doubts about whether the role of an MP in Canada today is of much consequence. The reasons for this are many – and hard to admit. Hard because it means that for thirty-nine years I may have been on the wrong trajectory and that all those who have worked loyally to support me may have shared not a dream but an illusion. Hard because I believe that those of us in public life, no matter how desperate we feel or how bleak the circumstances, have a duty to foster hope.

My late mother and I agreed that the best approach to life is a blend we called "optimistic realism." In many respects I have had a dream about Canada that is at once nostalgic and futuristic – or should I just say idealistic, that is, motivated by an ideal – and I have dreamed that I could be a part of this special Canada. I realize now that I sound alienated from the very system of Canadian government that I had for so long believed in. I came to understand, in writing this book, my disappointment at having learned that the role of being a member of the Parliament of Canada is like that of a Canadian soldier in the 1942 Dieppe Raid: a feeling that one is no more than fodder in an intended ambush to satisfy the larger workings of the system's grand design.

I also realize that if you want to go along with this system, it can be a fine life being an MP. If you care strongly about trying to make things happen through the system, however, frustration results and you conclude an MP really *is* a nobody.

Accepting that the role of an MP is really not what I had for so long hoped it would be has, ironically, given me a liberated feeling. I now recognize many of the so-called parliamentary crises as tempests in a teapot. The present workings of Parliament Hill mean that the urgent – or the illusion of what is urgent as portrayed by television – crowds out the important. This new perspective is as helpful as it is healthy. More than that, it has made me realize that the quest that I have been on for so many years has really hardly begun. There is a political system within our people that is waiting to be born, and I can work towards making that happen. Its shape is not yet fully known, but like the Inuit carver who chips away at a piece of stone to free the animal or bird whose shape is within, I have a new goal, and it has to do with the reformation of Canadian democracy.

Cecil Emden, on the final page of his 1956 book on the history of the people's influence on British government, wrote:

> If the people's mandate is not organized so as to provide the people with a genuine opportunity to express their views on the broad outlines of policy, democracy will suffer a serious set-back. An electorate like ours, growing rapidly in their ability to understand political factors, must not be allowed to discover that their alleged influence on politics is ineffective because it is too frequently disclosed as indefinite and disputable. Democracy is too frail a system to survive such a shock. The present makeshift means of enabling the people to have some influence on affairs of State might, even though left unreformed, continue haltingly for a period. But eventually the people's growing disillusionment would probably result in their insufficient co-operation with their rulers. Politicians often say that the people must be made partners in government if there is to be maximum efficiency, welfare, and happiness. But we have not yet gone very far towards achieving this ideal. We must confront the facts. If we should allow the people's part in government to lapse into futility, we might lose democracy beyond recall.[5]

I understand and share the contradictory feelings of Canadians who are disenchanted by the workings of our system of government, though they are aware of so much that is good and of permanent value in it. The problem is that democratic theory is premised on citizens' playing an active and informed role in the political system, but theory is not being met by opportunity. In part, suggests Joseph F. Zimmerman, "the relative lack of public participation can be attributed to the limited opportunities for playing a meaningful role in the governance process beyond voting in elections."[6]

Along with the lack of opportunity for meaningful participation have been parallel developments that undercut the respect that citizens have for our legislatures, and the credibility of these institutions. For instance, the number of decisions from the Supreme Court of Canada that strike down as unconstitutional laws made by elected representatives cannot help, cumulatively, but leave the impression that some people are not doing their job properly. To those who support the political system and still find it credible, criticism will be directed to the Supreme Court justices and the Charter of Rights, which they use to strike down existing laws; to those who are distrustful of legislatures, the Supreme Court and the Charter will be seen as champions and the respecter of individual citizen's rights. Either way, Canada is not so much the "peaceable kingdom" it once was.

Citizens will also no doubt conclude, the more they watch television and read newspaper accounts about the increasing role of lobbyists and interest groups, that their own chance to influence public decisions grows slimmer and more remote with each passing day. As chairman of the Parliamentary Committee on the Status of Disabled Persons in 1988, I raised the concern of those trying to speak up for the interests of disabled Canadians who found themselves shouldered to the sidelines by much more influential and powerful players. The often amateur groupings of individuals speaking for disabled persons stood little chance against the highly organized juggernaut that represented major industrial, commercial, union, sports, and other interests with their professional media advisers.[7]

Dissatisfaction with decision making by elected and appointed officials is also reflected in suggestions for community forums and town hall types of meetings that can form part of the ongoing government process in our country. Whether in the many submissions to the Citizens' Forum on Canada's Future or articles in Canadian periodicals dealing with policy alternatives, this is a recurring theme, heard with increasing frequency. "Canada calls itself a democracy," says G.E. Mortimore in one such article, "but every recent major change or attempted change in its structure of government has been haggled out in secret by cliques of politicians and bureaucrats, and pressed on the people by propaganda campaigns financed with their own tax money."[8] Contending that there "is no real evidence that elected politicians (whose horizon is bounded by the next election) take any longer or wiser view of events than the mass of their constituents," and that the mass media "handle political information-exchange badly because their chief purpose is to entertain," Mortimore advocates a "special independent agency, answerable only to the population as a whole, not to any government of the day." The independent agency would provide a systematic, coherent and continuing flow of lively information. The agency would recruit "all or most voters as power-wielding students and participants, not as passive spectators of a political circus."[9] People, of course, do not advance such alternatives unless they feel dissatisfied with the operation of the existing arrangements.

The illusion has been that the strength of a country lies in its leaders. The reality is that it resides in its people. Too much history has been written from the perspective of kings and emperors and presidents and prime ministers – rather than from the view of the people themselves. The ideal that forms the core of our democracy – and that must now be chiselled free – is more than trust in the people by those who are in government, although that is an essential stage whose achievement will be welcome. Trust of the people in our system of government, and in those whom they elect, is the nobler vision. Mutual trust is the ideal for a democracy because it embraces the perspective, not only of those in government, but also of the people themselves. Pierre Trudeau was groping for this idea when he said of Canada: "The land is strong." Had he pushed further, he would have realized the truth: "Canadians are strong."

"Like a mechanically religious person repeating a litany by mere rote, a Canadian may speak glowingly of our democratic system of government with neither question nor critical thinking about whether the forms of behaviour still really match the substance." I wrote that a decade ago. Rereading it today, I realize that something valuable has happened since then. Many Canadians now *are* questioning the gap between rhetoric and reality in our country's governmental operations. Critical thinking is more widespread in our society than ever before. While the language of our classical parliamentary arrangements continues to be used, a great many Canadians – I would now say a substantial majority – understand that the meaning has changed. What we now await is for the system itself to be transformed – into one based upon trust of the people.

Appendix

Record of Canadian Direct Votes

Electoral Jurisdiction	Date of Voting	Issue
Canada	September 29, 1898	Prohibition of liquor
	April 27, 1942	Releasing of government from its 1940 promise of no conscription for overseas military service
British Columbia	November 25, 1909	Local Option Policy for Liquor Control
	September 14, 1916	Women's suffrage
	December 16, 1916	Prohibition of liquor
	October 20, 1920	Temperance
	June 20, 1924	Beer-by-the-glass
	June 1, 1937	Public Health Insurance
	June 12, 1952	Daylight saving time
	June 12, 1952	Regulating sale of liquor
	August 30, 1972	Daylight saving time (provincially conducted plebiscite, but voting in five electoral districts only)
	October 17, 1991 (two questions)	Recall Initiative
Alberta	July 21, 1915	Prohibition of liquor
	October 25, 1920	Prohibition of liquor
	November 5, 1923	Temperance
	August 17, 1948	Ownership of power companies
	October 30, 1957	Additional outlets for sale of liquor
	May 23, 1967	Daylight saving time
	August 30, 1971	Daylight saving time

Electoral Jurisdiction	Date of Voting	Issue
Saskatchewan	November 27, 1913	Approval of the Direct Legislation Act
	December 11, 1916	Abolition of liquor stores
	October 25, 1920	Importation of liquor into Saskatchewan
	July 16, 1924	Prohibition of liquor
	June 19, 1934	Sale of beer-by-the-glass
	October 31, 1956	Choice of local time zones
	October 21, 1991 (three questions)	Balanced budget legislation
		Ratification of constitutional amendments by referendum
		Government funding of hospital abortions
Manitoba	July 23, 1892	Prohibition of liquor
	April 2, 1902	Prohibition of liquor
	March 13, 1916	Temperance Act
	June 22, 1923	Government control of liquor sales
	July 11, 1923	Amendments to Temperance Act
	June 28, 1927	Three questions on the sale of beer
	November 24, 1952	Marketing of course grains
Ontario	December 4, 1902	Prohibition of liquor
	October 20, 1919	Four questions respecting repeal of the Ontario Temperance Act and sale of beer
	April 18, 1921	Liquor importation referendum

Appendix

Electoral Jurisdiction	Date of Voting	Issue
Quebec	April 10, 1919	Prohibition of beer and wine
	May 20, 1980	Sovereignty-Association
	October 1, 1987	Constitution future of Northern Quebec (voting in the region only)
Nova Scotia	October 25, 1920	Regulation of liquor sales
	October 31, 1929	Retention of Prohibition
P.E.I.	1878	Prohibition
	1901	Prohibition
	1929	Prohibition
	1940	Prohibition
	June 28, 1948	New Temperance Act
	January 18, 1988	Fixed-Link Crossing
Newfoundland	November 4, 1915	Prohibition of liquor
	June 3, 1948	1) Responsible Government
		2) Join Canada, or
		3) Stay under Commission Government
	July 22, 1948	1) Join Canada, or
		2) Responsible Self-Government
Northwest Territories	April 14, 1982	Territorial Division

233

Notes

Introduction

1 From Professor Frye's address to the Social Sciences and Humanities Research Council of Canada at the University of Toronto, as published in *The Globe and Mail,* April 15, 1991.

2 Robertson Davies, "Keeping Faith," *Saturday Night,* January 1987.

3 John Godfrey, "A Call for National Unity," *The Financial Post Magazine,* Summer 1991, 61

4 David Butler and Austin Ranney, eds., *Referendums: A Comparative Study of Practice and Theory* (Washington: American Enterprise Institute for Public Policy Research, 1978), 223.

5 W.L. Morton, "The 1920s," in *The Canadians,* edited by R. Craig Brown and J.M.S. Careless (Toronto: Macmillan, 1967), 206.

6 Address by The Right Honourable Joe Clark, President of the Privy Council and Minister Responsible for Constitutional Affairs, at a Canada Day luncheon hosted by the Empire Club of Canada and the Royal Commonwealth Society in Toronto, June 27, 1991.

Chapter 1: Our Democratic Instinct

1 Dankwart A. Rustow, "Democracy: A Global Revolution?" *Foreign Affairs* 69, no. 4 (Fall 1990): 90.

2 John Dafoe, "The West," *The Globe and Mail,* July 20, 1991.

3 Patrick Watson and Benjamin Barber, *The Struggle for Democracy* (Toronto: Lester & Orpen Dennys, 1988), xvii, 261–62.

4 Vernon Bogdanor, *The People and the Party System: The Referendum and Electoral Reform in British Politics* (Cambridge: Cambridge University Press, 1981), 259.

5 Ibid., 259–60.

6 See Patrick Boyer, *Political Rights: The Legal Framework of Elections in Canada* (Toronto: Butterworths, 1981), especially chap. 7, "The Nature of Political Rights in Canada."

7 For a general discussion, see David Spitz, *Patterns of Anti-Democratic Thought,* rev. ed. (New York and Toronto: Macmillan, 1965).

8 *The Harper Dictionary of Modern Thought,* edited by Alan Bullock and Oliver Stallybrass (New York: Harper & Row, 1977), s.v. "democracy."

9 See, for instance, the recent Canadian offering on this thesis by William D. Gairdner, *The Trouble with Canada* (Toronto: Stoddart, 1990).

10 Watson and Barber, *Struggle for Democracy,* xvii.

11 From a speech to the Vancouver Board of Trade, January 18, 1991.

Chapter 2: The Meaning of Direct Democracy

1 Jean-Marie Denquin, *Référendum et Plébiscite* (Paris: Librairie générale de droit et de jurisprudence, 1979).
2 Butler and Ranney, *Referendums*, 4.
3 The Committee on the Process for Amending the Constitution (often called the Beaudoin-Edwards Committee after its co-chairmen Senator Gerald Beaudoin and MP Jim Edwards) had the mandate of recommending improvements in the amending process, after the sad experience of the failure of the Meech Lake Accord to be ratified according to existing procedures. One of the items the committee was expressly directed to examine was the use of a referendum. The committee had consulted a Swiss authority on the subject, Jean-Francois Aubert (and also experts from Australia, Germany, Belgium, and the U.S.), but had expressly refused to call as a witness the only Canadian who had written a book about our own experience with referendums. The British Columbia Referendum Office in the fall of 1991, on the other hand, issued background papers to all the province's voters, which cited my book *Lawmaking by the People: Referendums and Plebiscites in Canada*. When I wrote on February 18, 1991, to committee co-chairman Jim Edwards requesting an opportunity to appear before the committee, I enclosed a copy of my book. On February 27, 1991, he replied saying the committee had decided to hear the party leaders (all of whom were specifically invited; none of whom in fact appeared) but no other parliamentarians, and he asked me to submit something in writing instead. The fact that I'd already done so – in book form – seemed to have escaped him! It is ironic, too, that politicians complain about how they're denigrated, disparaged, and dismissed by the public when it is politicians who are hardest on each other, who discount the contributions of other politicians, and who from Question Period to most other public arenas give the lead to the public on how to undermine the authority and credibility of those in public office. I agreed with the observation of Rob Nicholson, MP for Niagara Falls and a member of the Beaudoin-Edwards Committee, who told me later that if I'd been a professor or other "expert" on referendums, the committee would have asked me to appear and paid my expenses to travel to Ottawa to do so, but being an MP, I was considered by other MPs as an inappropriate contributor to their proceedings. Co-chairman of the committee Gérald Beaudoin tried to have me appear to discuss the subject of referendums with the MPs and senators on the committee, but the committee members decided if that was done for one MP it would have to be done for all. Beaudoin said that this decision was "wrong" and "unfair." Thus it was the politicians' own verdict that politicians be categorized as one-dimensional elected representatives, with no credit for working to achieve a level of knowledge in a specialized area.
4 S.N. 1948, c.9.

5 S.Q. 1978, c.6.
6 Regarding the question of *referendums* versus *referenda*: although both forms are used, the former Anglo-Saxon form is favoured by contemporary authority. The editor of the *Supplement to the Oxford English Dictionary*, for one, gives as his reason that the Latin plural gerundive, *referenda*, meaning "things to be referred," necessarily connotes a plurality of issues (R.W. Burchfield, ed., *A Supplement to the Oxford English Dictionary*, 1982).
7 R.S.O. 1980, c.178.
8 See *Eastview Public School Board v. Gloucester* (1917), 41 O.L.R. 327, 40 D.L.R. 707; *Re West Missouri Continuation School* (1912), 25 O.L.R. 550, 3 D.L.R. 195, varied 25 O.L.R. 554 (C.A.); *C.P.R. v. Winnipeg* (1900), 30 S.C.R. 558; *Re Stratford Local Option By-law* (1915), 35 O.L.R. 26, 25 D.L.R. 774.
9 Joseph F. Zimmerman, *Participatory Democracy: Populism Revived* (New York: Praeger 1986), 119; see also Thomas E. Cronin, *Direct Democracy: The Politics of the Initiative, Referendum and Recall* (Cambridge, Mass.: Harvard University Press, 1989), and Referendum B.C. Office, *Background Paper on Recall* (Victoria, 1991).
10 S.A. 1936, c. 82. Repealed by S.A. 1937 (3rd Sess.), c. 7.
11 Agar Adamson, "We Were Here Before: The Referendum in Canadian Experience," *Policy Options* 1, no. 1 (March 1980).
12 Ibid., 53.
13 R.S.C. 1979, c. 14 (1st Supp.).
14 Adamson, "We Were Here Before," 51.
15 Joseph Schull, *Ontario Since 1867* (Toronto: McClelland & Stewart, Ontario Historical Studies Series, 1978), 236.
16 Peter Studer, "The Limits of Direct Democracy," in *Sovereign People or Sovereign Governments*, edited by H.V. Kroeker (Montreal: IRPP, 1981), 95.
17 *Maclean's*, January 7, 1991, 10.
18 Ibid., 1.
19 Referendum B.C. Office, *Background Paper on Recall*, 2.
20 *Times Colonist* (Victoria), September 10, 1991.

Chapter 3: The Pros and Cons of Direct Democracy

1 (1889), 17 O.R. 554, 561.
2 See *Gaulin v. Ottawa* (1914), 6 O.W.N. 38 at 39, 26 O.W.R. 21; *Darby v. Toronto* (1889), 17 O.R. 554 at 561; *Davies v. Toronto* (1887), 15 O.R. 33; *King v. Toronto* (1902), 5 O.L.R. 163.
3 In *King v. Toronto, supra.*
4 *Davies v. Toronto, supra.*
5 William Bennet Munro, *American Influences on Canadian Government* (Toronto: Macmillan, 1929), 96.
6 Bogdanor, *People and the Party System*, 2–3.
7 Martin Gilbert, *Churchill: A Life* (London: Heinemann, 1991), 845.

8 Clement Atlee, letter to Winston Churchill, quoted in Gilbert, *Churchill*, 845.
9 Gilbert, *Churchill*, 845.
10 Atlee, letter to Churchill, quoted in Bodanor, *People and the Party System*, 35.
11 Ibid., 36–37.
12 Ibid., 39; see also Philip Goodheart, *Referendum* (London: Tom Stacey, 1971).
13 Bogdanor, *People and the Party System*, 41.
14 Clifford D. Sharp, cited in Butler and Ranney, *Referendums*, 26.
15 Butler and Ranney, *Referendums*, 28–29.
16 Ibid., 25.
17 This point is further considered in Chapter 5, which deals with the traditional notion of a "mandate" given by voters at election time.
18 Audrey Marilyn Adams, "A Study of the Use of Plebiscites and Referendums by the Province of British Columbia," M.A. thesis, University of British Columbia, 1958, 4–5.
19 Kenneth Grant Crawford, *Canadian Municipal Government* (Toronto: University of Toronto Press, 1954), 157.
20 Butler and Ranney, *Referendums*, 29–33.
21 Adams, "Use of Plebiscites and Referendums," 5.
22 Butler and Ranney, *Referendums*, 34.
23 Ibid., 223.
24 Butler and Ranney, *Referendums*, 34.
25 Ibid., 35.
26 Elizabeth Chambers, "The Referendum and the Plebiscite," in *Politics in Saskatchewan*, edited by Norman Ward and Duff Spafford (Don Mills, Ont.: Longmans, 1968), 74.
27 Crawford, *Canadian Municipal Government*, 157.
28 Butler and Ranney, *Referendums*, 36; see also C.F. Strong, *Modern Political Constitutions: An Introduction to the Comparative Study of Their History and Existing Form* (London: Sidgwick and Jackson, 1963), especially chap. 10, "The Legislature," 222–32.
29 Adamson, "We Were Here Before," 51.
30 Butler and Ranney, *Referendums*, 226.

Chapter 4: Some Fundamentals of Fair Referendums

1 Butler and Ranney, *Referendums*, 3.
2 Ibid., 8.
3 For more on the Quebec situation, see Chapter 5, "Mandate, Mandate – Who's Got the Mandate?"
4 *Encyclopaedia Britannica*, 1971 ed., s.v. *"Plebiscite."*
5 See, for instance, *Helm v. Port Hope* (1875), 22 Gr. 273; *King v. Toronto* (1902), 5.O.L.R. 163.
6 1957 O.R. 20, [1947] 2 D.L.R. 125.

7   69 C.C.C. 299, [1938] 1 D.L.R. 374.
8   Of the Municipal Act, R.S.O. 1937, c. 294.
9   1953 O.W.N. 687.
10   Ibid., 688.
11   Ibid., 689.
12   [1949] O.W.N. 30, [1949] 1 D.L.R. 520.
13   30 O.R. (2d) 748.
14   *Greenwood v. Board of School Trustees, District 13* (1965), 54 W.W.R. 432, 55 D.L.R. (2d) 663 (B.C. C.A.).
15   In *Re Wetmore and Timmins,*[1952] O.R. 13, [1952] 2 S.L.R. 854.
16   For legal analysis of those steps beyond the voters' participation, such as matters of failure to submit by-laws to a vote, enforcing the submission, restraining the submission, non-compliance with statutory provisions, and enactment of a by-law after it has been assented to in a direct vote by municipal electors, see, for instance, Ian MacF. Rogers, *The Law of Canadian Municipal Corporations,* 2nd ed. (Toronto: Carswell, 1971), especially chap. 13, "By-laws Requiring Electoral Assent," 521ff.
17   *Allan et al. v. City of Toronto* 46 O.R.(2d), 641–644.
18   Documentation to this effect was attached as Schedule 'A' to the petition in the *Baird v. Oak Bay* case.
19   Of the Municipal Act authorizing referendums.
20   *Baird v. Corporation of the District of Oak Bay,* 21 M.P.L.R. 278–280. For a further discussion of the issue, see Heather McDonald, "Using the Municipal Referendum as a Community Expression Against Nuclear War in British Columbia," 18 M.P.L.R. 283.
21   30 O.R. (2d) 748.
22   *The Globe and Mail,* November 9, 1982, 9.
23   *The Newspaper* (Toronto), September 29, 1982.
24   *Daley v. London, supra; Taprell v. Calgary* (1913), 5 Alta. L.R. 377, 3 W.W.R. 987, 10 D.L.R. 656.
25   Crawford, *Canadian Municipal Government,* 156.
26   S.S. 1956, c. 74.
27   *Saskatchewan Sessional Papers,* no. 75, 1957. See, generally, Chambers, "Referendum and Plebiscite."
28   Chambers, "Referendum and Plebiscite," 73.
29   Adams, "Use of Plebiscites and Referendums," 158.
30   *The Ottawa Citizen,* October 26, 1983.
31   See, for example, a publication by the Dominion Alliance called *The Prohibition Plebiscite: Is It to be Untrammelled and Fair?* an eight-page pamphlet, published in 1898 (copy held by Library of Parliament, Ottawa).
32   Resolution of Ontario Provincial Branch Dominion Alliance, Toronto, July 14, 1897.
33   Resolution of June 17, 1897.
34   R.S.O. 1980, c. 171.

35 For a further discussion of this point, and of the nature of general and specific mandates given by the people in a general election, see Chapter 5.

36 (1921), 21 O.W.N. 264.

37 *Harrigan v. Port Arthur* (1909), 14 O.W.R. 973, 1 O.W.N. 169; affd 14 O.W.R. 1086, 1 O.W.N. 216 (C.A.); *King v. Toronto* (1902), 5 O.L.R. 163; *Daley v. London*, [1953] O.W.N. 341.

38 "No Telling People How to Vote, Council Warned," *The Globe and Mail*, July 16, 1991.

39 Ibid.

40 Broadcasting Act, 38–39 Elizabeth II, Ch. 11.

41 R.S.C. 1970, c. B-11, as amended.

42 The blackout rule, which applied to federal, provincial, and municipal elections, was extended in 1968 to all referendums in Canada, regardless of whether they occurred at the federal, provincial, or municipal level. Specifically, s. 28(1) of the Broadcasting Act stated that, on the day of a referendum and on the day preceding it, no broadcaster was to broadcast and no cable television operator was to receive a broadcast of a program, advertisement, or announcement of a partisan character in relation to a referendum being held in the area normally served by the licensee. Under the new Broadcasting Act of the Mulroney government, which became law in 1991, all blackout provisions for referendums and plebiscites have been dropped. The Department of Justice in Ottawa felt that the blackout rule was unconstitutional (or would be viewed as such if tested under the Charter) because, in their opinion, it unfairly discriminated against broadcasting in relation to other forms of advertising.

43 Austin Ranney, "Regulating the Referendum," *The Referendum Device*, edited by Austin Ranney, 90–97 (Washington and London: American Enterprise Institute for Public Policy Research, 1981).

44 See, generally, Patrick Boyer, *Money and Message: The Law Governing Election Financing, Advertising, Broadcasting and Campaigning in Canada* (Toronto: Butterworths, 1983).

Chapter 5: Mandate, Mandate – Who's Got the Mandate?

1 "Opposition Parties Plan Thorough Debate on Free Trade," *The Globe and Mail*, December 6, 1988.

2 Letter to the editor, *The Globe and Mail*, December 14, 1988.

3 Ibid.

4 Richard Gwyn, *The Northern Magus* (Toronto: McClelland & Stewart, 1980), 365.

5 Robert Sheppard and Michael Valpy, *The National Deal: The Fight for a Canadian Constitution* (Toronto: Fleet Books, 1982), 22–23.

6 Ibid., 23.

7 Ibid.

8   Michael Adams, *Environics, Election Report 1988, No. 3* (Toronto: Environics Research Group, 1988), 4.
9   A. Kornberg, W. Mishler, and H.D. Clarke, *Representative Democracy in the Canadian Provinces* (Scarborough: Prentice-Hall, 1982), 261.
10 Ibid.
11 Harold D. Clarke et al., *Absent Mandate: The Politics of Discontent in Canada* (Toronto: Gage Publishing, 1984), 7–8.
12 Ibid., 100–1.
13 Joseph Wearing, "The Phenomenon of the Canadian Voter: Recent Attempts to Explain Patterns of Voting," *Journal of Canadian Studies* 22, no. 3 (Fall 1987) 145. For further discussion of brokerage politics in theory and practice, see also Joseph Wearing, *Strained Relations: Canadian Parties and Voters* (Toronto: McClelland & Stewart, 1988), especially 227–33.
14 Bogdanor, *People and the Party System*, 47.
15 Jon H. Pammett, "Political Education and Democratic Participation," in *Political Education in Canada*, edited by Jon H. Pammett and Jean-Luc Pépin (Halifax: Institute for Research on Public Policy, 1988), 211.
16 Clarke et al., *Absent Mandate*, 182.
17 Ibid.
18 André Siegfried, *The Race Question in Canada* (1906; reprint, Toronto: McClelland & Stewart, Carleton Library series, 1966), 150.
19 See principally Herring's *The Politics of Democracy: American Parties in Action* (New York: Peter Smith Publisher, 1940).
20 Frank H. Underhill, "The Canadian Party System in Transition," *Canadian Journal of Economics and Political Science* 9, no. 3 (August 1943).
21 Frank H. Underhill, *In Search of Canadian Liberalism* (Toronto: Macmillan, 1960), 199.
22 John Porter, *The Vertical Mosaic: An Analysis of Class and Power in Canada* (Toronto: University of Toronto Press, 1965), 377.
23 Gad Horowitz, "Towards the Democratic Class Struggle," in *Agenda 1970: Proposals for a Creative Politics*, edited by Trevor Lloyd and Jack McLeod (Toronto: University of Toronto Press, 1968), 241–55.
24 Ibid., 242–43.
25 Ibid.
26 See the following works by Janine Brodie and Jane Jenson: "The Party System," in *Canadian Politics in the 1990s*, edited by Michael S. Whittington and Glen Williams, 3rd ed. (Toronto: Methuen, 1990), 249–66; *Crisis, Challenge and Change: Party and Class in Canada Revisited* (Ottawa: Carleton University Press, 1988); and "Piercing the Smokescreen: Brokerage Parties and Class Politics," in *Canadian Parties in Transition: Discourse, Organization, and Representation*, edited by Alain Gagnon and A. Brian Tanguay (Toronto: Nelson, 1989), 24–44.
27 H.D. Forbes, "Absent Mandate '88? Parties and Voters in Canada," *Journal of Canadian Studies* 25, no. 2 (Summer 1990), 5.
28 Ibid., 6.

29 Underhill, *In Search of Canadian Liberalism,* 136–37.
30 Forbes, "Absent Mandate '88?" 9–10.
31 Ibid., 10.
32 Ibid.
33 Porter, *Vertical Mosaic,* 374.
34 Clarke et al., *Absent Mandate,* 14.
35 Ibid., 10, 13, 180–81; see also Forbes, "Absent Mandate '88?" 7.
36 Forbes, "Absent Mandate '88?" 9.
37 Ibid., 11.
38 Ibid.
39 Ibid., 9.
40 John Roberts, *Agenda for Canada* (Toronto: Lester & Orpen Dennys, 1985).
41 Robert A. Mackay, *The Unreformed Senate of Canada,* rev. ed. (Toronto: McClelland & Stewart Limited, 1963), 172.
42 Quoted in Mackay, *Unreformed Senate,* 168
43 Arthur Meighen, "The Canadian Senate," *Queen's Quarterly* 44 (Summer 1937): 152–63.
44 Ibid.
45 Ibid.
46 Ibid.
47 Mackay, *Unreformed Senate,* 170–71.
48 Ibid., 171.
49 Quoted in Mackay, *Unreformed Senate,* 171.
50 Ibid., 171.
51 Senate, *Debates,* October 9, 1962.
52 Senate, *Debates,* October 10,1962; see also Mackay, *Unreformed Senate,* 171–72.
53 Ibid., 172.
54 Ibid.
55 Ibid., 173.
56 Robert J. Jackson and Doreen Jackson, *Politics in Canada,* 2nd ed. (Scarborough: Prentice-Hall, 1990), 490.
57 Forbes, "Absent Mandate '88?" 15.
58 Ronald Blair, "What Happens to Parliament?" in *Agenda 1970: Proposals for a Creative Politics,* edited by T. Lloyd and J. McLeod (Toronto: University of Toronto Press, 1968), 220.
59 Ibid.
60 Cecil Emden, *The People and the Constitution: A History of the Development of the People's Influence in British Government,* 2nd ed. (Oxford: Clarendon Press, 1956), 8.
61 Ibid.
62 Bogdanor, *People and the Party System,* 6.
63 Quoted in ibid., 60.
64 Ibid.

65 Ibid., 7.
66 Ibid.
67 Ibid., 13.
68 Ibid., 14.
69 A.V. Dicey, "Ought the Referendum to Be Introduced into England?" *Contemporary Review*, 1890, 504. See also Bogdanor, *People and the Party System*, 14.
70 Susan Delacourt, "House Rules to Change as Tories Plan to Revamp System," *The Globe and Mail*, August 3, 1991.
71 Peter Dobell, "The Alienation of Canadians from Their Political System" (Ottawa: Parliamentary Centre, 1992), 22 (unpublished at date of writing).
72 Bogdanor, *People and the Party System*, 15.
73 Dicey, "Ought the Referendum?" 505, 507.
74 Bogdanor, *People and the Party System*, 15.
75 Quoted in Bogdanor, *People and the Party System*, 17.
76 Ibid., 17–18. See also Patricia Kelvin, "The Development and Use of the Concept of the Electoral Mandate in British Politics, 1867–1911" (Ph.D. thesis, University of London, 1977).
77 Patrick Boyer, *Election Law in Canada*, vol. 1 (Toronto: Butterworths, 1987), 160–61; see also Henry Borden, ed., *Robert Laird Borden: His Memoirs*, 2 vols. (Toronto: McClelland & Stewart, 1969), 6–8.
78 Elizabeth Armstrong, *The Crisis of Quebec 1914–1918* (Toronto: McClelland & Stewart, 1974), 178.
79 D. Owen Carrigan, *Canadian Party Platforms 1867–1968* (Toronto: Copp Clark, 1968), 36.
80 House of Commons, *Debates*, May 3, 1898, 4713–18.
81 Bogdanor, *People and the Party System*, 23.
82 Ibid., 20.
83 Emden, *People and the Constitution*, 10.
84 Ibid., 11.
85 "When in doubt, put it to a vote," *The Globe and Mail*, November 17, 1987.
86 House of Commons, *Debates*, July 21, 1988, 17829.
87 See John Godfrey, "Letting the People Decide," *The Financial Post*, August 29, 1988; Jack McArthur, "A Referendum Needed on Free Trade," *The Toronto Star*, June 14, 1988; Claire Hoy, "Leave It to People Power," *The Toronto Sun*, November 20, 1987; Réjean Pelletier, "Un Référendum sur le libre-échange?" *Le Devoir*, September 10, 1987; Harvey Schachter, "Let the People Decide," *The Whig-Standard* (Kingston), November 14, 1987; and "People Power," *The Whig-Standard*, November 17, 1987.
88 J. M. Beck, *Pendulum of Power* (Scarborough: Prentice-Hall, 1968), 120.
89 Ibid., 129.
90 Ibid.
91 See, for greater detail, Patrick Boyer, "Robust Democracy: The Cana-

dian General Election of 1988," *The Parliamentarian* (London, England), April 1989, 72–75.

92 Richard Johnston and André Blais, "A Resounding Maybe: Voters Weighed the Free Trade Options and Gave the Clear Mandate to No One," *The Globe and Mail*, December 12, 1988; see also Frances Russell, "Tories Lack a Mandate to Ram through Trade Deal," *The Winnipeg Free Press*, December 14, 1988.

93 Rick Salutin, "The Voters' Revolt: The Biggest Upset in the Federal Election?" *Toronto Life*, February 1989, 23–26.

94 "Let's Vote on It," *The Economist*, November 10, 1990, 13.

95 Ibid., 13–14.

96 Ibid.

Chapter 6: Referendums Initiated by the People

1 Referendum B.C. Office, *Background Paper: Initiative* (1991), 2.

2 Quoted in Deborah Wilson, "Referendum Law May Spawn Huge Industry," *The Globe and Mail*, October 15, 1990, A7.

3 Letter to the author from Susan Ormiston, October 24, 1991.

4 Charles M. Price, "The Initiative: A Comparative State Analysis and Reassessment of a Western Phenomenon," *Western Political Quarterly* 28 (June 1975): 260–61.

5 *Blueprint for Our Future: Increasing Voter Participation and Reforming the Initiative Process* (Sacramento: California Senate Office of Research, January 1991).

6 Bogdanor, *People and the Party System*, 85.

7 Ibid., 86.

8 J. St. L. Strachey, *The Referendum* (London: Fisher Unwin, 1924), 29.

9 Bogdanor, *People and the Party System*, 86.

10 S.E. Finer, *The Changing British Party System, 1945–1979*, quoted in Bogdanor, *People and the Party System*, 86.

11 See summation and analysis of this, for instance, in Bogdanor, *People and the Party System*, 86.

12 Alan C. Cairns, *Constitution, Government and Society in Canada*, edited by Douglas E. Williams (Toronto: McClelland & Stewart, 1988), 156.

13 Ibid.

14 Ibid.

15 Bogdanor, *People and the Party System*, 87.

16 Finer, *Changing British Party System*, quoted in Bogdanor, *People and the Party System*, 88.

17 Hugh Bone, Senate Judiciary Committee on the Voter Initiative Constitutional Amendment, quoted in Bogdanor, *People and the Party System*, 90.

18 Eugene C. Lee, "California," in Butler and Ranney, *Referendums*, 117.

19 See, for example, *Initiative and Referendum Report*, edited by Patrick McGuigan, a monthly publication of the Free Congress Research and Education Foundation, Washington, D.C.,

20 Zimmerman, *Participatory Democracy*, 170.

21 Bogdanor, *People and the Party*, 88.
22 Lee, "California," 120.
23 Bogdanor, *People and the Party System*, 86–87.
24 Duff Conacher, "Power to the People: Initiative, Referendum, Recall, and the Possibility of Popular Sovereignty in Canada," University of Toronto, *Faculty of Law Journal* 49, no. 2: 193.
25 As has happened in the United States where minority rights are protected by the constitution and a number of successful initiatives were later ruled unconstitutional by the Supreme Court.
26 Conacher, "Power to the People," 203–5.

Chapter 7: Ratifying Constitutional Changes by Referendum

1 Austin Ranney, "The United States of America," in Butler and Ranney, *Referendums*, 68.
2 Alex Mesbur, "The Making of Federal Constitutions: A Study of Constitution-making Processes in the United States, Australia, India, Pakistan, Malaysia, and the West Indies," in *The Confederation Challenge*, vol. 1, background papers and reports of the Ontario Advisory Committee on Confederation (Toronto: Queen's Printer, 1967), 211.
3 Cairns, *Constitution, Government, and Society*, 27.
4 Mesbur, "Making Federal Constitutions."
5 See Jeffrey Simpson, "Those lazy, hazy, crazy days of constitutional amending formulas," *The Globe and Mail*, July 3, 1991.
6 C.B. Macpherson, *The Real World of Democracy* (Toronto: CBC Publications, 1965), 18.
7 *Encyclopaedia Britanica*, 1971 ed., s.v. "Constitutional Convention (U.S.)"; Charles A. Beard, *An Economic Interpretation of the Constitution of the United States* (New York: Macmillan, 1913); Robert E. Brown, *Charles Beard and the Constitution* (Princeton: Princeton University Press, 1956); Forrest McDonald, *We The People: the Economic Origins of the Constitution* (Chicago: University of Chicago Press, 1958); Mesbur, "Making Federal Constitutions," 210–11.
8 See generally, Geoffrey Sauer's two-volume work, *Australian Federal Politics and Law, 1901–1929* and *Australian Federal Politics and Law 1929–1949* (Melbourne: Melbourne University Press, 1956 and 1963); see also Don Aitkin, "Australia," in Butler and Ranney, *Referendums*, 123–137.
9 Alex Mesbur, "Making of Federal Constitutions," 209–10.
10 In Canada's case, some 90 percent of our people live along a 200-mile southern strip of the land; in Australia's, the largest portion of the people by far live around the perimeter of the continent. Our empty spaces tend to be in the north of our country, theirs in the centre.
11 Don Aitkin, "Australia," 123.
12 Ibid., 125–28.
13 In the same year, 1981, this status was also achieved by Antigua and Belize, whose populations were 77,000 and 167,000, respectively.

14   See the editorial in the Fall 1987 issue of the *Journal of Canadian Studies,* "Starting Over: The Reconstruction of Canada." It deals with the charter, free trade, and privatization, among other topics
15   Jean-Louis Roy, *Le Devoir,* July 1, 1981.
16   Alan Cairns, "The Politics of Constitutional Renewal in Canada," in *Redesigning the State,* edited by K.G. Banting and R. Simeon (Toronto: University of Toronto Press, 1985).
17   See Cairns, "Politics of Constitutional Renewal."
18   House of Commons, *Debates,* October 20, 1977, 53.
19   Stephen Clarkson and Christina McCall, "Trudeau's Great Paper Chase," *The Globe and Mail,* October 27, 1990, D1, D5.
20   Ibid., D5.
21   Ibid.
22   Ibid.
23   Alan Cairns, "The Process of Constitution Making" (Paper presented at the conference "The Canadian Mosaic: Democracy and the Constitution," University of Ottawa, April 28–29, 1990), 1.
24   Ibid.
25   Ibid., 2.
26   Ibid. *The Taking of Twenty-Eight* is a book (Toronto: Women's Press, 1985) by Penney Kome that describes how Section 28, which guarantees the legal equality of women with men, came to be added to the Charter.
27   Cairns, "The Process of Constitution Making," 2–3.
28   *The Globe and Mail,* July 9, 1990, A4.
29   Eugene Forsey, *The Gazette* (Montreal), "Let the People Decide on Meech Lake," November 28, 1989.
30   Ibid.
31   Willard Estey, "Canada's Political System Needs Big Changes," *The Ottawa Citizen,* September 26, 1990, A9.
32   Ibid.
33   Professor Howard McConnell, from a speech presented at the conference "The Canadian Mosaic: Democracy and the Constitution," University of Ottawa, April 28–29, 1990.
34   Susan Delacourt,"National Referendum Urged," *The Globe and Mail,* February 20, 1991.
35   Ibid. See also testimony presented to the committee by Professor Smith on February 19, 1991, and by Professor Lemieux on the same day (*Proceedings of the Committee* [Ottawa: Queen's Printer, February 19, 1991, vol. 2, 38–60 [Prof. Smith], 61–87 [Prof. Lemieux]).
36   Special Joint Committee of the Senate and the House of Commons, *The Process for Amending the Constitution of Canada (Beaudoin-Edwards Report)* (Ottawa: Queen's Printer, June 1991), 33.
37   Ibid., 36.
38   Ibid.
39   Ibid., 42.
40   Ibid.

41 Gérald A. Beaudoin, from a speech presented at the conference "The Canadian Mosaic: Democracy and the Constitution," University of Ottawa, April 28–29, 1990. See also, Gérald Beaudoin, "Les Aspects Constitutionnels du Référendum," *Etudes Internationales* (Université Laval, Québec) 8, no.3 (June, 1977): 197–207.

42 *Beaudoin-Edwards Report*, 42.

43 Ibid.

44 The proposed legislation was subsequently debated through second reading before dying on the Order Paper when the 1979 general election was called.

45 *A.G. Nova Scotia v. A.G. Canada* (1951), S.C.R. 31

46 David Butler, "The World Experience" in *The Referendum Device*, edited by Austin Ranney (Washington: American Enterprise Foundation, 1981), 75.

47 Jean Chrétien, *Straight from the Heart* (Toronto: Key Porter Books, 1985), 185.

48 Woodrow Wilson, quoted in Cronin, *Direct Democracy*, 38.

Chapter 8: The Quest for a Canadian Direct-Vote Statute

1 *The Toronto Sun*, August 29, 1986, 5.

2 Michel Gratton, "What's Brian Up To?" *The Ottawa Sun*, March 19, 1991, 18.

3 Ibid.

4 William Johnson, "Trudeau admits he leaned toward UDI: Former PM's plan would have made people sovereign," *The Gazette* (Montreal), May 29, 1991, 7.

5 "Politics of Anger," *Maclean's*, January 7, 1991, 12

6 *The Toronto Star*, June 20, 1990, A12.

7 *The Economist*, November 10, 1990, 70.

8 Ibid., 70.

9 Transcript of press conference, National Press Club, July 21, 1988, National Archives of Canada, Ottawa.

10 *Political Rights, Lawmaking by the People, Money and Message, Election Law in Canada* (2 vols.), and *Local Elections in Canada*.

11 House of Commons, *Debates*, June 18, 1991, 1974.

12 Ibid., 1975.

13 Ibid., 1975–76.

14 Ibid., 1976–77.

15 Ibid., 1977–78.

16 Ibid., 1978–79.

17 Statutes of U.K., 1975, c. 33

Chapter 9: Reflections Upon the Trust of the People

1 Patrick Boyer, "The Delicate Balance," *The Northern Institute Quarterly* 2, no. 1: 5, 7.

2 Northrop Frye, interviewed by David Cayley, "Inside Mythology," *The Idler*, March–April 1991, 28.

3 Boyer, *Election Law in Canada*, xlix.

4 Citizens' Forum on Canada's Future (Keith Spicer, chairman), *Report to the People and Government of Canada* (Ottawa: Queen's Printer, June 27, 1991), 107.

5 Emden, *People and the Constitution*, 316.

6 Zimmerman, *Participatory Democracy*, v.

7 See, Report of the Standing Committee on the Status of Disabled Persons, *No News Is Bad News* (Ottawa: Queen's Printer, August 1988).

8 G.E. Mortimore, "Why We Need Radical Democracy," *Policy Options*, June 1991, 27–30.

9 Ibid., 28–29.

Bibliography

Adams, Audrey Marilyn. "A Study of the Use of Plebiscites and Referendums by the Province of British Columbia." M.A. thesis, University of British Columbia, Department of Economics and Political Science, April 1958.

Adams, Michael. *Environics Election Report 1988 No. 3*. Toronto: Environics Research Group, 1988.

Adamson, Agar. "We Were Here Before: The Referendum in Canadian Experience." *Policy Options*, March 1980, 51.

Alderson, Stanley. *Yea or Nay: Referendums in the United Kingdom*. London: Cassell, 1975.

Anderson, Dewey. *Government Directly by the People*. Stanford: Stanford University Press, 1942.

Armstrong, Elizabeth. *The Crisis of Quebec, 1917–1918*. Toronto: McClelland & Stewart, 1974.

Banting, K.G., and R. Simeon, eds. *Redesigning the State*. Toronto: University of Toronto Press, 1985.

Beck, J.M. *Pendulum of Power*. Scarborough: Prentice-Hall, 1968.

Blueprint for Our Future: Increasing Voter Participation and Reforming the Initiative Process. California Senate Office of Research, January 1991.

Bogdanor, Vernon. *The People and the Party System: The Referendum and Electoral Reform in British Politics*. Cambridge: Cambridge University Press, 1981.

Bonjour, Felix. *Real Democracy in Operation*. New York: Frederick A. Stokes Co., 1970.

Borden, Henry, ed. *Robert Laird Borden: His Memoirs*, 2 vols. Toronto: McClelland & Stewart, 1969.

Boyer, J. Patrick. *Political Rights: The Legal Framework of Elections in Canada*. Toronto: Butterworths, 1981.

———. *Lawmaking by the People: Referendums and Plebiscites in Canada*. Toronto: Butterworths, 1982.

———. *Money and Message: The Law Governing Election Financing, Advertising, Broadcasting and Campaigning in Canada*. Toronto: Butterworths, 1983.

———. *Election Law in Canada*, vol. 1. Toronto: Butterworths, 1987.

Boyer, J. Patrick, et al. *No News Is Bad News*. Report of the Parliamentary Committee on Status of Disabled Persons. Ottawa, Queen's Printer, 1988.

Brodie, Janine, and Jane Jenson. *Crisis, Challenge and Change: Party and Class in Canada Revisited*. Ottawa: Carleton University Press, 1988.

Bullock, Alan, and Oliver Stallybrass, eds. *The Harper Dictionary of Modern Thought*. New York: Harper & Row, 1977.

Burchfield, R.W., ed. *A Supplement to the Oxford English Dictionary*. Oxford: Clarendon Press, 1982.

Butler, David, and Austin Ranney, eds. *Referendums: A Comparative Study of*

The People's Mandate

Practice and Theory. Washington, D.C. and London: American Enterprise Institute for Public Policy Research, 1978.

Cairns, Alan C. *Constitution, Government and Society in Canada,* edited by Douglas E. Williams. Toronto: McClelland & Stewart, 1988.

Canada Gazette, January 1, 1921, 2644.

Canadian Annual Review, 1917, 303.

Careless, J.M.S., and R. Craig Brown, eds. *The Canadians, 1867–1967.* Part 1. Toronto: Macmillan, 1968.

Carrigan, D. Owen. *Canadian Party Platforms 1867–1968.* Toronto: Copp Clark, 1968.

The Challenge of Abundance. Toronto: Queen's Printer, 1969.

Chambers, Elizabeth. "The Referendum and the Plebiscite." In *Politics in Saskatchewan,* edited by Norman Ward and Duff Spafford. Don Mills: Longmans, 1968.

Chrétien, Jean. *Straight from the Heart.* Toronto: Key Porter Books, 1985.

Clarke, Harold D., Jane Jenson, Lawrence LeDuc, and Jon H. Pammett. *Absent Mandate: The Politics of Discontent in Canada.* Toronto: Gage Publishing, 1984.

Cleverdon, Catherine. *The Woman Suffrage Movement in Canada.* Toronto: University of Toronto Press, 1950.

Conacher, Duff. "Power to the People: Initiative, Referendum, Recall, and the Possibility of Popular Sovereignty in Canada." University of Toronto, *Faculty of Law Journal* 49, no. 2.

Crawford, Kenneth Grant. *Canadian Municipal Government.* Toronto: University of Toronto Press, 1954.

Cronin, Thomas E. *Direct Democracy: The Politics of the Initiative, Referendum and Recall.* Cambridge, Mass.: Harvard University Press, 1989.

Denquin, Jean Marie. *Référendum et Plébiscite.* Paris: Librairie générale de droit et de jurisprudence, 1976.

Deploige, Simon. *The Referendum in Switzerland.* London: King, 1898.

De Witt, Benjamin Parke. *The Progressive Movement.* New York: Macmillan, 1915.

Dicey, A.V. "Ought the Referendum to Be Introduced into England?" *Contemporary Review,* 1890.

The Dominion Alliance, *The Prohibition Plebiscite: Is It to Be Untrammelled and Fair?* Eight-page pamphlet, 1898.

The Economist (London), November 10, 1990.

Encyclopaedia Britannica, 2nd ed., vol. 18, p. 41. Chicago: Encyclopaedia Britannica Inc., 1968.

Finer, Herman. *Theory and Practice of Modern Government.* New York: Henry Holt, 1949.

Finer, S.E. *The Changing British Party System, 1945–1979.* Washington: American Enterprise Institute, 1980.

Foreign Affairs (New York) 69, no. 4 (Fall 1990).

Gagnon, Alain, and A. Brian Tanguay, eds. *Canadian Parties in Transition: Discourse, Organization and Representation.* Toronto: Nelson, 1989.

Gairdner, William D. *The Trouble with Canada.* Toronto: Stoddart, 1990.

Bibliography

Garland, Rev. M.A., and J.J. Talman. "Pioneer Drinking Habits and the Rise of the Temperance Agitation in Upper Canada prior to 1840." *Papers and Records of the Ontario Historical Society* 27 (1931): 341.

Gilbert, Martin. *Churchill: A Life.* London: Heinemann, 1991.

The Globe and Mail (Toronto), October 26, 1977, 6; November 8, 1977, 7; September 20, 1978, 2; October 16, 1979; August 5, 1980; April 29, 1981.

Goodhart, Philip. *Referendum.* London: Tom Stacey, 1971.

Gould, Lewis L., ed. *The Progressive Era.* Syracuse: Syracuse University Press, 1974.

Granatstein, J.L. *The Politics of Survival: The Conservative Party of Canada, 1939–1945.* Toronto: University of Toronto Press, 1967.

Gwyn, Richard. *The Northern Magus.* Toronto: McClelland & Stewart, 1980.

Hahn, Harlan. "Voting in Canadian Communities: A Taxonomy of Referendum Issues." *Canadian Journal of Political Science* 1 (1968): 462.

Herring, Pendleton. *The Politics of Democracy: American Parties in Action.* New York: 1940.

Hofstadter, Richard. *The Age of Reform.* New York: Random House, 1955.

Honey, Samuel Robinson. *The Referendum among the English.* London: Macmillan, 1912.

Hughes, C.J. "The Referendum." *Parliamentary Affairs* 11 (1958).

Jackson, Robert J., and Doreen Jackson. *Politics in Canada.* 2nd ed. Scarborough: Prentice-Hall, 1990.

Journal of Canadian Studies 22, no. 3 (1987); 25, no. 2 (1990).

Keith, Berriedale. "Notes on Imperial Constitutional Law." *Journal of Comparative Legislation and International Law* 4 (1922): 233.

Kelvin, Patricia. "The Development and Use of the Concept of the Electoral Mandate in British Politics, 1867–1911." Ph.D. thesis, University of London, 1977.

Kroeker, H.V., ed. *Sovereign People or Sovereign Governments.* Montreal: IRDP, 1981.

Link, Arthur S. *Woodrow Wilson and the Progressive Era.* New York: Harper & Row, 1954.

Lloyd, Trevor, and Jack McLeod, eds. *Agenda 1970: Proposals for a Creative Politics.* Toronto: University of Toronto Press, 1968.

Mackay, Robert A. *The Unreformed Senate of Canada.* Rev. ed. Toronto: McClelland & Stewart. 1963.

Maclean's, January 7, 1991.

Macpherson, C.B. *The Real World of Democracy.* Toronto: CBC Publications, 1965.

Mesbur, Alex. "The Making of Federal Constitutions: A Study of Constitution-Making Processes in the United States, Australia, India, Pakistan, Malaysia, and the West Indies." In *The Confederation Challenge.* Vol. 1, *Report of the Ontario Advisory Committee on Confederation.* Toronto: Queen's Printer, 1967.

Mortimore, G.E. "Why We Need Radical Democracy." *Policy Options,* June 1991.

Mowry, George. *The California Progressives.* Berkeley: University of California Press, 1951.

―――. *Theodore Roosevelt and the Progressive Movement.* Madison: University of Wisconsin Press, 1946.

Munro, William Bennett. *The Initiative, Referendum and Recall.* New York: D. Appleton, 1912.

―――. *American Influences on Canadian Government.* Toronto: Macmillan, 1929.

Neidhart, Leonard. *Plebiszit und Pluralitare Demokratie.* Bern: Franke, 1970.

The Newspaper (Toronto), September 29, 1982.

Oberholtzer, Ellis P. *The Referendum in America.* New York: Scribner's, 1911.

Pammett, Jon H., and Jean-Luc Pépin, eds. *Political Education in Canada.* Institute for Research on Public Policy, 1988.

The Parliamentarian (London, England), April 1989.

Pope, Joseph. *Confederation: Being a Series of Hitherto Unpublished Documents Bearing on the British North America Act.* Toronto: Carswell, 1895.

Porter, John. *The Vertical Mosaic: An Analysis of Class and Power in Canada.* Toronto: University of Toronto Press, 1965.

Queen's Quarterly 44 (Summer 1937).

Ranney, Austin, ed. *The Referendum Device.* Washington, D.C. and London: American Enterprise Institute for Public Policy Research, 1981.

Rappard, William E. "The Initiative and Referendum in Switzerland." *American Political Science Review* 6 (1912): 345–66.

Richardson, J.E. *Patterns of Australian Federalism.* Canberra: Australian National University, 1973.

Roberts, John. *Agenda for Canada.* Toronto: Lester & Orpen Dennys, 1985.

Rogers, Ian MacF. *The Law of Canadian Municipal Corporations.* 2nd ed. Toronto: Carswell, 1971.

Saskatchewan Sessional Papers 75 (1957).

Sauers, Geoffrey. *Australian Federal Politics and Law 1901–1929.* Melbourne: Melbourne University Press, 1956.

―――. *Australian Federal Politics and Law 1929–1949.* Melbourne: Melbourne University Press, 1963.

Schull, Joseph. *Ontario Since 1867.* Toronto: McClelland & Stewart, 1978.

Scott, Stephen A. "Constituent Authority and the Canadian Provinces." *McGill Law Journal* 12 (1966-67): 528.

Sharpe, Clifford D. *The Case against the Referendum.* London: Fabian Society, 1911.

Sheppard, Robert, and Michael Valpy. *The National Deal: The Fight for a Canadian Constitution.* Toronto: Fleet Books, 1982.

Shortt, Adam, and Arthur George Doughty, eds. *Canada and Its Provinces.* Vol. 19, 130–31. Toronto: Publishers Association of Canada, 1914.

Siegfried, André. *The Race Question in Canada.* Reprint. Toronto: McClelland & Stewart, Carleton Library Series, 1966.

Smith, Gordon. "The Functional Properties of the Referendum." *European Journal of Political Research* 4 (1976): 1–23.

Spence, Ruth E. *Prohibition in Canada*. Toronto: Ontario Branch of the Dominion Alliance, 1920.

Spicer, Keith, et al. *Report of the Citizen's Forum on Canada's Future*. Government of Canada, June 1991.

Spitz, David. *Patterns of Anti-Democratic Thought*. Rev. ed. New York and Toronto: Macmillan, 1965.

Sproule-Jones, Mark, and Adrie Van Klaveren. "Local Referenda and the Size of Municipality in British Columbia: A Note on Two of Their Interrelationships." *BC Studies* 8 (1970–71): 47–50.

Strachey, John St. Loe. *The Referendum*. London: Unwin, 1924.

Strong, C.F. *Modern Political Constitutions: An Introduction to the Comparative Study of Their History and Existing Form*. London: Sidgwick & Jackson, 1963.

Tallian, Laura. *Direct Democracy: A Historical Analysis of the Initiative, Referendum and Recall Process*. Los Angeles: People's Lobby, 1977.

Tellier, Robert. *Municipal Code of the Province of Quebec*. Rev. ed. Montreal: Wilson & Lafleur, 1975.

Torelle, Ellen, ed. *The Political Philosophy of Robert M. La Follette as Revealed in His Speeches and Writings*. Madison: Robert M. La Follette Co., 1926.

Underhill, Frank H. "The Canadian Party System in Transition." In *Canadian Journal of Economics and Political Science*, August 1943.

———. *In Search of Canadian Liberalism*. Toronto: Macmillan, 1960.

Wambaugh, Sarah. *Plebiscites Since the World War*. Washington: Carnegie Endowment for International Peace, 1933.

———. *A Monograph on Plebiscites with a Collection of Official Documents*. New York: Oxford University Press, 1920.

Watson, Patrick, and Benjamin Barber. *The Struggle for Democracy*. Toronto: Lester & Orpen Dennys, 1988.

Wearing, Joseph. *Strained Relations: Canadian Parties and Voters*. Toronto: McClelland & Stewart, 1988.

Western Political Quarterly 28 (June 1975).

Weyl, Walter E. *The New Democracy*. New York: Macmillan, 1915.

Whittington, S., and Glen Williams, eds. *Canadian Politics in the 1990s*. 3rd ed. Toronto: Methuen, 1990.

Whyte, John D., and William R. Lederman. *Canadian Constitutional Law: Cases, Notes and Materials*. 2nd ed. Toronto: Butterworths, 1977.

Zimmerman, Joseph F. *Participatory Democracy: Populism Revived*. New York: Praeger, 1986.

Zurcher, Arnold J. *The Experiment with Democracy in Central Europe*. New York: Oxford University Press, 1933.

Index

Printed and bound in Canada by
Best Gagné Book Manufacturers